THESE
FOOLISH
THINGS

By

Ken Heather

DEDICATION

To those good friends and colleagues who have shared with me in the great privilege of teaching others.

You know who you are.

TABLE OF CONTENTS

CHAPTER ONE:
A LECTURER'S LIFE

"He who can, does. He who cannot teaches."

- George Bernard Shaw

"Those that know do, those that understand, teach."

- Aristotle

The dream occurs too frequently for comfort. He is surrounded by students, almost all of them in their late teens and early twenties, some of them beautiful young women. He is glad that he has an easy relationship with the great majority of them. Yet he is an outsider. In the dream, he is conscious of the age gap between him and his students and aware that it is growing larger with every passing term. Although he has no wish to be part of their set, he is envious of the casual intimacy they share together.

It takes Keith Stokes five minutes to wake from his dream. He doesn't like being disturbed when it's still dark outside, but he needs to get to his 9 a.m. class, which is twenty miles away and likely to have heavy traffic, so he has to get moving. He swats at the alarm button clumsily, almost missing it. The second attempt is better, and by the third try, he finally turns off the noise. A few minutes later, as he gets out of bed, he makes and drinks his first cup of coffee. "Why do I do this?" he asks himself, "I don't even like coffee that much." He says this out loud. He hopes his students never find out, but he talks to himself a lot. When friends who know about this habit ask him about it, he says he likes having smart conversations and gets too few of those, especially since he spends most of his day with students.

Keith's parents were strict tea drinkers, always preparing it the English way with cold milk, making it almost undrinkable. He grew up with no coffee at home. It was only when he started university that he switched from tea to coffee. Now, he only drinks tea once a week on Sunday afternoons. He has it with cucumber sandwiches, crusts removed, though he doesn't really like these either. He just feels a need to maintain the English traditions he has always been conscious of. He loves the songs of Michael Flanders and Donald Swann and especially enjoys the line: "The English, the English, the English are best..."

He does need the coffee to wake up in the morning. Getting going feels like dragging himself through quicksand. It takes him about two hours after getting out of bed to feel fully awake. Drinking coffee, like his job teaching Economics at Barmouth University, has been a habit for the last twenty-five years and is hard to break.

He's becoming more aware that his years before retirement are quickly running out. A few years ago, he thought he'd be out of the job by his mid-sixties. Now, with the end of mandatory retirement at sixty-five, he has to decide for himself when to retire unless, of course, they fire him for incompetence. He reassures himself that this seems unlikely for now. He hopes it's because he's not actually incompetent rather than because it would be hard for the university to prove.

The idea of retiring at sixty-five is something his students can't even imagine. People are living longer and longer, and the retirement age keeps going up. By the time his students retire, the government may only be providing pensions to those who get to beat Methuselah.

Keith has a university pension to rely on, as well as a private pension, which is a large house that's much bigger than he really needs. Years ago, he made the decision that, since he can't live in shares, it's wiser to invest in a house. Over time, house prices have steadily risen. While the amount of land stays the same, the population keeps growing. He has to admit that maintaining the house comes with its expenses. While he dislikes small, cramped houses, this large one now needs a new boiler for the central heating. His recent conversation with the heating engineer didn't offer much reassurance.

Heating Engineer: "You are thinking about oil? You'd be burning it faster than they could ship it in."

Keith: "Well, maybe electricity?"

Heating Engineer: "Are you mad? You would create so much global warming that after five years, you wouldn't need any heating at all."

He had come to a conclusion about all this. He concluded that he really needs to make a decision.

Spending most of his time around much younger people, with the age gap between him and his students growing wider with each passing term, constantly reminded him of how quickly the years were slipping by. It won't be long before a student tells him, "My dad was one of your students, and he sends his regards." When that happens, it will really hit him how long he's been teaching. Keith does a quick mental calculation and realizes that it won't be long before a student says, "Hello" on behalf of their grandfather. This thought makes him fear how soon he might fall into a state of decline: In the words of Shakespeare: "My way of life is fallen into the sere, the yellow leaf." Life's autumn is approaching quickly.

Keith would like to be able to quote Shakespeare more often, but his knowledge of literature is quite poor. As a young man, he had spent most of his time playing football instead of studying. Ironically, he now finds football quite boring. Meanwhile, he needs to prepare for his classes and make the journey to make an assault on ignorance and indifference once again.

Keith has never married. He's not against the idea of marriage. He simply hasn't met the right person. Recently, thoughts about marriage have been on his mind again because he has just returned from a Greek wedding. At the wedding, he had the special role of "giving away" a former student named Anna. When Keith first met Anna in his class, he learned that she had lost her father when she was just eleven years old. Seeing her get married and being part of the celebration made Keith reflect on his own life and the concept of marriage. He had then become her personal tutor and had assisted Anna with various problems during her time as a student. They had stayed in touch when she had left Barmouth and Keith had kept a good relationship with her. So, Anna had asked Keith if he would play a fatherly role at her wedding, should she ever get married, and give her away. Keith had agreed to this request. To keep his promise, he recently travelled to Greece for the weekend to attend her wedding and fulfil his role.

Keith hadn't anticipated that Anna would marry someone in Greece, but he didn't mind the travel. The wedding was a delightful and happy occasion, but it also highlighted how much older he was compared to his students. It was another reminder that he was from a different generation as he watched Anna, someone he had once taught, begin this new chapter in her life with someone from a different culture.

At the wedding he had spoken to a fellow guest who was a businessman. The businessman suggested that a marriage between a man and a young, beautiful woman is unlikely to be beneficial. The woman would bring her looks to the marriage, while he would contribute his wealth. However, the man's wealth would grow over time, while she would become less attractive as the years passed. In making a marriage proposal he would be offering something that would increase in value, while she was offering something that would lose value over time.

He understood the businessman's idea but Keith remains doubtful. He feels that he himself is in danger of losing value quickly, not financially but in most other ways. Now at fifty-four, although he's still able to move around without a walking frame and still has most of his teeth, he wonders how long this will remain the case. He finds it hard to believe that while he is still fit, he'll be struck by Cupid's arrow. Even his finances are moderate. While his salary at Barmouth is enough to keep him out of poverty, it has never really given him the chance to save or build a substantial nest egg. Apart from owning his house, his income hasn't allowed him to grow his savings quickly or securely.

He takes a quick shower. He catches a glimpse of himself in a full-length mirror. He is a shade less than six feet tall. He would like to be thinner, but the self-discipline needed is too much. He isn't very much overweight. The body mass index, it is said, should not be more than twenty-five. Keith's BMI is around 25.2, especially when he breathes in. He would also like to be a bit taller. When he visits the theatre, it always seems that there is a woman in the seat in front of him wearing a hat. Since he rarely goes to the theatre, it doesn't bother him so very much. Now, it's time for a shave. Keith is always clean shaven. Designer stubble is so uncomfortable. Just once in his life, he had tried something different by growing a full beard. It was a short-lived experiment. When he decided to shave it off, he had tried leaving just the moustache in place. Still sporting his new moustache, he had called around to the house of his friend Ben to give the family a bag of apples from his garden. Ben's wife had answered the door. She had taken one look at him, screamed and ran back into the house. Keith took this to mean that she didn't like the new form of facial growth. He had returned to the house and examined his face with care. No wonder she was appalled. A great hairy caterpillar should be munching its way through a cabbage on someone's allotment, not crawling across the top lip of a neighbour at the front door. He had shaved the moustache off immediately, and neither the beard nor the caterpillar had ever returned.

His clothes are reasonably smart but somewhat informal. In the past, university lecturers were expected to wear a jacket and tie as part of their professional attire. But now, he's joined the trend of dressing casually, which is popular among many people today. Although he enjoys the relaxed dress code, he wonders if there's a connection between the shift in academic dress styles and the decreasing respect for academics. He notices that the wealthy businesspeople he often mentions in his lectures still dress in a formal manner, which contrasts with the casual clothing worn by him and most of his colleagues.

After getting dressed, he leaves his house and gets into his second-hand Lexus. The car starts smoothly and without any issues. Keith drives a Japanese car now because he values reliability. When he was younger, he had bought a British car, despite his training in economics which should have made him cautious about such decisions. The nature of the British car meant that he had spent many Saturday mornings developing a relationship with the local garage. Over time, Keith grew tired of the constant issues with his British car. He now prefers a Japanese car because it starts smoothly every time and only stops when he decides to stop it: "The English, the English, the English are best...." Well, perhaps not at manufacturing things. In the past, when Keith was a boy, there was an attempt to improve British cars through a joint effort: the Japanese provided the engines, and the British made the car bodies. Unfortunately, this collaboration didn't work out well. The car body could not be relied upon to move in sync with the engine.

As Keith drives on the motorway, he sees a woman pulled over with a flat tire. He slows down, thinking about stopping to help her, but then decides against it and speeds up again. One reason he doesn't stop is that the woman is on her mobile phone, so she can call someone for help. But there's another, bigger reason: Keith has noticed a cultural shift since he started working as a lecturer. In the past, when he first began teaching, he would have stopped to help a stranger like her and even changed the tire himself, as he had done before. However, he now feels that stopping might make the woman uncomfortable or scared, as she might find it unsettling to have a stranger approach her while she's alone. In many ways relationships with women are now fraught with more difficulties. He finds this change in social norms troubling. Society has improved in some ways, but he feels that it has also become worse in other respects. Although he continues driving, he feels a sense of guilt about not stopping to help.

The rest of Keith's drive is uneventful, and he arrives at his classroom, Room B.1.09, by three minutes past nine. By this time, nearly half of his students have already arrived. He double-checks the room number to make sure he's in the right place. He knows that mistakes can easily happen, especially when he's still groggy from waking up.

A few years ago, Dan Billings, one of Keith's colleagues, had a mishap at the start of his teaching career. He arrived on time at Floor Eight, Room Three, and gave what he thought was a great lecture. The students seemed to like it. However, Dan had made a mistake, he was supposed to be on Floor Seven, Room Three, not Floor Eight. The lecturer who was supposed to be on Floor Eight, Room Three hadn't arrived, but the students in Dan's lecture hadn't appeared to notice.

Persuading some students to attend classes is challenging. For example, some of his students don't like Thursdays and Fridays because the weekend has started. Mondays and Tuesdays are problematic, being seen as the last part of the weekend. That leaves Wednesdays. However, any class scheduled before noon is difficult because they might still be asleep. Also, Wednesday afternoons are often set aside for sports and other activities, so this is not the best time for classes either. Asking the timetable to schedule all classes for that hour is more than a little problematic. However, for some students it's not about being lazy. Getting through a three-year degree can be financially overwhelming. Many students work part-time to make up for their low income so attending classes can have a financial cost.

Even though it's tough, some students have managed to come to Keith's class this morning. He has only just begun his lecture when a student raises his hand and asks, "Can you please repeat that explanation? It's a tricky part of the theory."

Keith, still feeling the effects of waking up early, finds himself responding in a way that feels like he's listening to someone from another planet. He says: "Um, sorry, I wasn't actually listening." Waking up early and starting work in the morning can be hard for him. Teaching is a demanding job that needs him to have a good understanding of the subject, be able to explain it clearly, and know if the students are understanding the material. Keith finds it easier to manage these tasks later in the day when he's more alert. He starts to think that one reason he chose teaching as a career might be because he hoped it would be a job that doesn't start too early in the morning.

After the class, Keith reflects on how his own answer to the student's question was still preferable to a response he had received as an undergraduate. When he had asked his lecturer for a more detailed explanation of a concept, the lecturer had simply looked at his notes and repeated the exact same words in a monotonous tone. This approach hadn't helped Keith understand the concept any better.

Keith wonders if that kind of teaching might be why, despite graduating with an excellent degree, he left university with a limited understanding of what economics truly involved. He realizes that his own experience of being on the other side of the classroom has made him more aware of how important it is to explain concepts clearly and help students genuinely understand the material.

Unfortunately, Keith feels that his challenges extend beyond just his students; he sometimes feels like he's also in conflict with other staff members in the Business School. Many of his colleagues who are not economists seem to have a strong dislike for economics, often based on their misunderstanding of the subject they criticize.

After the lecture he walks past the shared staff photocopier and notices a handout created by a lecturer from a different discipline. It happens to be an accountant. The handout is titled "Four things that economists believe that are not true." Keith finds this remarkable because none of the four things listed are actually believed by any self-respecting economist. This only adds to his frustration, as it highlights the lack of understanding and misrepresentation of his field by those outside of it. He feels disheartened because this kind of misunderstanding makes it even harder to get students excited about economics.

In the past, Keith used to go to the photocopier to pick up his own materials for class. But recently, he's been more interested in finding and collecting anything that catches his attention. Perhaps, in a spirit of academic enquiry, he should follow this up, but he decides that the handout criticizing economists isn't worth his effort. He can't be bothered and chooses to ignore it.

Keith realizes he might be overreacting. Just a few months ago, he had his students debate whether accountants are more boring than sociologists. Unsurprisingly, this discussion was much livelier than the one about endogenous growth theory, which is a topic associated with the former politician Ed Balls. The theory, which Ed Balls had introduced to the Labour government, was not very convincing to many. Because of this, someone had pointed out that since Ed Balls was the only one who had proposed it and it wasn't very convincing, the theory was "all Balls."

In his second class of the day, Keith is about to meet some second-year students for the first time. He starts with a question: "Now, you all remember the basics of supply and demand?" The response he gets is predictable: "No, never heard of that." Keith isn't surprised, as he knows that students often deny knowing basic concepts, even if, on occasion, they are familiar with them. He suspects that the students are either not being truthful, lacking understanding, or, more likely, both.

However, Keith recalls an incident from a few years ago when a similar situation turned out to be genuinely true. In that case, the students really didn't know the basics of supply and demand, despite it being fundamental to their studies. This memory adds a layer of frustration to his current experience, reinforcing his scepticism.

A former head of the department had faced a situation where the demand for courses taught by economic historians had dramatically dropped. This led to some of the historians becoming unemployed while still being paid. To address the issue, the head of the department assigned one of these economic historians to teach a basic first-year introduction to economics. When Keith took over the class to delve deeper into the subject, he found that the students had not been taught any of the fundamental concepts of economics. Instead, they had spent the entire course focusing on Japanese multinationals, which was the lecturer's personal research interest.

Keith found it amusing, if frustrating, that the students had learned very little about economics, but they might possibly have gained some insight into why Japanese cars start reliably in the morning, something related to the lecturer's research.

Keith greets the students and scans the room, taking in the diverse group before him. To his surprise, he recognizes one or two of the students. One of them is Andy Wilde, who had been one of his tutees in the first year. At Barmouth, first-year students are given a designated time in the first week to meet with their tutor for an hour. Previously, this meeting had been scheduled for week four, allowing students to settle in before their first individual session with the tutor. This timing led to an interesting outcome, as it gave

Keith a chance to see how students had adjusted to university life and provided a more accurate picture of their academic needs and interests. The relatively few high maintenance students needing support failed to receive it early enough and so went off and committed suicide.

To address this, Keith's department decided to make changes. Now, Keith meets with all his new students during the first week of their studies, rather than waiting until later. During this initial meeting, he runs an icebreaker activity. For this activity, each student must share two statements about themselves: one true and one false. The other students then guess which statement is true and which is false.

To help them understand what was needed and to make the icebreaker activity more effective, Keith started by sharing two statements about himself. One of Keith's statements was about a notable achievement from his past: he had scored all ten goals in a football match for his school team. This accomplishment was one of the very few highlights he had from his somewhat mediocre school days, although he is reluctant to admit this to the class.

His other statement was that his name, Keith, comes from a Scottish place name meaning "large woods or forest." He then claimed that he had come to Barmouth from Scotland, where he had played the bagpipes in a regimental Scottish band. To his surprise, most of the students guessed that the story about playing the bagpipes was the true statement, even though it was pure fiction.

When it was Andy's turn to participate in the icebreaker activity, he said, "First statement: I have a dog. Second statement: I have a rabbit." Oh dear, clearly this student had no idea of the purpose of the activity. If Andy were just a little brighter, Keith thought, he would be stupid. Despite this, Keith noted that Andy had managed to pass his first-year exams. He thought that anyone with a basic level of intelligence would pass, considering that removing Andy from the course would result in a loss of income for the university. Barmouth, like many UK universities, faces financial challenges and sustains an annual loss. The university relies on students' fees to help cover the costs of employing staff, including its highly paid administrators and so does all it can to hang on the Andy Wildes of this world.

As Keith looked at Andy again, he was reminded of his own experience as a tutee during his undergraduate years. In the first few weeks of university, he had received a note asking him to come for a tutorial session with his tutor. Eager and optimistic, Keith had arrived on time, ready to engage. He knocked on the tutor's door, and when he was told to enter, he found his tutor sitting behind a desk. The tutor didn't get up or make any effort to greet him. Instead, he simply looked up and said, "I am your tutor. Now look, if you don't bother me, I won't bother you, okay?" Keith, somewhat taken aback, responded with a brief "okay," which turned out to be the last communication he had with the tutor.

Over the following thirty-five years, Keith's opinion of that encounter remained unchanged. He felt that it had been an ideal arrangement for him at the time. As an eighteen-year-old, he was independent and didn't feel he needed much tutorial support. Looking back, he realized he could have been working in a paid job during those early years, a job in which tutorial support was probably not provided. Keith noted that even today, the situation is similar. Most students, perhaps ninety percent, view such tutorial systems as a waste of time. However, for the remaining ten percent, these sessions are crucial and provide essential support.

Apart from Andy, who had already shown his unique approach, almost all the other students in the class were new to Keith. He observed that, as is now common, there were an equal number of women and men in the room. This was a significant shift from when he first started teaching economics and business students about thirty years ago. Back then, his typical class would consist of twenty-eight men and only two women.

Despite these changes in the classroom demographics, Keith found that the process of engaging with students and encouraging them to think critically remained the same. The old French saying, "Plus ça change, plus c'est la même chose," which translates roughly to "the more things change, the more they stay the same," still resonated with him. However, Keith's preferred take on the saying is: "Nothing changes as fast as women's shoes." While certain aspects of teaching and student dynamics evolve, some things, like fashion, change rapidly and unpredictably.

Keith values the presence of women in his classes, believing they bring a civilizing influence on the male students. However, coming from a more conservative generation, he finds some of women's fashion choices a little odd. One student is dressed in jeans with large rips, so much so that it looks like she's wearing more holes than fabric. Another student has bright pink hair, which he finds interesting because the hair changes colour frequently. Last week it was green, and the week before, royal blue. This student clearly wants to stand out, although the bold exterior may hide an inner insecurity. Keith finds himself looking forward to seeing what colour she'll choose next.

Some of the older, more traditional female staff members are more shocked by these modern styles than he is. They prefer their own conservative appearance, although this more restrained dressing can include blue-rinsed hair and criticize the latest trends as dreadful. Despite his own reservations about the hairstyles, Keith is more interested in what's going on inside the students' minds rather than their outward appearance.

Keith struggles with a particular student who has an earring. He finds it hard to deal with for two main reasons. Firstly, the sight of the earring reminds him of his own experience with ear-piercing, although the circumstances were somewhat quite different. As a student, Keith had spent part of his summer working at a cattle market. He remembers vividly using a special punch to create holes in the ears of cattle for identification purposes. He can still recall the sensation of the punch pressing through the soft flesh of the cattle's ear. The thought of this process makes him cringe. He wonders if the student's earring has a similar purpose, although he doubts the university has started using earrings as a new form of student identification.

Secondly, the earring reminds Keith of a shop sign he recently saw that read, "Ears pierced while you wait." What did the shopkeeper think was an alternative? "If you could just drop off your ears here on Wednesday you can pick them up by the weekend."

Keith values the increase in the number of women in his classes. He believes that this change has raised the overall level of intelligence and dedication among students. For him, having bright and committed students is what makes teaching rewarding and enjoyable.

An hour later, Keith is back in his office. He needs to create a multiple-choice test for his first-year students and has a few more questions to write. However, he feels too tired to start working on it right now. Instead, he decides to go shopping before his afternoon class. As he gets his coat to leave, he notices Aydin, a Turkish student, standing outside his office looking very unhappy.

Keith isn't surprised by Aydin's sad expression. Aydin has had a lot of trouble with his studies. Foreign students often pay higher fees, so the department feels pressure to admit them, even if they're struggling academically. Unfortunately, while some foreign students are outstanding, Aydin is a clear example of someone who hasn't been doing well. Keith, despite not feeling very motivated, calls out to Aydin with a forced cheerfulness, "Come in, Aydin." His outward enthusiasm doesn't match how he feels inside.

Aydin says, "I got only ten percent on the test you gave. I didn't expect to get a top grade, but ten percent? How could I have done so poorly?"

Keith thinks that it might be best to be straightforward with him. "Well, that's because you don't know anything."

Aydin pauses, looking deeply thoughtful. After a moment, he slowly nods his head. Ah, so this is the explanation. Clearly the student has come to understand this for the first time. It takes Keith a while to help Aydin address some fundamental misunderstandings about the material. He suggests some additional reading to help Aydin improve his grasp of the subject. After Aydin leaves, Keith decides, on a whim, to Google the name "Aydin." He discovers that "Aydin" is a Turkish name meaning "enlightened." Keith chuckles to himself, thinking, "Well, perhaps Aydin is now enlightened, but probably not just yet."

Before Keith can leave for the day, another student, Carrie Davis, appears outside his office. She looks very distressed. Keith greets her with concern, "Hello Carrie, what's the problem?" Carrie immediately starts to cry. Her tears flow freely as she tries to speak.

"I've done something really stupid. I don't know what to do about it."

Keith starts to wonder what kind of trouble she might be in. Is it a problem with a boyfriend? Has she found herself pregnant? Or perhaps she's had an argument with her landlord and is facing eviction? Keith has heard many troubling stories from students over the years, so he is no longer easily surprised by these personal crises.

Carrie explains, her voice trembling, "I got caught cheating in an exam. I brought some notes with me to help remember the basic points, and the invigilator caught me with them."

Keith nods, understanding that the invigilators did exactly what they were supposed to do. They had crossed out her exam work and recorded the incident on the script. Keith asks gently, "Carrie, you would have passed the exam easily without cheating. Why did you feel the need to do it?"

Carrie replies, looking regretful, "Yes, I know. I can't believe I was so foolish."

Carrie's tears continue to flow, and Keith realizes that dealing with students in the 18-20 age range often requires a lot of patience. They often project an image of confidence but are much more insecure behind closed doors. Keith assures her, "I'll speak to the head of the appropriate department and get back to you. Even though this was a foolish mistake, the world won't end because of it. The sun will still come up tomorrow." Carrie leaves the office feeling somewhat comforted by his words. Keith is relieved to see that, despite her distress, she does not appear to be suicidal.

Keith hurries out of his office, eager to escape the possibility of encountering more students. His plan is to buy ingredients for dinner at the local co-op, hoping that this small errand will offer a much-needed break from the chaos of his day.

However, his relief is short-lived. At the co-op, he finds himself fourth in line at the checkout. In front of him are an old lady, who is being served at the register, and an even older man who is next in line. Just in front of Keith stands one of his students, Selenia. She is a strikingly attractive mature student, pursuing a master's degree. Selenia, who lives alone in Barmouth without any family nearby, is a familiar face to Keith.

As Keith waits, the older man begins to mutter repeatedly, "Fifty years. Fifty years. Fifty years." Oh, no. What is he rambling on about? Keith fears that he may be looking at himself in a few years' time. Unable to endure this any longer, Keith asks him what he means.

The old man explains that he is thinking about the price of cheese from fifty years ago, which he recalls was much lower than it is today. Keith is somewhat taken aback by this observation. He wonders if the man truly believes that the state pension has remained at the same level over the past fifty years. Keith smiles, choosing not to delve into an explanation about inflation. After all, that's not part of his job description, and he's not inclined to educate random strangers in the grocery store.

Keith, feeling increasingly exasperated, turns his attention to the old lady at the register. It appears that she is having a difficult time. She has just been informed of the total cost of her groceries, which seems to shock her. She looks dismayed at the idea of having to pay for the items. Despite her frustration, she decides against complaining about what she seems to view as an unreasonable expectation of payment. Instead, she begins a slow and methodical search for her purse.

After some effort, she finds her purse in her bag. She then opens it and starts looking for money. The cashier, displaying patience, waits as she fumbles with her purse. The old lady's struggle to find the correct amount of cash drags on, and the cashier appears to tolerate the delay with practiced forbearance.

As the transaction proceeds, Keith, unable to tolerate the drawn-out process any longer, decides to step in and help. He notices that the old lady does not have enough money to cover her purchase. With a sense of relief at having a way to escape the tedium of the conversation about cheese, Keith discreetly adds a couple of pound coins to make up the difference. He is well versed in the principles of monetary economics but finds himself alarmed that one day he may struggle to find the right money to buy a few groceries. Finally, the old lady, now able to pay for her groceries thanks to Keith's assistance, leaves the store. Keith, feeling a mixture of satisfaction and relief, prepares to continue with his day.

Now it is the turn of the elderly man to make his purchase. He approaches the checkout with his cheese and a few other items. Unlike the old lady, he doesn't need to search for his purse; he simply reaches into his trouser pockets. Keith assumes this transaction will be straightforward, but he quickly realizes that his optimism was misplaced.

The elderly man presents a couple of vouchers. One of the vouchers is outdated, and the other is for a discount on fish fingers, which he is not buying. Selenia, still in line and observing the situation, turns to Keith and asks why the Co-op doesn't simply lower the prices of their products instead of issuing vouchers. Keith explains that such vouchers are a form of price discrimination. They attract lower-income customers who are willing to use them, while higher-income customers, who don't bother with vouchers, end up paying more. Selenia, who is both intelligent and perceptive, quickly grasps the logic behind this practice.

Soon, the elderly man completes his purchase and leaves the store. Selenia, efficient as ever, uses her mobile phone app to pay for her groceries and exits the shop within seconds. Keith, meanwhile, is left with his own purchases, which total eleven pounds and twenty-three pence. As an economist, he is irked by these pre-set prices and is tempted to negotiate: "I'll give you ten pounds for the lot." However, he decides against it, feeling a twinge of sympathy for the cashier, and pays the full amount without protest.

Before leaving the shop, Keith is struck by a thought and casually asks the cashier, "Gosh, isn't that girl gorgeous? Do you know who she is?" The cashier smiles and responds, "You think she's gorgeous? You should see her twin sister." Keith is taken aback, wondering how the twins could possibly be more beautiful if they are indeed twins. He considers whether he should share this incident with Selenia, who, as far as he knows, does not have a twin sister. He doubts that he will mention it to her, as such a disclosure might not be well-received by the university, which might not approve of staff making personal comments about students. As Keith leaves the shop, he reflects on how unfair it is that he was born twenty years too early to ask Selenia out for a meal. He ponders the university's formal policy on relationships between staff and students and decides that he is less concerned about it than he probably should be.

There is a brief opportunity for Keith to grab a quick snack at the staff canteen before his afternoon class begins. He feels fortunate as he finds himself second in the queue at the canteen. The only person ahead of him is a woman he recognizes vaguely. She has recently arrived in Barmouth and is named Dawn. Keith is surprised that he remembers her name at all, given the university's custom of not formally introducing new staff members.

At Barmouth Business School, the usual practice is that new staff members are not introduced to anyone directly. Instead, their names and faces are learned through a process of academic osmosis, where existing staff gradually become aware of new colleagues through casual interactions and observations. Dawn, a sociologist, is currently inspecting the vegetables used in the soup, trying to discover if they are organic. Keith is reminded of his own background. Growing up in a modest household, his father maintained a large allotment where he was accustomed to eating organic vegetables long before the term "organic" became popular. As an economist, Keith is aware that organic vegetables often require significantly more of the earth's resources compared with conventionally grown ones. He contemplates whether he should mention that the higher prices of organic produce reflect the increased resources needed for their production. He knows that if the world adopted organic farming on a large scale, it could lead to widespread hunger due to the increased costs that many people could not afford. He considers pointing out that organic farming might be a delightful hobby for those like Dawn who can afford it, but might not be practical or sustainable for everyone. Despite these thoughts, Keith decides to remain silent and simply smiles.

Keith now moves towards the serving counter, where Joan is stationed to hand out soup. Joan, who has served him for the last fifteen years, looks up from her duties. With her thick Hungarian accent, she informs Keith that the soup "needs a little salt and pepper, sir." Keith, though appreciative of the suggestion, is inclined to ignore it. This is because Joan has made the same recommendation for every bowl of soup she has served him over the years, regardless of its actual taste.

Joan is wearing her usual heavy makeup, which includes the same rouge and lipstick she always uses. However, something catches Keith's eye. Joan is winking at him, or so he initially thinks. Upon closer inspection, Keith realizes that she isn't winking at all. Instead, she has only applied mascara to one eye. Keith finds himself struggling to suppress a laugh.

He decides to ask Joan a question about the sausage rolls. "Do you think that the sausage rolls are (a) fresher than last week, (b) about the same as last week, (c) staler than last week, or (d) a misshapen Cornish pasty?" Joan looks at him with confusion and asks, "I beg your pardon, sir?" Realizing his attempt at humour may have missed the mark, Keith quickly responds, "Oh, it's nothing, thank you, Joan," and moves on, still thinking about his incomplete test questions.

It's time for Keith's last class of the day, which is more of a lecture than a typical class. Today, he has to speak to a group of eighty students. Although this is a sizable number, it is relatively small compared to some of his larger classes. The largest group he has ever taught was a staggering six hundred and ninety-seven students. For that class, he had to give the same lecture three times a week. It was still preferable to standing on Barmouth common with a megaphone.

Keith looks out over the sea of faces before him. Some students look eager and attentive, but he notices one student at the back who appears to be asleep. Initially, it seems like the student is waking up, but then Keith realizes it's just a false alarm. The student is merely turning over in their seat. By the end of this lecture, Keith hopes that his students will have a good understanding of the relationship between monetary policy and unemployment. He is realistic, though, and knows that it is possible only a few students will grasp the concept fully.

Some of the students find it hard to concentrate but it isn't easy for Keith to concentrate on his lecture either. He is distracted by the front row, where several things catch his attention. One of these distractions is a girl who always sits right at the front. She has long legs and is wearing a very short skirt. Keith knows that being twenty years old, she probably doesn't care about what he thinks. However, even though he is older, he is still aware of her appearance. He tries hard to ignore this distraction and stay focused on his lecture.

Another distraction is quite different. This distraction is also a woman. She is wearing a short skirt and a very tight top that shows off her figure. Her figure is a living testimonial to fish and chips and jam roly-poly. He pictures her ordering a double Big Mac, extra fries, and a diet Coke. Keith swims regularly. Why does he now start thinking about water wings? Perhaps if he could view her through the wrong end of a telescope, things might seem different.

In the past, seeing a woman with a substantial figure would have been unusual. Now, it's so common that only something really extraordinary can capture attention. An email he received recently didn't help him focus on monetary policy. A friend had sent him a joke about his mother-in-law. The joke was that she was so big she got run over. The driver said he had enough room to go around her, but he didn't have enough petrol.

Despite his tendency to see the funny side of everything, Keith feels that there are serious issues with obesity. Although more women are becoming obese, men are also affected, and the problem is growing rapidly. The National Health Service is under a lot of pressure because of this issue. If healthcare were private, people with obesity would have to pay for their own treatments.

Instead, overweight people are adding extra costs for everyone else. This is just one example of the complex problems that economists deal with. Keith is relieved that he doesn't have to discuss this topic today, especially with the distracting audience in the front row.

Another distraction is a girl in the audience who looks quite frighteningly powerful. She has muscles in places where Keith does not even have places. Recently, he had visited a swimming pool where the Health and Fitness club was advertising a talk. The talk was titled: "Do strong, muscular men make placid husbands?" Keith had been tempted to add a note underneath that said, "I don't know, but I suspect strong, muscular women do."

The lecture passes without incident and before heading home, he stops by the library. The excellent staff there wish him a good afternoon. Still preoccupied with finishing the multiple-choice paper, he finds himself wanting to reply: "Do you think I look (a) very tired, (b) somewhat tired, (c) not very tired at all, or (d) do you think you should call the undertaker now?"

Keith thinks about how libraries have changed over the last thirty or forty years. When he was a student, he would study in a university library that was very quiet. You could hear a pin drop because everyone was focused and studying alone. Now, university libraries are much different. Students often work in groups, and there is a lot of talking. People discuss their ideas and work together to solve problems. Keith likes that students can collaborate and share ideas, but he is also worried about group assignments. He thinks that when students work together on projects and turn in joint work, it can create problems. Some students might not do much work and just let others do everything. This can be frustrating for those who are trying hard and want to learn because they end up doing all the work for the group.

Keith knows that teamwork is important for jobs, and companies want graduates who can work well with others. But he believes that too much group work can be unfair and might stop some students from fully learning and developing their own skills. One of his students, named Megi, had stayed up all night to do the work for another student who hadn't done anything. This made Keith feel bad because he could see how unfair it was for Megi to have to do all the work alone.

He also felt sad that the change in the library's atmosphere made one of his favourite jokes no longer funny. The joke goes like this: a man walks into a library and approaches the librarian. He speaks in a loud and cheerful voice, saying, "Three bags of fish and chips, please." The librarian is shocked and quietly tells him, "Sir, this is a library." The man replies in a whisper, "Oh sorry, sorry, three bags of fish and chips, please."

This joke was only funny because it played on the idea that libraries are usually very quiet places where you shouldn't speak loudly. Keith thinks that now, with the libraries being noisier, younger people wouldn't get the joke because they are used to the louder environment and don't understand how quiet libraries used to be.

The trip home is taking longer than the trip to work. A thick fog has settled in, making it hard to see. The traffic on the motorway is moving slowly because of the poor visibility. As he drives, he squints through the fog and notices a flashing sign ahead. At first, he thinks the sign might be warning about an accident or a closed lane. As he slows down even more to get a better look, he finally reads what the sign says. It says "FOG." How useful How would he have known otherwise? Despite the fog he arrives home safely.

Although Keith tries to keep up friendships, he often spends his evenings at home by himself. He is very introverted, so that he feels a strong need for quiet time alone, especially after a long day. During his workday, he has to talk and interact with many people, which can be exhausting for him. Sometimes, to relax, he will put on some music at home. But there are times when even music feels like too much, and he just wants complete silence to feel calm again.

Many of his friends are the opposite; they are very extroverted. They feel more energized and happier when they are around other people. After a busy day, they don't want to be alone—they want to go out and spend time with others. Occasionally, one of these friends will invite Keith to hang out in the evening. While he appreciates their invitations, he often feels the need to turn them down, especially during the school term when he is very busy. He tries to be polite when he declines, as he prefers to spend his free time recharging quietly at home.

Keith feels frustrated when people assume that, because he is introverted, he must also be shy. But this isn't true at all. He has no trouble approaching people and starting conversations when he needs to. In fact, he finds interacting with others an important and sometimes even enjoyable part of his job. However, he can only handle this kind of interaction for so long before he needs to be alone. That time alone helps him regain his energy. The only exception to this rule is when he occasionally gets chance to spend time with someone special like Selenia — he feels differently about spending time with her.

Some of Keith's friends who aren't teachers have a hard time understanding how he, as an introvert, can stand in front of an audience of three hundred students and lecture with ease. They think it must be hard for him. But actually, he finds it easier to speak to a large audience than to teach a small group of just six people. He enjoys the energy he feels from a big crowd and finds it exciting. Once the lecture is over, though, he looks forward to being by himself, enjoying the peace and quiet that helps him feel balanced again.

After finishing his meal, Keith decides to check his email. As he does so, he once again thinks about how people often say that emails are great for saving trees. They believe that because emails reduce the need for paper, it helps protect forests. But Keith sees things differently. He has explained this to his students many times. He points out that if the need for something is reduced, less of it will be produced. For example, if people don't buy as many tomatoes, farmers will plant fewer tomato plants. In the same way, if we stop using as much paper, fewer trees will be planted to make that paper. Keith finds it a bit sad because he really likes trees. To him, emails reducing the demand for paper could mean that fewer trees are planted, which might not be as helpful to the environment as people think.

Although Keith often finds reading emails to be very boring—like counting the spots on his wallpaper—he genuinely enjoys receiving messages from former students who share updates about their lives.

He notices that many students graduate with degrees in subjects like Welsh Mythology or needlework, and after finishing their studies, they sometimes struggle to find jobs. In contrast, students who study economics usually have a better chance of landing interesting and well-paying jobs after they graduate. These economics graduates can even afford to shop at Waitrose. Hearing from his former students brings him much pleasure. It's nice for him to see how they are doing and what paths they have taken in their careers, especially when they share good news about their successes.

Most of the time, he just deals with the usual stuff on his computer and eventually turns it off. He tries to read different kinds of books so he doesn't get stuck thinking about the same thing. Sometimes, he reads a bit of poetry. Keith didn't learn much poetry in school, but one poem has always stuck with him. Since he was fifteen, he has been trying to memorize it. The poem is called *The Highwayman*. It tells the story of an 18th century highway robber and his love for Bess, who is the daughter of a landlord. He speaks to Bess at the inn before his planned robbery:

"Yet, if they press me sharply and harry me through the day,

Then look for me by moonlight,

Watch for me by moonlight,

I'll come to thee by moonlight, though hell should bar the way."

Keith is no marauding adventurer, but he wonders whether he could love a woman in that way, promise her that kind of devotion. Bess is later tied up by soldiers who have put a musket beneath her breast. The ill treatment of women by men is not a problem confined to the twenty first century. The soldiers then wait for the highwayman to return to the inn and to come into the trap they have prepared. But Bess sacrifices her life to warn him.

Tlot-tlot, in the frosty silence! Tlot-tlot, in the echoing night!

Nearer, he came and nearer. Her face was like a light.

Her eyes grew wide for a moment; she drew one last deep breath,

Then her finger moved in the moonlight,

Her musket shattered the moonlight,

Shattered her breast in the moonlight and warned him—with her death.

The highwayman later learns of what has happened to the one he loves.

Back, he spurred like a madman, shrieking a curse to the sky,

With the white road smoking behind him and his rapier brandished high.

Blood red were his spurs in the golden noon; wine-red was his velvet coat;

When they shot him down on the highway,

Down like a dog on the highway,

And he lay in his blood on the highway, with a bunch of lace at his throat.

After a long day filled with work and chores, he finally gets into bed. As he lies there, he reflects on the poem. He feels that, in some ways, a common robber might be more honourable than some of the people who are supposed to help others. He thinks of Bess and wonders if a woman could ever love him like that.

CHAPTER TWO: CONFRONTING MORTALITY

"A professor is someone who talks in other peoples' sleep."

- W.H. Auden

Tuesday morning presents a dilemma for Keith. There are no early classes on his timetable, so a lie in to recover fully from the rigours of the previous day is a temptation. On the other hand, with a little discipline, he can get it in an early morning swim before the journey to Barmouth. The feelings of virtue associated with the swim are just sufficient to get him out of bed.

He takes his customary morning shower, shaves, dresses himself and takes a quick look at his appearance in the mirror. Although his face is hairless, he still retains hair on his head. This is important to him, for he retains a streak of vanity. When he was a boy, he had very blond, almost white, hair. It had darkened to a more normal blond over the years and now, the grey streaks are appearing with a vengeance. Keith tries to tell himself that the grey hair simply makes him look distinguished and insists on thinking of himself as basically blond, though he acknowledges that the proportion of hair to air is slowly changing. The bald patch is far enough to the back that he doesn't have to think about it much. At least the hair colour is a match for his blue eyes. He still feels reasonably good about himself, whilst recognizing that a half hour trip to the gym each week would not be sufficient to cause a stream of women to beat a path to his door. The laughter lines around the eyes don't help to create an impression of youthfulness, but he hopes that this is offset by the basically cheerful disposition that caused them.

He dresses. He tends to favour clothes that are mostly black, grey or blue. Blue brings out his eye colour. The style of his clothes can best be described as Marks and Spencer. It will do to face the world, although he doesn't think that George Clooney will be beside himself with envy.

By 8.30 he has turned the lock on the front door of his pension fund, he is out of the house and on his way to the pool. He feels that swimming is good exercise and will, at least marginally, help him to obtain that sylph like figure that was always been tantalisingly out of reach. Ben is about to get into his car, and they meet briefly. Ben is a young carpenter who frequently does jobs for Keith. It isn't that Keith has no time to do odd jobs. It's just that his relative abilities lie elsewhere. He can teach, but changing a light bulb may well result in the need to get a builder in to put up a new ceiling.

Ben disagrees with Keith's analysis of the benefits of swimming, and a conversation takes place that is not dissimilar to others who have gone before.

"Off to the pool again, Keith?"

"Your powers of observation and deduction are remarkable, Ben. All you had to go on was the towel around my neck and the swimming trunks in my hand. It's great to have such a smart neighbour. Are you sure you wouldn't be well advised to do a degree at Barmouth?"

"I can't afford it. It's not the cost of the tuition. People actually need carpenters. Why don't you ever listen to your clever neighbour? How can swimming possibly keep you in shape? Have you never looked at a whale?"

Keith smiles at him. Perhaps he should use this neighbourly comment with his students and explain that correlation is not causation. Could it be that swimming is not the primary cause of the whale's somewhat bloated shape? Some of his students have trouble with the distinction between causation and correlation. Maybe this neighbourly chat will help. The illustration he usually uses to highlight the distinction concerns Barmouth beach. It has been observed that when there are more ice creams sold, more people drown. He invites his students to consider whether we can therefore prevent some loss of life through drowning by banning ice cream sales. Only some of the students see that the reason for both the higher rates of drowning and the increased ice cream sales is the weather. Warmer weather increases ice cream sales and causes more people to go swimming in the sea. Today, he will try the whale illustration and see if it works better.

He enters the leisure centre and buys a ticket for his swim. Now that he is fifty-four, he dreads more and more that the girl at the desk will think him a senior and offer him a reduced rate senior citizen ticket. Such an event would make it harder for him to maintain the conviction, shared only by him, that he looks less than half a century old. "Vanity of vanities, saith the preacher, all is vanity". Still, sixty is the new fifty, right? More and more frequently, he finds himself looking into the future. Often, it does nothing to cheer him, although he recalls hopefully the words of Bob Hope when the comedian reached seventy.

"I still chase women – but only downhill."

Last year he had gone to the cinema and, on checking his change, found that there had been a mistake. He had been given too much. That is, until with his lightning-fast mathematical brain, he realised the teller had given him a senior ticket. Outrageous. How could such a ridiculous error occur? He is defying the passing of the years, is he not? He is being sensible about his increasing years. Only a few years ago, he decided that he was twenty-eight. Now, he is happy to acknowledge that he is thirty-six. This ambivalence about himself and approaching senility is distracting him ever more frequently.

When Keith started university lecturing in his early twenties, he was asked what arrangements he wished to make about his pension. He had thought the question irrelevant. He had no plans to be really old, say twenty-eight or thirty. How his perspective has altered. Sometimes he feels that life is good. At other times he does not think it can last much longer.

October in Southern England is often beautiful. The weather is pleasantly warm. Sitting in his garden at that time of the year, with a book in his hand and the sun on his back is such a delight. Yet there is still a background awareness that the cold dark days of November and December are not far away. That's how he has begun to feel about his life in general, privileged to be able to enjoy the October days of life and, at the same time, increasingly conscious that life's winter is fast approaching when he may be unable to do things which now make him feel that life is worthwhile. He can enjoy October on his own. When November and December come will he feel a sense of loneliness as never before?

He enters the locker room, undresses, puts on his costume and deposits his clothes in locker number 182. He picks this locker whenever it is free because the number is easy for him to remember. It's the age that Keith feels on completing his swim. Early mornings are a good time to swim since there is lane swimming available and the pool is not crowded.

Within a few minutes, he is in the water. Twenty lengths of a slow crawl are sufficient to quieten his conscience about taking exercise, although it does require a pause to recover every five or six lengths. The pause is not just to recover. It is strategic. Even such a simple event as a swimming session has its potential for disaster. He has to be careful not to be seen being overtaken by seventy-year-old ladies doing the breast stroke. Even more problematic is the possibility of a conversational nightmare. During one of his pauses, he looks up and, to his despair, sees that the Chinese guy has arrived. The Chinese guy is friendly and always ready for a chat. Keith is no racist. The problem is the accent. This particular Chinese accent is so strong that he can understand nothing of what is being said and is too embarrassed to admit it.

"Hwa Naa aso kwa ha na".

Keith smiles and hopes that he hasn't just been told that his friend has broken his arm.

"Water cold today."

What? Could he be hearing this correctly? Keith understands the second sentence. These are the first words of his swimming companion that he has ever understood. He smiles, agrees enthusiastically and makes an inane remark comparing the water temperature with other occasions in a desperate attempt to communicate that he has comprehended the last sentence. He then resumes thrashing at the water in his inelegant style before any further incomprehensible discussion can take place.

Showering and changing at lightning speed lest his Chinese friend catch him with additional incomprehensibility, he makes for the car and then heads towards Barmouth. He is careful these days to keep close to the speed limit. Only a few months ago, he had been caught speeding. He was mortified. His Lexus had warned him of approaching speed cameras, but only those of the fixed variety. A policeman with a hand-held device had picked him up, doing 35 miles an hour at a thirty-mile speed limit. The fact that the roads were entirely deserted was no defence. The police had offered him a choice: either £100 fine and three points on his licence or attending a four-hour speed awareness course at a cost of £90. At first, he decided that his time was worth more than £2.50 per hour, but the lure of a clean driving licence and a possibly lower annual insurance premium had convinced him to take the course. When he had attended the course, he found that a large number of other miscreants had clearly reached the same conclusion. There was a mix of men and women, older and younger, affluent and poorer. Some of them could easily have been his students. Fortunately, none of them was. The age range was, perhaps, no surprise. The speed camera is no respecter of persons. The course, however, did surprise him. He had found it quite instructive. At one point, the instructor had said that someone was seriously injured on Hampshire's roads every five days. It was all that he could do not to respond with, "And he is getting fed up with it".

Given his recent experience, he checks his speedometer and makes sure that he is driving within the speed limit. He is in the slow lane, travelling at seventy miles an hour, and a stream of vehicles overtakes him. Even if technology makes some jobs redundant in future, the guys running the speed awareness course have little to fear. Seventy seems to Keith to be adequate. Even at that speed, an accident can make a serious mess of a frail human body.

Reflecting yet again on his mortality, he wondered again how he had gotten started on his career. To him, it was amazing that he had come to be lecturing in economics at all. He had grown up on a council estate in a family where no one had ever been to university. Indeed, his parents had both left schools remarkably early to look after younger brothers and sisters. Father grew up in a family of fourteen, so getting to the end of the day was an achievement in itself. Often, he would be sent to buy a bag of broken biscuits, and this would constitute a significant part of the day's nourishment of the family. Both mother and father had been so very kind to him but he had received from them no encouragement to pursue a university education. They barely knew what a university was. Somehow, he passed at eleven years old, an exam that meant he finished up at a grammar school for boys from eleven to eighteen years old. Being far more interested in football than other forms of knowledge, he had managed to pass a few exams at sixteen. Lacking any alternative, he stayed on to do A levels, but what subjects should he choose? He was only sixteen, but he was cunning. With almost any subject he picked, he would be behind others in the class before the A level course even began. Such was his enthusiasm for football. Study had come at too high an opportunity cost. However, there were two subjects, economics and economic history, that had not been taught lower down the school. He could pick these and begin on what had later come to be called in the jargon, a level playing field. His third choice was German. Well, yes, he was behind some others, but he could say Jawohl and Berlin, even if not much else. The time had passed so quickly, and soon his friends were making University choices. Keith, like his parents, barely knew what a university was, but the school system was such that they all filled in their forms during class time. Thus, he barely made a decision to apply. Rather, he was simply sucked up by the school's system.

For many, grammar schools were regarded as elitist. For Keith, they had probably rescued him from a life working on the dustcart. At the time, the cost to a student of university education was tolerable, even to a boy from a council estate background. Tuition was free, and grants were given on the basis of the income of the parent. How different for his students nowadays. Many of them now expect to leave with debts of around £40-50,000, having paid something around £30,000 for tuition fees. At that time, about five percent of British 18-year-olds went to university. Now, the figure is around 45 percent, and the cost of free tuition is enormous. It is Keith's view, although given his job, he rarely articulates it, that it could still be free. To make this possible, access should be restricted to those with the mental capacity to gain from it. There are far too many Andy Wildes and far too many universities trying to teach them. He carefully avoids considering whether Barmouth is one of the "far too many universities".

Arriving later than he had the day before, he expects to struggle to find a precious car parking space. There has been a proliferation of the enormous 4 x 4s in recent years so any available space often feels small. Why do people buy these enormous things? Maybe they want to compete with his father in family size. Ah, there is an empty space behind a Range Rover. Oh no. It isn't a free space at all. Now he is close to it he can see that what he thought was a space is taken by a smart car. It is so small it was hiding behind the Range Rover. Why do people buy these tiny things? Perhaps the advantage is that you can pick it up and throw it over the hedge rather than use up a space? When, almost in despair he finds a place. He feels very fortunate.

Feeling energised by his earlier swim, he decides to use the stairs rather than the lift. His office is on floor six, so the decision to walk is not to be taken lightly. At least in his building, walking is often just as fast as using one of the two lifts. This is especially true today, for one of the lifts is still out of action as it has been for two weeks. The notice apologising for the inconvenience includes at the bottom the words:

"WORKING TOGETHER TO IMPROVE OUR CAMPUS"

Working in order to improve the campus does not seem to include fixing the lift. The queue includes young, fit looking students who would rather wait forever than take even one flight of stairs, up or down. It would use up precious seconds, during which time they would not be able to tap furiously those life-saving messages on their mobile phones.

He had observed many times that pressing the lift button never seemed to reduce the sum of the two numbers. Now, there is only one number, and it is changing very slowly. Since Keith can manage not to tap a mobile phone for several minutes at a time, when necessary, for him it is definitely going to be the stairs today. Once, we might have run up six flights at one go. Now, he can only manage to walk as far as floor four without stopping. At that point he pauses, not for the first time, to catch his breath. Others using the stairs pass him, so he finds something interesting to look at out of the window and smiles meaninglessly at them whilst holding his stomach in.

He is pretty sure that there is an unarticulated and informal arrangement that the less well thought of the staff member, the higher the floor to which that staff member is allocated. His office is on floor six, the top floor. There should have been seven or eight floors. While the University is poor, the Business School is rich and highly profitable. However, the bean counters had decided in their wisdom to limit the building to six floors, resulting in an inevitable shortage of accommodation. This included the need to repeat lectures several times a week as the lecture theatres were of an inadequate size, and more recently, the placement of two or three staff members into an office that had been designed for one. The place had been too small on the day it opened. Planning for the future is not one of the strengths of the University of Barmouth.

When Keith reaches floor four for his break, he sees a sign on the window sill. Reading it could be today's excuse to get his breath back. However, reading it doesn't take long. It says just a few words.

"BROKEN WINDOW. DANGER. BEWARE."

Keith had travelled a great deal in Europe and had noticed a fairly consistent response to things which were broken. In Eastern Europe, they were usually left broken. In Western Europe, they were fixed. In England, a sign would appear saying that something was broken. Easier and cheaper than fixing the problem, Keith supposed.

Inevitably, there is a trickle of late students, apologising with miserable excuses about missed buses etc. He wishes he was brave enough to do what a former teacher, Professor Evans did. He would lock the door behind him when he entered the room and then unlock it when he left at the end. There is only one time a student has ever offered him an explanation for lateness that he could appreciate. It was from a girl.

"I am very sorry, but the man who was following me walked so slowly."

He had believed her. She was French. When the class is finally underway Keith uses examples from current events to illustrate the principles, he wants his students to understand. He recalled being a student himself. On the rare occasions that his lecturers did this it would really aid understanding and occasionally even produce in him an intellectual orgasm. However, illustrating economic events with reference to examples and people has its problems. The memory of an eighteen-year-old is necessarily short. Even talking about the recession of 2008, so vivid in Keith's memory, doesn't work. The 18-year-old student is too young to know or care. As an illustration, 2008 is about as updated as a reference to the sailing of the Spanish Armada. Soon this will be true of the events surrounding covid.

Afterward the class Keith gets to speak to the head of business department about Carrie's cheating. Derek is an ex-lawyer and is familiar with all the university's rules.

"Actually, it isn't the end of the world for her. It is a first offence. It will be treated as a failed paper. She will simply have to sit the exam again. Of course, a second offence is a whole new ball game. Send her to me, and I will deal with her."

Keith is relieved that he will be able to reassure her that she can put this foolishness behind her if she is sensible from now on.

In his second lecture, he decides to try the whale example. To begin with, a homely illustration about whales and swimming would help establish the idea that because two things were connected, it did not prove causation. The students seem to get the point, so he tries a much more difficult illustration directly related to economics. Increases in land prices go together with increases in house prices. However, rising land prices do not cause higher house prices as so many people think. It is rather that when demand pushes up house prices, the inevitable increased competition among builders for the land results in a rise in the price of land. He looks at the group before him. Oh gosh, some of them now think that an increase in the demand for housing makes whales fatter.

After the lecture, there is a chance to catch up on a few other things. Keith has several students to see and a couple of references to write for those in their final year. One reference is straightforward enough. The tutee is a sensible, solid student who will do well in his chosen profession. The other one is of a very different order. Barry Gold has claims to a place in the Guinness book of records as the laziest student ever to grace an English University, even though the competition from Barmouth students alone is fierce. Eight weeks into Barry's first term, the student had knocked Keith's door asking for a copy of a handout that he had not picked up at the lecture.

Keith: "Which handout is this?"

Barry: "The one you gave out at the last lecture."

Keith: "I didn't give out a handout then."

Barry: "Yes, you did; you must have forgotten."

Keith: "I rather think I would have remembered."

Barry: "You are Dr Dan Billings, aren't you?"

Oh goodness, nearly at the end of the term, and he doesn't know what his lecturer looks like.

Now Keith has to produce a reference for this idle moron. Keith thinks very carefully and then begins to type. The days are long gone when he could hand write and ask a typist to make it look like a professional document. Computers had arrived with a promise of an easier workload. In fact, they had simply replaced secretarial support and increased the lecturer's workload. He types his carefully chosen words:

"You will be very lucky to get Barry Gold to work for you."

One of the tasks Keith least enjoys is the supervision of Master students' dissertations. As part of the master's degree, the student is expected to write a ten-thousand-word original thesis under the guidance of a tutor. Ludicrously, the university thanks that 20 minutes per week is sufficient time for the lecturer to meet with the student, discuss the work, read and comment upon drafts and mark the finished assignment. The process is to begin today with a first meeting of a Chinese guy. He enters the office shyly and politely, and Keith greets him with his warmest smile.

"Hello, how can I help with your dissertation?"

"Hwa Naa aso kwa ha na".

Keith smiles and looks at him carefully. No, it isn't the lad from the swimming pool, but perhaps it's his brother. Their language is remarkably similar.

"I'm sorry, I didn't catch that."

"Hwa Naa aso kwa ha na".

Keith wonders, as he has so often in the past, what kind of English Language course such students have taken. If he was a tourist, it would be rather impressive, but he is supposed to be getting a qualification that says he has a master's level qualification in the English language. Fifteen minutes later, Keith ends the conversation.

"Good, well I think the way to proceed is for you to set these thoughts down in an email and send them to me. Then, when I have read it, I will get back to you for further discussion.

Much bowing later, the student leaves. At least Keith is confident that the student hasn't broken his arm. Waiting outside his office is Alison. She is an undergraduate, also writing a dissertation, but this is not the first time that they have discussed her progress. The timetable allowance for supervising an undergraduate dissertation is more pitiful than for a master's student. Keith thinks Alison to be an attractive girl, but his awareness of her attractiveness is about to be reinforced. Before their discussion begins, Mike Andrews knocks the door and enters. He takes a quick look at Alison and asks Keith if they could have a word immediately. He apologises to Alison and steps outside of his office. He soon realises the urgency of Mike's visit. Mike has a story to tell about something that happened to him three months ago, a story Mike has only just remembered. It clearly won't wait. Keith listens patiently. They have been friends for many years, so nothing of this comes as a surprise. Just as Keith is about to return to his office, Mike asks who the girl is that he has just seen. Keith explains that she is his supervisee.

"Are they really giving you a positive allowance for talking to her? It should be a negative one!"

Maybe the people who decided upon the allowances for supervision of projects have a case after all.

Alison has always been conservatively dressed. Today she is wearing a boat neck jumper and jeans without holes. The discussion on her project concludes, and she leans forward to put her notes into her bag. The boat neck jumper is quite loose and gapes forward alarmingly as she spends a while positioning her papers. It becomes very obvious to Keith that, conservatively dressed as she is, she has no underwear under her jumper. Alison is quite unconscious of having made this revelation, and Keith finds it all the more disturbing as a result. It takes him several seconds to avert his eyes. He often sees female students in lectures and classes dressed to tell everyone, "Look at me; I have legs and breasts." Such displays leave him largely unmoved. With Alison's unconscious movements, he realises that although he is old enough to be her father, he is acutely aware that, at least for the present, he is not so old that his male instincts are in any way diminished.

When she has gone, he reflects upon the changes in culture that have occurred in recent years. The increased awareness of how badly women have been treated by men is appearing all around the campus. Willingness by staff to have students in their offices is decreasing, and more and more staff/student discussions are taking place in communal areas. This is fine for academic matters, but Keith is aware that this arrangement reduces student willingness to discuss more private things. In some institutions, he has heard of groups of staff being encouraged to take separate trains and planes to conferences, stay in separate hotels and not have meals together. This saddens Keith hugely. For many years, he has kept his hands to himself and his trouser zipped up. Is it so unreasonable to expect other men to do the same? He is glad, though, that no one has made accusations of impropriety against him, accusations that would be hard to deny even though completely false.

The next student is Andrew. He is a bright, hard-working student, and Keith has no idea what he wants. It turns out that Andrew is in some distress. He has chosen a dissertation topic on an area of sociology about which Keith knows nothing. Andrew is not getting on well with the dissertation supervisor, who keeps offering contradictory advice. How can Keith help a student when the subject is such that he is out of his depth himself? Asking Andrew to wait in his office, he finds Angela, an able and kindly sociology lecturer. She is willing to help Andrew immediately. With relief, Keith passes Andrew on to Angela.

Peter Fischer is next through the office door. Keith barely knows him. He looks nervous and uncertain.

Peter: "I have been talking to my friend Carrie about her exam cheating."

Keith: "I am sorry, but I can't possibly discuss this with you even if she is a friend of yours. These things are confidential."

Peter: "Yes, I understand, but I am here because I was also caught cheating, although in a different exam."

This is beginning to feel like an epidemic. Cheating in exams is quite rare. Plagiarism in coursework is rather more common, but generally, an exam session will pass off without any such case, so two instances during the same exam period are very unusual. It sounds a similar case to Carrie, and so Keith promises to refer it to the appropriate head of department. He is fortunate to find Derek very quickly, expecting Derek to react much as he had with Carrie. It is not to be.

"What this student has not told you is that this is his second offence, so this is extremely serious. Leave it with me. Just tell him he must come and see me. I will deal with it."

Keith leaves with the feeling that this student may well be removed from the University.

He is worn out by the conversations of the morning and is happy to have lunch on his own. Today it's a quick pub sandwich and a pint, anything to get away from the academic fug for half an hour and to think about or read about something else.

On his way to the pub, he passes one of the staff canteens. There is no point stopping there. It is closed anyway. He recalls the story. Sometime after he had arrived in Barmouth, it became clear, even to the directorate, that the staff canteen facilities were grossly inadequate. After some, doubtless lengthy, consideration with highly paid external consultants to assist, they had decided to include a Staff Canteen which comfortably seated about 20-25 people. This could be argued to have been surprising given that it was to accommodate 4-500 staff. Of course, there was also an open seating area outside the canteen. This area was about ten times the size of the canteen itself, unheated, and included a huge pair of north-facing double-doors which swung to admit a freezing howling gale coming directly from The Urals, plus an occasional blast of horizontal sleet. It was known to staff as Siberia. The fact that the Staff Canteen could easily have been extended to at least five times the size to use up some of this useless space seemed to have been lost upon the Senior Post Holders, known with no affection at all as SPH.

Apart from the building itself, the serving lady has her own particular charms. There is only one person to run it because the SPH had decided that the Staff Canteen only needed sufficient counter space to serve one person at a time. With 500 staff, this seems so obvious a conclusion that one wonders how it could ever have been called into question.

Doreen had been specially recruited for the job. She combines the IQ of an amoeba living in a puddle on Saturn with the disposition of Captain Bligh and the energy levels of a tree sloth. She also nurses a deep and visceral loathing of the teaching staff. She makes it her life's work to make each and every one of them wait as long as humanly possible for whatever service they are unwise enough to request. It takes her between six and eight minutes to provide a helping of salad, a slice of quiche and a coffee. Hence, at best, she serves around eight people an hour. Many had spent their whole lunch hour standing in Doreen's queue. This incensed the staff and, eventually, the directorate agreed to consider the matter. After lengthy deliberation, they decided that the solution was clear. The problem was that too many members of staff wished to eat their lunch at lunchtime. This ridiculous and inexcusable staff behaviour created excess demand and placed a pressure on people like Doreen. The way to ensure that no queue built up outside the Staff Canteen was to close it at lunchtimes. The doors were bolted; Doreen ate her own lunch there in peace and quiet, and a sign on the door read, "This canteen is closed between 12 am and 2 pm." It remains closed to this day. As an economist, he is not entirely convinced that the geniuses in the directorate got things right. When there is excess demand for a service, to eliminate the supply is not the obvious solution. But wait, perhaps other problems in Barmouth could be tackled in this way. Keith sees all kinds of possibilities of extending this principle to other problem areas. Sometimes, there is excess demand for some of the lifts. The problem could be eliminated by closing them. There is not enough room in the car parks for all staff cars. They could be permanently shut. There are inadequate facilities for teaching students. Perhaps they can be banned from classes. He must raise his ideas at a future staff meeting.

At the pub, the attempt to give his mind something else to dwell on is a failure. As he begins to peruse his copy of the Times, he is unable to avoid overhearing a conversation on the table next to him. Two ladies are having a discussion, and it quickly becomes clear that one of them has a son of about seventeen.

"My son was even saying he might not go to university at all."

"What made him say that?"

"He is worried about the debt he might end up with. He has a few friends who are wondering if they will ever be able to repay the loans they have taken out."

"What did you say to him?"

"I told him that you are only young once, so you should go on and enjoy yourself."

Oh, how depressing. Another youngster is bound for £50,000 of debt without the least understanding or insight into the decision he is taking. In his experience, Keith feels that young people often ignore the advice of their elders. In some cases, that's exactly what they should do.

One of the most eccentric lecturers in the business school is Joe Carter. For reasons that no one seems to know, he has very few lectures, perhaps one a term. The best guess for this tiny amount of student contact is that his lectures are so bad that any greater frequency would lead to a student riot. However, they are something of an event, for he brings a pistol along and, at some point in each lecture, points it up into the balcony area of the lecture theatre and fires a blank. If this is to make a point, none of the students has the remotest idea what it is. Keith is hearing some news spreading around the building of this morning's events in Joe's lecture. The students had decided to make their own point and a few of them had secreted themselves in the balcony before the lecture began. As Joe fired his pistol, a dead pigeon came out of the balcony onto the floor in front of him. Apparently, he was the only person in the room not to find this hilarious. The students reported that he looked mystified, but when he had recovered, he fired a second blank. Right on cue, a second dead pigeon hit the ground before him. He staggered out of the lecture room to wild applause. Although Keith finds such occurrences beyond ludicrous, there is a little corner of his mind where he rejoices that in such a conformist world, such eccentricity is not as dead as the pigeons.

In his afternoon class, the discussion centres on the idea of business efficiency, and Keith realises that the episode with Alison has left its effects upon him. One of his better students, Karen, has been reading about the subject beforehand. This is almost unique in Keith's experience. She has seen a variant of the story about the optimist and the pessimist. The optimist thinks the cup is half full, and the pessimist thinks the cup is half empty. Karen has read that the economist thinks that this is an inefficient waste of resources because the cup is bigger than it needs to be. Keith decides to introduce some further ideas about efficiency rather than express what is in his mind. He attempts to distinguish different kinds of efficiency. He wants to say:

"If the cup is only half full.... you probably need a different bra."

Only the brighter students leave better informed. It was ever thus.

One of the key concepts in economics is specialisation. The standard of living most of us enjoy is made possible because we each specialise in the thing; we are comparatively good at rather than trying to do everything for ourselves. In his last class of the day, Keith tries a joke to illustrate the principle.

"Men have a variety of needs, but what woman can provide for them all? A man needs a woman who will take care of his needs by ironing and mending etc, a woman who will talk with him and provide companionship, a woman who will care for his children, a woman who will meet his needs in the bedroom. Most important of all, he needs to ensure that these four women never meet one another. "

When the penny drops, it seems to be a joke that meets the approval of at least some of the students, even if the link to specialisation is a little tenuous. Although it is a joke that Keith has always appreciated, it makes him ever more wistful as he reflects how he has never known a woman who would share any of these things with him. Like many teachers, Keith is an introvert. He can entertain 300 students in a lecture theatre, and yet he is very near the introvert end of the introvert/extrovert spectrum. It is easy to speak to others when there is a structure to the interaction, as there is with lectures and classes or indeed, with individual student discussions. He seems lost, however, in an unstructured environment where he so often becomes tongue tied. He often dreams of a woman with whom he can just relax and be himself.

The department is to make a new appointment, and he has been asked to spend a half hour showing the candidates around. There are four of them, and they all look nervous. As part of the tour, he shows them the main, three hundred seat, lecture theatre. There is an entrance to it from the back so that if there is a lecture currently running, they can look into the room without disturbing the lecturer in full flow. When the five of them arrive, it becomes clear that the lecture is not a flow. It is barely a trickle. The words are slow, disjointed, dull and largely meaningless. They seem designed to fill up the time until the lecture can be respectably brought to a close. The few minutes in which they listen are acutely embarrassing. In academic circles, the lecture as a vehicle of communication is increasingly despised. No wonder. Some of its practitioners can't teach. Keith looks at the four people he is showing around. In a sane world, new appointments would be made partly on the ability to communicate to students. In the increasingly insane world of academia, an appointment is decided upon the number of articles published in journals. The articles need have no value in the real world. It does not even matter if they are never read. They simply need to have been published. Lecturing is an unimportant side activity.

According to some recent estimates, half of all jobs globally, around two billion of them, are under threat from AI and other technological advancements. Maybe this will include robots giving lectures in future. Keith thinks but doesn't say, that they won't need to be up too much to improve upon some efforts like the one they have just been listening to. Keith is aware, though, that such predictions have been made several times in the last eighty years or so and have been wildly inaccurate. Technological innovations have destroyed some existing jobs but created new ones. As Keith listens, however, he thinks that the sooner this one is destroyed, the better.

As they leave the room, he discusses the flipped classroom idea with his four potential colleagues. Flipped learning is an approach where conventional lecture-based learning is inverted. The classroom time is used for discussion, which is facilitated by teachers. The four seem positive about it. To Keith, the driver of this kind of approach had been standing before him. Lousy lecturers would prefer an approach where their incompetence is hidden. Flipped classrooms fulfil this purpose beautifully. He looks at the four aspiring lecturers and feels very old and curmudgeonly.

Keith says goodbye to the visitors and wishes them every success. He returns to his office and looks at a few more emails before leaving for home. One, he is unable to read with a straight face. All staff, he discovers, receive a bonus after twenty-five years' service and in the next year or two he will qualify. As a result, he is to receive £100! Oh, joy. At last, his services to Barmouth are recognised. He is to receive £4 for each year of service. Will he spend it all at once? Take a trip to the Caribbean? Do a further extension on his house? In fact, the bonus is worth somewhat less than £100. If he had been granted £4 at the end of each year of service, he could have invested it and turned it into more than £100. Further mathematical calculations suggest that it is still unlikely that this would have gotten him his Caribbean cruise, or even a day trip around the Isle of Wight.

Ready to go home, he finds one more student waiting to see him. Belinda is a lovely, intelligent girl who needs to do some thinking about her dissertation topic, which is about firm efficiency. It quickly becomes clear that Dan Barker is the best man to advise her. Dan has made a careful study of the topic and has written extensively about it. Dan is about the same age as Keith. He is not only highly intelligent but also a very gentle character and can quickly put students at their ease. When Keith suggests a visit to Dan, Belinda is very happy with the idea.

"Oh, yes, I like him. He is so very debonair. I will look for him tomorrow."

He closes his office to begin the slow journey home. Dan is still in his office, so Keith knocks his door and tells him of the impending visit of Belinda.

"Belinda says that she finds you very debonair."

Keith waits for the warm glow to appear on Dan's face. He is surprised when it doesn't come.

"Debonair? Debonair? I don't want to be debonair. I want to be...... dangerous."

Keith smiles. Dan is the gentlest of gentlemen. The chances of Dan being dangerous are somewhat less than Keith's chances of finding the lady of his dreams.

After he leaves Dan, before he walks down the stairs, and then he remembers something he wished to do before going home. He retraces his steps to his office. By the time he has unlocked the door, he has forgotten what he came back for. Oh, is this feeble mindedness or absent mindedness? He goes back to the top of the stairs and by now he has remembered what it was. He wanted to take a book off his shelf to look something up when he got home. Maybe this incident is an indicator of the early onset of senility?

If it is, at least he has the comfort of knowing that it hasn't got any worse in the last twenty-five years when he first noticed himself doing this kind of thing. As a young man, the stereotypical image of the absent-minded professor had always appealed to him as an ambition for which to strive. Well, he has now achieved fifty percent of that. Since he is unlikely ever to obtain the other fifty percent, he will have to accept what he already has and make the best of it.

The fog has cleared for the return journey, but the traffic queues on the motorway are considerable. At the end of the evening, the journey home is still on his mind. It seems that traffic conforms to its usual pattern. In a motorway queue, the traffic in the other lanes always moves faster. Was his life moving into the slowest lane?

As he drives home Keith Reflects on the lives of the students that he teaches. Have they made a sensible decision in coming to university, a decision which will probably involve them in an enormous debt that might take twenty or more years to pay off? His own decision, taken so long ago now, was not one that he had carefully weighed. He had arrived in academia more or less by accident. How many of those he now teaches, Keith ponders, have been similarly sucked up by the system?

At least he had graduated free of debt. Government policy towards higher education had been much more generous at that time, with a grant system covering the costs. On the other hand, perhaps many of his students will find a partner. Regretfully, this was something that had not happened to him. But he still wonders whether some of them would have been better starting a career at eighteen. Well, the decision has been made and he will do his best to give them every opportunity to gain a meaningful University qualification.

When they have graduated, few, if any, will choose a career in academic life. When, twenty years ago, he had suggested such a possibility to his students, they had unanimously said that they would not do so. Now, twenty years later, student reaction is different. They laugh at such an absurdity.

But he had not regretted his choice. At least, only occasionally. He finds it deeply satisfying when he explains a concept and the eyes of the understanding light up. He wishes that this happened more often but whenever it does, he finds it hugely rewarding.

He cannot retain friendships if he spends every evening alone. This evening, he is visiting a couple he has known for many years. He can eat with them and even, at the end of the day, take pleasure in their company. Johnny and Cleo are about his age and have several delightful teenage children. One of them, Hannah, has begun a master's dissertation in social work, a topic in which Keith has no qualifications at all. Hannah is struggling, unable to see how to structure her material into a thesis. Johnny and Cleo are both highly intelligent, but neither has had any university training and so they feel helpless to assist their daughter. Keith spends an hour with her, showing her how to create a structure for her dissertation. The subject matter is so different from economics but the methodology of constructing a dissertation is remarkably similar. Hannah feels much better at the end of the hour. Keith feels better too. Being a teacher of economics, it's easy to feel one is essentially useless. Hannah's father Johnny, by contrast, is an engineer. He fixes things, including sometimes, Keith's car or his washing machine. Keith can't fix anything mechanical. Maybe fixing a dissertation counts as a kind of fix. Cleo is a great cook, so by the end of the meal, he feels relaxed. Maybe he is too relaxed. He and Johnny play cards. He gets beaten easily at crib.

At home with his glass of milk, he thinks about the lovely Hannah. She has so much to offer during her life. If he has been able to play a tiny part in making that possible, he is delighted. What is true of his feelings for Hannah is true of his feelings towards many of his students. They are setting out at the beginning of their adult lives. His job is so rewarding. He is thrilled to be able to add to their stock of knowledge and thus improve their chances of making the world a better place. He hopes he still has many opportunities left to do something similar for others. Despite his introversion, he feels better for having spent the evening with his friends. There is time for one more glass of milk before bed.

CHAPTER THREE: MEMORIES

"Never be afraid to try something new. Noah was an amateur; the Titanic was built by professionals."

- Anon

This morning, Keith decides to let the train take the strain. The house he owns is within walking distance of the station, and this proximity adds significant value to his property and therefore, effectively, to his private pension. He shuts the door of his private pension pot and arrives at the station during the rush hour. He has to buy a ticket. His enthusiasm for online purchases is close to zero, although online purchases are the only way of operating for his students. He knows that there are three ticket windows. As ever, two of them are closed. At the one open window, a potential passenger is seeking information. It isn't entirely clear what is being said, but it sounds something like:

"How much is a return to Zurich via Stockholm with a dog on the outward part of the journey? "

The response of the rail employee is, inevitably, as long and as complex as the question, but after what seems an eternity, the enquiry is sorted out and several others, who, mercifully, just wish to buy a ticket, are dealt with. Each of them has a railcard, warrant officer token, or some kind of pensioner discount. Keith seems to be the only one paying a full contribution to the network's overheads. He quickly checks his account on his mobile. Yes, he has both an arm and a leg in his account, so he is able to afford the fare. He passes through the barrier. Waiting for the train, he catches sight of a sign:

Toilet out of order. Please use the stairs below.

He decides he isn't desperate enough to relieve himself on the stairs and would prefer to cross his legs until a more suitable opportunity presents itself. Soon, the train arrives, and it's hardly late at all. He begins the journey by looking at the emails. At least he can manage to do this on his mobile.

Keith's hold on modern technology is at best tentative. He had enjoyed the days when he could teach with just a blackboard and a piece of chalk. He had only slowly adapted to modern teaching methods. The covid era he had found to be particularly unsettling. Online classes were the only possible way of teaching at that time. Drawing diagrams at home on a computer for class members scattered across Barmouth was a nightmare. He had somehow managed it but was delighted when it was over.

One of the latest emails to arrive warms his heart more than he would have believed possible. It's from a student of about twenty years ago. It reads:

Dear Keith,

It's getting on for nearly twenty years since I left Barmouth. I wonder, do you remember our Economics and Business Studies group from all that time ago? You took us for various subjects in Economics in every year of our course. Some of us managed to stay in touch with each other after graduation, and we have decided to get together for a reunion meal on Friday evening at a pub near where you once told me you lived. It's only nineteen and a half years really, but everybody is so busy with their own lives now that it seems the best chance. If you are still living around that part of the world, we would love to have you join us if you could. Please email me if it's possible. You were my favourite teacher and I am sorry that we ever lost contact. It would be a delight for me personally if we could meet up again.

Ellie James

Does he remember that group? He certainly does. He has not had another group like it since. The huge increase in the proportion of young people entering into higher education in the last twenty or more years has resulted in a considerable fall in the average level of intelligence. This lot was very bright. Their group, he remembers telling them, was his carnival group. The jokes would fly, and the atmosphere was a remarkable mix of academic progress and great fun. He never minded their jokes, even those at his expense. They had been a hard-working group that was an absolute pleasure to teach. He has generally enjoyed his teaching career, but that particular bunch of students was special and never to be forgotten.

Does he remember Ellie in particular? Of course, he does. He remembers her as one of the brightest and a very attractive girl at the same time. He had come to know her a little because he had also supervised her project for which she had been awarded an outstanding mark. With the enormous grade inflation that had taken place in recent years, it would no longer stand out in that way now. At the time, it had been exceptional. Her eyes also stand out in his memory. They were the bluest he had ever seen. He had overcome his natural shyness and told her that he had noticed them. She had laughed and told him they were blue tinted contact lenses! Keith had never heard of such things at the time.

Now, he has an unexpected chance to meet some of that group again, and he is surprised how much he is already looking forward to it. He allows himself to acknowledge that he is especially looking forward to seeing Ellie. She had left Barmouth at the time when email was only just becoming commonplace. He thought that had she left five years later, he might have retained a contact with her and with a few others in the group. As he searches his memory, he seems to recall that she had a boyfriend, and that she was quite serious about him. Or maybe that was a different girl altogether. Keith, you poor old chap, is your memory falling apart too? Sometimes, he enters a room to do something and realises that he has completely forgotten what he had come for. By the time he has retraced his steps, though, he has often remembered. Is this something else to be concerned about, or does it happen to everyone? He makes a mental note to ask a few people. Keith is not an unfriendly guy, but there are few with whom he would share a concern about his mind falling apart, and he has no wish to confess to university colleagues that he has started to think he may be on the road to senility.

He emails a reply to Ellie from the train.

Dear Ellie,

What a joy to hear from you. Of course, I remember you and the group. It was such enormous fun teaching you all. Yes, of course, I would love to meet up with you and the other members of the group after all this time. Please send the details. I will certainly be there.

Keith

The journey to Barmouth is not a long one, but he has to change trains. He expects this to be a simple process. He steps out of the train and across to the adjoining platform, something he has done many times before. As almost always the connecting train is waiting for him. He is surprised at how empty it is. Indeed, there is no one else in his carriage at all, but the rush hour is coming to an end and he thinks little of it. Before he boards the train, he checks with a rail employee to be sure he has the right train. A rail employee is a rare sight. He makes a note to give himself 100 points in his Eye-spy book of railways. Minutes later, the train pulls away from the station.

The journey is familiar to Keith, but as he glances out of the window a few minutes later, the scenery seems unfamiliar. Has he somehow boarded the wrong train? He stands up and pulls down the window. He puts his head out and is greeted by a sight he can't quite believe. A large, very wet sponge the size of an elephant is just a few feet away from his face and getting closer by the second. He closes the window fast and is almost in time so that the washing machine that the train has entered has only a small chance to make him wet. Perhaps after all, it was not so lucky that he had found a rail employee.

The train returns from the cleaning shed to the platform and if Keith is a little damp from the train washing episode, his spirits are not damped at all. Ellie's email is still on his mind. Finally, he is on his way to Barmouth in the correct train. Lecturing is a service industry. It is essential not to miss classes so he has allowed himself plenty of time to cope with the vagaries of the railway system. There are several copies of a newspaper scattered on the seats. He picks up one copy and scans it. It takes little time to come to the conclusion that it is overpriced. Remarkable, given that it's a free paper. Maybe he should put the newspaper down and read that article on homogeneous production functions, but he can't face the idea. Ellie's email has disturbed him, albeit in a most pleasant way. Then he sees a women's magazine that someone has left on a nearby seat. He hasn't looked at anything like this since about five years ago when he was last in the doctor's waiting room. There had been an endless supply of such magazines, all of them three years or more out of date. Maybe the culture has changed in recent times and reading the magazine might help to bring him up to date. He looks at the list of contents. One article that catches his eye is titled:

LOVE RATS UNCOVERED:
WHY YOU SHOULD **NEVER** TRUST A MAN

He wonders whether Ellie looks at this stuff. The title of another article catches his eye:

TEN WAYS OF SNARING THAT
GORGEOUS MAN OF YOUR DREAMS. **REVEALED**!

He wonders if the same author has penned both pieces. He thinks that if women in their thousands are reading this kind of drivel, then maybe his chances of finding a woman to whom he can relate are not small after all. They are virtually non-existent. Is it the case that all such magazines focus on these two big themes? Why men are such rats, and how to snare one.

Arriving in Barmouth and entering the building to get to his office, he passes the inevitable small gang of smokers outside. Once, it was a mix of staff and students, but now it is almost always just students. Keith finds it all very depressing. His own experience of smoking is confined to two cigarettes when he was twelve years old. This was the age at which he decided that it was time he was a man. The adverts made it quite clear to this impressionable youngster that the best way to demonstrate his masculinity was to suck smoke, tar and related substances into his lungs. He found the experience so appalling that he decided he would have to remain a boy for some time to come. At fifty-four, he has made no further progress in growing up. As he has explained in classes, the students he sees smoking are not irrational, just stupid. To be irrational means to take a decision to do something where the perceived costs are greater than the perceived benefits. Somehow, these students feel that the benefits of smoking outweigh the costs. However, it is still colossally stupid. To decide that the pleasures of smoking are greater than the costs of rotting the lungs, coughing to death and having skin that looks fifty when just thirty years old is beyond belief. Putting a gun under the chin and pulling the trigger seems a much faster and probably cheaper suicide option.

The day passes quite peacefully and then, towards the end of the day, Keith decides to face the feedback forms. He finds parts of such forms bordering on the laughable. In these forms, the students are invited to give feedback on the lectures and classes that they have received. Keith sees a benefit in this process. The students are paying a great deal for their tuition. They should have a means of conveying their views as to whether they feel they receive value for money. Yes, agreed. However, despite getting generally favourable feedback himself, Keith thinks that, at least in part, it's a fatuous exercise. A number of questions particularly irritate him. One question asks the students to say whether they think the course is at the right level. How can they possibly know? The reason they are doing the course in the first place is that they do not have sufficient knowledge to make such judgments. He resists the temptation to throw the forms in the bin and scans them. He soon discovers that the students think the lectures are rather easy.... and, at the same time, bordering upon the impossible. The classes are a little dull...... and, at the same time, very interesting. The content of the course is too narrowly focused.... and, at the same time, so broad that it lacks depth. Oh right. Now, he is clear on what his students are thinking.

Oh, for an element of wit in the usual turgid drivel. One student has been a little more original. Keith has let his hair grow rather too long, and he has just begun to experiment with wearing glasses. A student has written:

"Good stuff. And he looks like Gerry Springer. Go Gerry, go Gerry, go!

Amazing. What an unusual student. Gerry Springer was a popular TV character years ago when the student was hardly born. Maybe Keith knows even less of student thinking outside of the class than he had thought.

As he reads the stuff from the students, some of whom are not very interested in the subject Keith calls to mind the story he had heard about a preacher in a church service. The preacher was seriously long winded and was going on and on. Finally, a member of the congregation could stand it no longer and stood up to leave.

"Where are you going?" said the preacher.

"I am going to get my haircut".

"Why didn't you go before I started to preach?"

"Well, I didn't need one then".

Perhaps it is asking too much of Barmouth students to match this kind of line. He sometimes thinks it is asking too much of some of them to write their names properly. He has a first-year class this morning before attending the open day lunch. The students change throughout their three years. Teaching first year, second year and third year students are different experiences One difference is in the reaction when Keith arrives and says a cheery good morning. The third year respond by saying good morning. The second years tend simply to smile. The first years....... write it down.

Keith has asked this group to come prepared with stories that illustrate some features of life under a non-market system like communism or socialism. He explains first that European countries all have a "mixed" economy, where some goods like clothing, are provided through markets and some things are provided by the state out of taxation, such as roads and street lighting. What he is now after is an appreciation of what they think life is like when the vast majority of goods and services are produced by the state and where the distribution of the goods is controlled by that state.

Craig offers the first story. Keith likes him. He is a bright lad from a working-class background, making a good showing of his first year at university. Keith's own background, he suspects, is very similar, and he knows the difficulties of being placed in an environment of largely middle-class people. He well remembers feeling in the first year that he was in the presence of intellectual giants and that he had no place at university at all. He is so keen for Craig to do well. In the second year, Keith had grown in confidence to the point where he realized that some of those fellow students he had seen as "intellectual giants" were middle class idiots. He hopes Craig will grow in confidence too during his years in Barmouth.

"Here is a story I found to illustrate the inefficiency of the Soviet Union in the Gorbachev era of the 1980s." says Craig.

"In those days and in that society, people had to be on a waiting list for ages to get many goods and services. Even if you could afford a car, the wait was ten years. Ivan goes to put his name down and is told he must wait the full ten years to collect it."

"The appointment is for ten years to the day." says the car provider.

"Ten years from today, eh?" says Ivan. "Well, can we make that in the afternoon?"

The man in charge of ordering the car is somewhat taken aback.

"Well, yes. But why in the afternoon?"

"Well," says Ivan, "I've got the plumber coming in the morning."

The class appreciates the joke. It was actually told some years ago by a former USA president, Ronald Reagan. Keith has many friends in Eastern Europe who have experienced something of what Craig has only read about, but he wants to challenge him to realise that inefficiency, although on a considerably smaller scale, can be part of a Western type of market economy too. He tells the class of his own experience last year with trying to get his old gas central heating repaired.

"I reported to a local gas company that the central heating was not working and there was a possible gas leak. Three different people came, spread out over a period of ten days. The third man came three times to look at the problem, sucked his teeth, shook his head, stroked his beard and completely contradicted what the second gas man had said previously. He went away again, saying that they could do the job next month when the parts he needed would have arrived from Isleworth. These are parts which the first gas man had said would not be needed, but there is a four-week lead time on a maintenance docket unless there is a leak, in which case it is it is raised directly from Brentford. But this is only possible, he had explained, if at least two deaths have been directly attributed to it by the coroner. This, however, does not apply in the case of double entry valves unless they are right angled."

"The second gas man in June came, shook his head, sucked his teeth, completely contradicted what the first gas man had said the previous month and went away to raise a Form 42 from Wembley. The first man had said exactly what the third man was now saying. He, of course, was contradicted by the second gas man, who in turn was contradicted by the third gas man. Is this all clear so far, class?"

"However, the second man had raised a contract Form 111 from the Maintenance Department in Staines, which Keith had signed. The parts, he was told, would probably come down from Isleworth at the beginning of next month. They would try to get someone from Harwell to come and fit them the following week but could not promise anything. Eventually, the repair was made some months after the boiler had broken down."

He cannot resist also telling them of a conversation that he has had this morning when passing Ivailo on the stairs. Ivailo is a student from Europe who is in Barmouth to do a master's degree. He has a flat on a housing estate a mile or so from the University. He had shown Keith a letter he had just received from the water company that was addressed correctly in every particular, including the post code. The letter explained how the water company was unable to get in touch to sort out a problem because they didn't have Ivailo's address!

There follows a discussion of the relative merits of capitalism and communism in which Keith makes the point that we shouldn't generalise from one story but look for evidence across a broad spectrum. The overwhelming evidence is that non-market societies have a level of inefficiency even greater than in market economies. Toby is next with his story. He is from a middle-class background and oozes the confidence that Craig is yet to develop.

"My story involves the concept of 'Perestroika,' so I would like to explain what this and the related term 'Glasnost' means. Perestroika was the policy or practice of restructuring or reforming the economic and political system of the Soviet Union. It came to involve the use of markets rather than the failed system of central planning. Glasnost was the policy of having a more open and less secret government which Gorbachev wanted to introduce."

Keith thinks this is a pretty good effort for a first-year student and finds himself looking forward to Toby's story. It goes like this. A Russian walks into a bar to order a beer. The bartender tells him it will cost one rouble. "How can it be one whole rouble?" says the customer." I saw that the price last week was just fifty kopeks!" "Ah," replies the bartender, "it's now fifty kopeks for the beer and fifty kopeks for the perestroika." The man hands over a rouble to the bartender and is surprised when he is given fifty kopeks back. "What's this for?" asks the customer. "We are out of beer," says the bartender.

There follows a short discussion on the expectations of what is achievable in a market and a non-market society. Keith points out that while the average British worker's real wage was, and is, much higher than that of the average Russian, there hasn't been much of an increase in average living standards here in recent years.

A French student, Dominique, always called Dommie, wants to tell her story. She is an exchange student, whereby a student from a foreign university comes to Barmouth without the need to pay a fee since a Barmouth student will study for a period in a French University. Such exchanges are now far fewer as a result of Britain's withdrawal from the European Union and its exit from the 'Erasmus Scheme', whereby such student exchanges were made possible with government assistance.

Keith is delighted that Dommie has found a story involving the French. This is the story she has found. It is about a British guy, a Frenchman and a Russian who are looking at a painting of Adam and Eve in the Garden of Eden.

"Do you see their calm and their shy reserve? "They must be British," says the Englishman.

"Ah non, non, ce n'est pas possible" argues the Frenchman. "They are beautiful, and they are naked. They are clearly French."

"They have no clothes and no shelter," the Russian points out, "they have just one apple to eat, and they are being told this is paradise. Clearly, they are Russian."

Although Keith has heard the story before, it sounds all the better for being told in Dommie's sexy French accent.

They discuss the role of expectations in obtaining happiness, and then Keith closes the class with a semi-relevant pun, which also involves nudity. It must be Dommie's influence. At a nudist colony for intellectuals, one guy says to the other: "Have you read Marx?" and the other one says, "Yes, I think it's these metal chairs we are sitting on. When he first came to teach, a lecturer had told him that every class should have three jokes: one to attract the attention, one in the middle to keep the attention and one at the end to bring them back next week.

After the class he decides to forgo lunch and take the opportunity to begin a sausage roll free diet and spend an hour going for a walk along the cliffs, before playing his part in the open day event. The University is only a short walk from the sea, so Keith is soon looking across at the ocean from his vantage point, high up on the cliffs. Opportunities of breaks in the day are fewer now. Even opportunities to reflect on the job become scarcer as pressures on teaching staff mount. He had recently had the great pleasure of interviewing Gary Becker, the Nobel Laureate in Economics. He had asked Becker what he did during his annual six weeks trip to a think tank in California. Becker had said: "I think." Six weeks for thinking? This is an activity which is virtually banned at Barmouth, where the directorate feels that such trivial considerations are no part of a lecturer's job.

When Keith began lecturing, the forecasts were that within a generation the biggest problem people would have would be filling their leisure time. Fifteen hours of work per week would be the norm. The forecasts were about as accurate as the weather forecasts. However, he has been reading of Swedish companies experimenting with cutting the workloads of their employees to see if the shorter hours will raise productivity to the point that the same amount of work is done in much less time. The early results are encouraging. He has little expectation that the directorate at Barmouth will be studying these results.

It's surprisingly warm, and Keith's thoughts turn from Swedish companies to a Swedish girl he once knew. When he began his teaching career, he was still in his twenties, not much older than the students he was then teaching. He had been attracted to this lovely Swedish blonde. They had walked together along these same cliffs a few times, but he was too shy to know how to develop the relationship, so nothing came of it. As each year passes, the gap between him and the students he is teaching becomes larger, and now he finds himself still unattached and looking at the current crop of students as a different breed. There are compensations, though. He finds that helping individual students to achieve their goals is perhaps an even greater source of satisfaction than many of his other activities, teaching, making academic films or writing books.

He wanders down the cliffs and along the beach. The tide is out, and he heads past the rock pools. He is looking for a secluded spot in which he has sometimes sat to read. It is surrounded by rocks and is invisible from the road or, indeed from the sea. For the first time ever, he finds that it is occupied. Two of his students are there, and it is immediately obvious that they are not discussing the merits of national income accounts. She is wearing, or in this case nearly wearing, a thin blouse, but all the buttons are undone. Their lips are locked on one another's, and his hand is massaging her breasts. Keith wants to tell him to slow down, to treat her more gently. He decides against offering his advice. He is fortunate that they are far too wrapped up in one another to notice him, and he quickly retreats. While he does not find her in any way exciting or desirable, he admits to himself a pang of envy that they should be sharing something that has passed him by.

Although he does not find the girl very attractive, she has a few features that remind him of Meg, a foreign student he helped a few years ago. Meg was very attractive indeed. What an amazing beginning to the story it was. She had emailed him and asked to meet him to discuss her future plans. They had agreed to meet at the University café. Having never seen her before, he had no idea what she looked like. In the event she didn't turn up. He received an email from her a few hours later. He can recall its contents fairly accurately even now.

Dear Keith,

I don't suppose you will ever be willing to speak to me again. I am so sorry I didn't come. I was just about to start out when a friend rang to say she needed me. She was pregnant, the baby was coming, and she had no way to get to the hospital. I felt that I had to drive her there. I just couldn't ignore her. I am so sorry.

Meg

Keith had thought the story so ludicrously unlikely that it must be true. If she had wanted to lie, she could easily have found something much more believable. He had replied, telling her that she had made the right decision. They had met again; she turned out to be a superb student; he had supervised her dissertation and found contacts for her with a London accounting firm where she was now doing brilliantly.

He is making his way through the rock pools, looking at the starfish and recalling a well-known story. The story is told of a man who used to do his writing near a beach. He had a habit of walking there before he began his work. Early one morning, he was on his walk after a storm had passed and found the beach full of starfish as far as the eye could see. Then he looked up and noticed a small boy coming towards him. As the boy walked, he would stop, occasionally bending down to pick up an object. He would then throw it into the sea.

"What are you doing?" the old man asked kindly.

"I am throwing starfish into the ocean". said the boy. "The tide has washed them up, and they are unable to get back to the sea by themselves. When the sun gets hot later, they will die unless I throw them back into the water."

"But there are thousands upon thousands of starfish on this beach. It's impossible to make much of a difference." pointed out the old man.

The boy bent down, picked up another starfish and threw it into the ocean. Then he turned to the old man, smiled and said, "It made an enormous difference to that one!"

Meg, Keith thinks, is a fine illustration of a starfish being thrown back into the sea. A small act of kindness, being willing to rearrange another meeting, made a huge difference to her. He walks on along the beach back towards the University. He passes a couple of people forlornly trying to sell horse and donkey rides to the handful of people on the shore. He smiles. He has never sat astride a donkey and only ever sat once on a horse. Gary, a student of his, had recommended it largely because his father owned stables. Keith had succumbed to the temptation, expecting it to be a failure. It wasn't. It was a disaster. The horse he was given to try had completely different ideas from Keith. The beast insisted on going up when Keith was coming down and coming down when Keith was going up. After an hour on the horse and a week with a sore behind, he was never willing to try again. Fortunately, both Gary and his father found it very funny. A sense of balance is not one of Keith's gifts. He had previously taken to the ice rink a group of young people from the local church. One of the people in the group was a tiny twelve-year-old, Karen, who had never been ice skating before. Twenty minutes after the session began, he had spent eighteen of them sitting on the ice, getting a wet backside. He had then looked up from the ice rink floor to discover Karen serenely gliding across the ice with all the elegance of Dame Margot Fonteyn at the Royal Ballet. Inevitably, dancing is not his forte either. On the rare occasions he tries he seems, at best, to have one less foot than he needs. At worst, he has two less.

He returns to the University. The hour alone with his thoughts is a delight for an introvert. He is sometimes challenged when claiming to be introverted. So many people find it difficult to believe since he often stands before large groups of people and addresses them without in any way feeling uncomfortable. He sometimes explains that many teachers are introverts. The structured atmosphere of the classroom is a different world from unstructured conversation. He occasionally feels that he has to attend a party where there is a room full of people he doesn't know. His strategy to get a glass of wine and keep moving around the room for ten minutes, trying to look as if he is just about to strike up a fascinating conversation with someone on the other side of the room. After ten minutes of this purgatory, when sufficient people have noted his attendance, he leaves. This is a strategy that he had developed a long time ago when he was in a group of volunteers to clean a church and the adjoining rooms. He found that if he picked up a bucket and kept walking, everyone thought he was on his way to doing something useful in a different part of the building.

The University runs open days in order to give potential students and their parents a chance to find out what life as a student would be like. There are usually about thirty young people and about the same number of parents and guardians. By now, they have been addressed by deans, heads of departments and other members of the great and the good. Now, they are assembling for lunch. Keith is to play his part this afternoon, and as a reward for his input, he is allowed to partake of a sausage roll alongside students and staff. He doesn't even have to pay for it. After conversations with visitors, it is time for him to perform. This is an experiment which he himself has suggested, and he is uncertain how successful it is going to be. If he isn't brave enough to take on challenges like horse riding, ice skating and dancing, he can at least try some new ideas professionally. This particular idea is to give a ten-minute lecture on a topic of interest to economists as a kind of taster of what it is like to have a full University lecture. Keith talks for ten minutes about fairness in society, using illustrations and stories profusely. He wants to encourage them not just to do a degree but to do an economics degree. All the evidence suggests that the income generated by a degree is heavily dependent upon the subject chosen, and by that criterion, economics is one of the very best to choose. Much lower income jobs are available to less demanding subjects.

"What did the economics graduate say to the sociology graduate?" He pauses. "I'll have the burger and fries, please."

However, honesty compels him to explain that whilst incomes are high for economists, respect for the profession is low in the eyes of the population at large.

"Everybody thinks they are an economist. If you sitting around in a group drinking coffee and an economics subject comes up, whether it's fairness, unemployment, inflation or whatever, if the economist explains what is happening, the others around the table will disagree and say what they believe. Your contribution as an economist is regarded as of no more value than that of anyone else. Now imagine that in the group of people is someone who has a serious eye condition. One of the members of the group is a professional consultant eye specialist. He says that the eye problem is a particular form of conjunctivitis and requires a special antibiotic. Can you imagine the others around the table saying that they don't think this is right and that it should just be treated with a salt water solution? It would be absurd. Everyone will acknowledge the expertise of the eye specialist. The respect for the eye specialist would be replicated for every profession except economists. Everyone thinks he/she knows as much or more than the professional economist. I suggest you do an economics degree, accept this lack of understanding on behalf of people, and just take the money."

He finishes by telling the potential students not to be frightened by the idea that there will be some mathematics in the course. To do so, he tells a final story.

A man in a suit is walking through the countryside and sees a shepherd with a large flock of sheep. "I bet you £10 to one of your sheep that I can tell you exactly the size of your flock," says the man.

"OK," says the shepherd, "you are on."

"There are 1257 of them."

The shepherd is amazed. The man in the suit is absolutely correct. The man in the suit, having won his bet, bends down, picks up an animal, puts it under his arm and begins to walk away.

"Wait," says the shepherd, "Let's play double or quits. I bet that I can guess your occupation."

"OK. Go ahead" says the man in the suit.

"You are an economist," says the shepherd.

"That's amazing!" says the man in the suit, "How did you work that out?"

"Oh, all right," says the shepherd, "put down my dog, and I'll tell you."

There is laughter from the audience, but it is very noticeable that the parents find it funny whilst the seventeen-year-olds look bemused. Keith feels again the gap between the generations. He will never use this story among students. He concludes by explaining that the economics lecturers at Barmouth are not like that. They live in the same world and try to explain this world rather than the one of mathematical theory. The audience claps at the end of his talk. He invites them not to clap but to throw money instead. There are no takers for his suggestion. Nevertheless, he feels that the experiment has been worthwhile.

When the open day events have come to an end, Keith travels part of the way back home with his friend and colleague Cliff Garston. They have always got on well together, although Keith looks at Cliff's family circumstances in awe. Cliff is married with six children. They live in an enormous, rambling old house where Keith had been entertained for a meal a while ago. Cliff will have to divide his inheritance between six. Keith has no offspring to whom he can leave any remains from his pension fund.

They discuss Cliff's house and what he might do with it in the future. Although Cliff has a large house, it also has a large garden, albeit in a fairly unkempt condition. It is therefore worth a great deal as a site for redevelopment.

"Cliff, when you retire, you can sell the house. You can then move to a smaller place and live comfortably on the proceeds in your dotage." suggests Keith.

"I can't do that. If all my six children get married and have six children, and they all come to visit my wife and myself, there will be fifty of us." Says Cliff. Keith's mathematical brain does the arithmetic. Wow, he is right.

They are travelling in an open carriage, and the train is moderately full. The atmosphere is quiet, with most people reading a book or newspaper. Suddenly, the silence is disturbed by a booming voice.

"And who's been eating MY porridge?"

Cliff and Keith look at one another in astonishment. They both recognise the very distinctive tones of James Wise, one of their colleagues. James is an eccentric bachelor in his fifties. What is going on?

"And who's been eating MY porridge? And who's been eating my porridge and eaten it all up?"

They peer around the seating to find a little boy of about six snuggled up with James as he reads in a voice loud enough to entertain the whole compartment the story of Goldilocks and the three bears. The book clearly belongs to the child whose mother sits opposite, somewhat bemused but relaxed because her little one is clearly being entertained immensely by John.

There is a mix of emotions in Keith as he tries to take in this astonishing sight. John is either unaware, or he doesn't care, that the whole carriage is now caught up in the story. Keith admires an ability to establish such an easy rapport with a family. He is also deeply impressed that John can focus on the child and ignore everyone else. Could he do that? He is also delighted that John is helping to instil into this child a love of books. The boy is enraptured by the story, as indifferent to the people around him as John seems to be. Instil in a child a love of books, and you give him the world. How much easier it would be to teach a group of students to delight in reading if they have learned to do so from an early age? He also, however, finds himself reflecting again, as he had with Cliff a few moments ago, on his relationship to children. He has no children to whom he can pass on this love of books or indeed, anything else. Cliff and Keith hide quietly behind their seats and enjoy the relief of hearing how Goldilocks eventually returns to the safety of her family. At the end of the story, Keith is disappointed. If his audience this afternoon rewarded him with a clap, surely John should receive a standing ovation for his story telling exploits. Alas, it is a British audience. People return to hiding behind their newspapers and pretend that they have heard nothing.

Keith arrives home and cooks himself a meal, and then settles down to read a book. As on many occasions, he accompanies this with a glass or two of milk. He drinks considerable quantities of it although he has never invested in a cow. He can't settle to reading this evening and decides to check his email. There is a new one from the senior management on "the need for greater efficiency in teaching." Before he can stop himself, he has opened it. Management, he discovers, has decided that all assets have to be seen to be fully utilised. This is deemed to be achieved when there are no spare seats in any classroom. The seating capacity must be 100% utilised. Hence, at the beginning of each classroom session, all unoccupied seats are to be removed from the classroom and stacked in the corridor. If there are not enough seats, spare ones must be brought in from the corridor. Latecomers, of course, must bring in their own seats.

Keith thinks this is the genius of senior management. 100% capacity utilisation is guaranteed. The Plan will then be achieved. Unbolting seats that are bolted to the floor in the lecture theatres should prove to be particular fun. Others may be surprised to read this stuff. Keith has been at Barmouth long enough not to be surprised at all. This Kafkaesque nonsense is par for the Barmouth course.

Among the other emails there is a reply from Ellie. It reads:

Dear Keith,

I am very glad you can join us. We are meeting at the Red Lion Inn, which I suspect you know, but I can send details if not. We plan to be there by eight and have a meal. Some of us are staying overnight. I plan to stay the Saturday night as well so I can spend Saturday re-visiting a few old haunts in the area. If you are free for some part of Saturday, we might be able to meet up then with more chance to speak than on Friday evening when everyone else is around.

Ellie

How delightful it would be to spend a day with Ellie in the Barmouth area. But Keith knows it is not possible. He has promised to spend the day in a prison on the Isle of Wight teaching economics to Open University inmates. He crafts a reply to Ellie immediately.

Dear Ellie,

Many thanks for sending the details. Of course, I know the place and will meet you all there. I would have been delighted to spend some time with you on Saturday, but I have a commitment during the day that I cannot break. I am teaching economics to a group of prisoners! Since I won't get much chance to speak to you on Friday evening when you have so many other people to catch up with, maybe we could have something to eat on Saturday evening. Please let me know if this works for you.

Keith

Before he has finished his second glass of milk, he has another email. It's from Ellie.

Dear Keith,

Saturday evening sounds great. We can arrange some details on Friday. I will be fascinated to know whether it's more fun teaching prisoners than teaching our lot all those years ago. See you very soon.

Ellie x

He is happy at the prospect of seeing a bunch of former students to whom he had related so very well, but he is thrilled at the prospect of gazing into Ellie's eyes over a meal on Saturday evening. He will see her when all the others are around, but the following evening, he will have her all to himself. He is so delighted by the thought that he decides to have another glass of milk to celebrate. At bedtime, as he falls asleep, he wonders how those former students have changed. A few had stayed in touch for a while with occasional Christmas cards, but with the passing of the years, he had lost contact with all of them. How quickly the years have gone by. Given his introversion, he is surprised to be looking forward to Friday evening. In particular, he finds himself thinking about Ellie. What is she doing now? Where does she live? And yes, he is keen to know if there is a man in her life. She was so very attractive so he is pretty confident that there must be. He will find out quite soon now.

CHAPTER FOUR: THE DAY OF THE STAFF MEETING

"Education is a method whereby one acquires a higher grade of prejudices."

- Laurence Peter

Keith wakes with the group reunion still on his mind. As ever, he takes a considerable time to come around and to prepare himself for another day. Before shaving and showering, he emails Ellie again.

Dear Ellie,

I can't remember if we ever discussed it, but I enjoy cooking as a way of relaxing. Since you will still be in the area, would you let me cook you a meal here at my place on Saturday evening? It may not be Michelin starred, but I promise it will be edible. You may have other plans, but if not, I would be very glad of your company. When you have a moment, let me know what you think.

Keith x

Oh gosh, can he really send this? They had always got on well but they had not been in touch for years. It is easier to write such an email than to send it. This boldness is rather unlike him. So, send? Or not? He presses the send button. It is done now. Since Ellie's first, entirely unexpected, email he has searched his memory to recall her. He remembers her more clearly than the vast majority of students he has taught, more, even, than the ones from recent times. She was not particularly tall, smaller than the average for her group, but she had radiated an intelligence and an energy that had made her an obvious leader of the group of which she was a part. She also had a smile that was infectious. Her figure was usually hidden by the loose-fitting student uniform of the time but he remembered her quite long hair that curled gently. He had no idea whether this was natural or whether it was a look she had strived to maintain. Whatever the case, he vividly recalled that she looked very good.

He cannot quite believe it but he realises that he is already thinking about looking the best he can when he meets the group. Oh, all right, when he meets Ellie. He decides that he had better get fit. There is one form of exercise that has appeals to him since it is supposed to have been designed with older people in mind, and although there are days when he feels twenty-eight, there are other days when he feels eighty-two. The exercise is particularly designed to tone up muscle in the arms and shoulders. He imagines walking through the door of the Red Lion with shoulders bulging from his jacket.

The exercise is supposed to be done every day. The way to begin is to stand on something like a carpet and to have plenty of room around. Next, it involves having a five lb potato sack in each hand and extending the arms straight out from the sides, holding that position for as long as possible. Ultimately, the aim is to sustain at least a whole minute in that position and then to relax. It should be possible after a week or two to move to ten lb potato sacks, then 50lb and eventually to 100 lb sacks. Finally, the exercise involves putting a potato in each sack.

To be fair to himself, something Keith is always inclined towards, he feels that he is still reasonably fit. Until recently, he was still playing squash, both at the University and at a club near his home. He was winning rather more games than he was losing. That was until a few months ago. He had happened to meet the Barmouth University's number one squash player, and they had agreed to have a game together. Keith had felt that he was under no illusion. He was expecting that he would be beaten easily, maybe 9-2 or 9-3. It had not worked out that way at all. It soon became clear that, however long they played, Keith was never going to get a single point. He hadn't played squash since.

Keith admits to himself that if he makes a start on the potato exercise immediately, his body is unlikely to have a full set of finely honed pectorals by any time soon. He settles for a shower, a shave and a drive to Barmouth. He has some filming work to do first thing this morning, then a couple of classes followed by a staff meeting to attend in the afternoon.

He doesn't like meetings much, but when there is just one, it is sometimes necessary to put in an attendance. He prefers it when there are two at the same time since it is only possible to attend one, and this saves time and his sanity. Occasionally, there are three meetings that have been arranged to take place all at the same time. This is ideal because he doesn't then feel the need to go to any of them. Everybody assumes that he is at one of the other two. His absence is never of significance. In all his time in higher education, he has yet to attend a meeting of more than three people in which anything worthwhile has been achieved.

After a relatively uneventful commute, he arrives at the entrance to the Business School building and glances towards the lifts. Of course, nothing much has changed. One of the lifts is still out of action. The only difference now is that graffiti is appearing on the notice enquiring, semi-politely, how much longer this state of affairs is expected to last. He has brought a small pork pie for his lunch. He makes a quick calculation and decides that if he waits for the working lift, the pork pie will be his dinner, or, more likely, past its sell by date.

This morning, Keith begins with the filming. He has been able for some years to get funding from various bodies to make films that illustrate key ideas in economics. The films are made available on the web free of charge. They have almost finished the current round of filming, but they need some shots over the city to complete the job. The University has an astronomy department, and he and the cameraman/producer, Billie, have permission to use their building. Keith is not looking forward to this. He finds film making enormous fun, but he has no head for heights. He meets Billie, and they walk with the filming equipment across to the astronomy building. The vice chancellor happens to be coming the other way. He knows of the filming work that Billie and Keith do, and he clearly intends to ignore them. Keith is not going to let that happen, so he adjusts his position on the pavement, forcing the VC to stop. Keith gives him a two-minute statement of what they are doing. The VC smiles politely, mutters something inane and looks utterly bored. Keith gives him a cheery goodbye as though the VC has just told him that he will be considered for a Nobel Prize and praised them warmly for promoting Barmouth's name. They take the lift to the top floor of the astronomy building and enter onto the roof. Keith is horrified. Because it is not a public building, there is no safety barrier. There is a pole just outside the entrance to the roof. Keith wraps his arm around the pole while Billie goes onto the roof to film. Keith is in awe and wonder of Billie, who is hanging over the parapet with the camera, inches from certain death. Keith's knees are knocking loudly. He is sure that the astronomy students who are fifteen stories below can hear the sound. After some while, Billie strolls over to Keith.

"While we are here, I need you to deliver a piece to camera that we can use in the film." Says Billie.

"Ok. Just point the camera at me, and we will do it."

Billie: "No, you need to be out on the rooftop, not clinging to a pole in the entrance. It just won't look right on the film otherwise."

"Have you gone raving mad? I am terrified."

Billie: "We can't do it from where you are, and it will only take a few minutes."

Keith emerges, heroically he feels, just a short distance from the pole, and Billie films him saying a few things to the camera. The shots are only from Keith's waist upwards. The lower half of his body is shaking uncontrollably. He tries not to have a face like a rictus while speaking. When Billie is satisfied, Keith runs to the pole and grabs it until they are ready to descend. At least, Billie seems moderately content. Keith is quite grateful that Billie is alive and very, very grateful to be alive himself.

When his heartrate returns to something approaching normal, he reflects on what has happened. Was he a coward? Was Billie brave or stupid? Is it wise to be courageous in some circumstances and cautious in others? Has his failure in matters of the heart been the result of a lack of willingness to take risks? There is one thing about which he is sure: he cannot overcome his problem with heights easily. His heart goes into overdrive in such circumstances. Can he control his heartrate when he meets Ellie?

Keith arrives back at his office with a few minutes to spare before his next class. He finds a small group of students waiting for him. They wish to complain about a course that Keith shares with another member of staff. The students are unhappy with the lectures given by Andrew Castle. This is politically tricky. Andrew is probably the dullest character that Keith knows. He has never heard Andrew lecture, although it is easy to imagine how an hour of his dull monotones must sound. Compared with that, the sound of a lawnmower would be exciting. However, Andrew is superbly organised, gives excellent handouts to accompany his lectures and, if students do as he suggests, they have everything they could want to be successful on the course. Keith encourages them to accept that they are fortunate to have Andrew teach them.

"You are here to learn. If you want entertainment, go to the circus." He manages to say with a straight face.

He then spends a few minutes scanning a load more emails. One catches his eye. The first half reads:

From The Directorate:

To all staff.

It has come to our attention that some members of staff have still not filled in their TRD. Please do this urgently. We cannot proceed with our PTS assessment until this is done. It is a simple matter to OBD the inputs on the NRQ. We will then be in a position to fulfil our obligations to NVH.

Thank you for your help.

Yes, thinks Keith, let's all do that. He has no doubt why some members of staff have failed to co-operate with this request. They, like him, have not the least idea what this bumf means. What is more impressive is that he doesn't care. Keith is one of the least computer literate members of staff and suspects this would be so even if everyone else in the department was under four years old. Ironically and ludicrously, he has the (completely meaningless) title of e-champion in the Business School. He has been appointed because of the filming work he has done. People see the films and say, look, there goes Keith. The reality is that although Keith gets the glory, it's Billie who does the work. Whilst Billie has an awesome knowledge of technology, Keith has technical knowledge at the level of a two-year-old. The films are useful for Keith. It keeps the management off his back because he can point to something that is clearly time-consuming. However, the insights the films convey are not always appreciated by all the audience. In one film, Keith asked Dan Billings to take part. Dan has given an excellent presentation of the intricacies of price discrimination. When Dan showed the film to his wife, he had sat back, waiting to receive a string of compliments from her for his smooth, presentational and communication skills. She had watched it and said:

"Dan, really! How could you have worn that tie with that shirt?"

Such is the fleeting glory of the film star. There is a follow up email from the directorate. It reads:

In response to requests for greater clarity with respect to PGNS, clearer guidelines will shortly be available from DAL. Your own ADR will address any uncertainties you have.

Well, that has cleared that up, and Keith now feels much more relaxed about life. He has time to look at one more email. It is headed:

Today's class

Hello Keith,

Sorry, I can't not come to the class today. I have another appointment.

Colin Carswell

His language skills are sufficiently refined as to enable him to translate immediately. The translation goes:

Hello Keith,

Your class is just not very important to me.

Colin Carswell

The appalling grammar is nothing he has not met a thousand times before. Keith is sufficiently old fashioned to think that precision of language is necessary to communicate properly. When it comes to exams and coursework, this is a battle he knows he has long since lost. Sloppiness in language in higher education is acceptable almost everywhere, for example, just as long as there is a pretty cover on the coursework document. The double negative in the student email reminds him of a story he heard from a class in the USA given by a linguistics professor there.

"In English, a double negative forms a positive. However, in some languages, such as Russian, a double negative is still a negative. However, there is not one language in which a double positive can express a negative."

A student voice from the rear of the class was heard to respond:

"Yeah, right."

In his second class, Keith attempts to show the group that a problem can be better understood with a simple piece of mathematics. He has seen a school syllabus and knows that the material he is using is something that one could reasonably expect an average fifteen-year-old to understand. Soon after he begins, one student stands up, throws his hands up in the air and gathers his file to leave.

"What's the matter?" says Keith.

"This is all beyond me. I am none the wiser now." says the student. Keith recalls the words of Frederick Smith, a lawyer and a friend of Winston Churchill. A judge had said to Smith that he had listened to him for an hour, and afterwards, he was none the wiser. Smith had replied:

"None the wiser, perhaps, my Lord, but perhaps better informed."

Keith thinks that there is no point saying this to the student, who will probably not be better informed, however long he remains in the class. He hopes the student will be back when he has calmed down a little. He is grateful that the other students remain. Keith has been called to jury service shortly and wonders whether the prosecuting or defence counsel will be as rude to the judge as Frederick Smith.

The last class of the day focuses on a few aspects of fairness and income distribution but with rather more content than his presentation at the open day. One bright student makes the point that the state provision of education and healthcare is a means of making the distribution of income more even. If people had to pay for these things at the point they use them, it would be beyond the means of most. Keith agrees but points out that those from higher socio-economic groups still tend to enjoy more than their share of such services. The students ask for illustrations. Keith starts with education.

"Two houses, identical in every respect, are on different sides of the street. One is selling for £30,000 more than the other. Why? It is because those with a higher income are purchasing a better standard of education through the housing market. The road divides the catchment area of two schools, one of which is more highly thought of than the other."

There follows a discussion of whether this is fair and whether it can or should be stopped. Keith always gets a kick out of students discussing a subject in a way which indicates that they actually care. He decides to make the same point in the area of health care. People from higher socio-economic groups find ways of getting more healthcare than those from lower socio-economic groups. The students are reluctant to believe this to be true. He illustrates his argument with a recent personal experience.

"Do you remember a few weeks ago that I was ill for a week and missed lectures and classes? I will tell you what happened. I had visited a friend, Ronnie, who is not very clever, and found him extremely unwell with flu or some related virus. He looked dreadful. I suggested that he make an appointment with the doctor."

"Oh, I tried that." Ronnie had responded. "They said there were no appointments for a week. By then, I thought I would be better or dead, so I gave the idea up." said Ronnie.

"Well, explained Keith," a few days later, I was feeling wretched with the same symptoms as Ronnie. I probably caught a bug off him. I rang the doctor for an appointment, but I come from a higher socioeconomic group. I am not so easily discouraged."

Keith goes on to describe the conversation that took place between him and the receptionist.

Keith: "Hello there, I would like an appointment to see the doctor."

Receptionist: "Certainly, he is free on Tuesday week at 3.30."

Keith: "Well, no, I am not ill next Tuesday; I am ill now. I would like to see the doctor now."

Receptionist: "I am sorry, but all his appointments are booked before that."

Keith: "Oh, I see, well, if you are happy to have my death on your conscience, I guess that's how it will have to be."

There is a pause.

Receptionist: "Well, if you are very ill, perhaps we should see what can be done. Can you describe the symptoms?"

Keith: "Yes, certainly doctor. Oh, you are not a doctor? You have no medical qualifications, and you are about to make a diagnosis of my condition over the phone. Is that correct?"

There follows another pause.

Receptionist: "Perhaps you had better see the doctor this afternoon at three thirty.

Keith: "Thank you".

Keith points out that such a result is not going to be achieved by one from a lower socio-economic background. He worries that the students will generalise too much from this particular example, but it does seem to make the point. It is now lunchtime, and his last class for the day has come to an end. Unable to face one of Joan's sausage rolls, he heads back to his office. Amazingly, there is no student waiting there for him.

Staff meetings are not Keith's favourite pastime. Knowing nothing about a topic is rarely something that discourages people from talking about it, so the meetings can sometimes seem to last forever. The staff meeting is being chaired by Dan Billings. The head of department, Nikos Ioannidis, widely known as Nick the

Greek, is away. In this, there is nothing unusual. Nikos delegates everything except his salary. This week, he is strengthening the relationship between Barmouth and a small University in the Greek Islands. Judging by the time he devotes to this task; the relationship must now be as strong as reinforced concrete. There are perhaps twenty people at the meeting from a staff of around thirty, which seems quite a respectable turnout. Before the meeting gets properly underway, Dan introduces Professor Dennis Creasy to everyone. He will be a visiting professor until the end of the summer. Dan begins to go through his list of very impressive qualifications and achievements, and Keith wonders why on earth he would come to Barmouth. As Dan is talking, he mentions that Dennis has a daughter in the area who has just given birth to a first child. Ah, so that is the mystery solved. By the time Dan has finished his eulogy, Keith is thinking how much he is going to hate this guy. Professor Creasy stands up to respond.

"Thank you, Dan, for that very kind introduction. If my father had been here to hear that, he would have been very proud. If my mother had been here to hear it.... she would have believed it."

The room breaks out in laughter, and Keith thinks that he is going to like this man after all. Professor Creasy makes it clear that he hopes to get to meet as many people as possible in the next few weeks and then leaves Dan to open the meeting. The formalities are quickly dealt with, including the acceptance of the minutes. Keith finds this formality difficult to take seriously. Minutes are not to record what was said or even decided but to record what *should* have been decided. These particular minutes record the substance of a rare contribution that Keith made at the last meeting. He is also recorded as sending his apologies for absence.

The first substantive item is the student satisfaction feedback. There is a general murmur of pleasure as people sit around congratulating themselves because students at the end of the course have indicated that they are pretty happy with Barmouth's economics department.

There is an elephant in the room. Keith wonders if anyone plans to comment on its presence. He is not surprised when no one does. One third of the students are awarded first class honours degrees.

When Keith began teaching, the figure was perhaps two or three percent. Could this have something to do with our satisfaction ratings? Are students satisfied that first class honours degrees are now scattered about like confetti? No one has an incentive to make the point. Indeed, no one in higher education has any incentive to change things, neither the staff nor the students.

Feeling good about it, the staff members move on to the next item. This is a report from the marketing people. Higher education is now a cutthroat business, and much time and effort is spent making Barmouth look good to potential students. One or two people offer criticisms of the tenor of the marketing material. In particular, there is an emphasis on the fact that Barmouth is one of the "new" Universities created by government edict in the 1990's. Why would anyone care that it is new? Why on earth would marketing make a point of this? The staff is invited to suggest ideas to improve the marketing for economics. Are there more attractive photographs that could be used?

"How about Marion's legs?" says Dan Billings sotto voce. Marion is a secretary whose long legs and short skirts make a wonderfully attractive combination for some male members of the department. Simon Stamford is appointed to say thank you to the marketing department for its efforts, but the decision is not to suggest pictures of Marion's legs. Keith is slightly surprised that Simon is still awake. He is coming up to retirement, and whenever Keith passes his office in the morning, Simon is avidly studying the Financial Times. When he passes Simon's door in the afternoon, Simon is asleep over the Financial Times.

Keith is primarily at the meeting for the next item. He is to show some clips from the films he and Billie have been making. Fortunately, someone else will press the buttons on the equipment, as Keith has very little idea of how to make it all work. The process runs smoothly. A guest in the meeting is the deputy Vice-Chancellor, Angela Ashton. She is a small, dour woman and speaks in a condescending way. Keith thinks she manages to do that even when ordering an egg sandwich. She has a reputation of bolstering her own ego by running down everyone else. He has heard her referred to as the 'poison dwarf'. She is also one of the leaders in the University in introducing meaningless jargon as a means of appearing to be up to the minute in educational philosophy and practice. Among the small minded, this creates the impression of great wisdom, understanding and cutting-edge educational pedagogy. When making the films, Keith had written a paper assessing their value as an aid to student learning. Just as he was about to send it for publication, Angela had started talking about the use of "blended learning" in Barmouth, a meaningless phrase that simply conveys the idea that mixing up means of learning can help students. Keith had, with a nearly straight face, changed the title of his paper to include the new jargon phrase. The paper was immediately accepted for publication. A selection of the films is shown at the meeting, and Angela is the first to comment.

"It's interesting," she says, "to see what my staff spend their time doing."

Keith screams inwardly. "I am not your staff. You don't own me, you arrogant woman. I am not your slave. Your university buys my labour services", he thinks but does not say. At this point, Angela drops her electronic diary on the floor, picks it up and looks concerned lest it be broken. He is tempted to drop his paper diary on the floor, pick it up, look at it and say, "Yes, mine's still okay. "He says nothing. Angela exits the room with a great flourish, this to make it clear to everyone that she has far more important things to do than spend her time with a bunch of academic staff. Her exit manages to convey an impression that she has to get up to Parliament in order to explain to the minister for higher education what changes the government should be making to educational policy.

He is delighted when the meeting finally moves on to another item on the agenda. This is a proposal from the Business Studies department. The item is presented by a member of their staff, Edward Stoneham, who wishes to suggest that a further course be added to the Economics degree, one which is suited to the modern dynamic world of business, perhaps in place of an older, more traditional subject such as International Economics. Edward does not have a reputation as a lively representative of the new thrusting world of business education. He is sometimes referred to as Mr. Death. Keith had heard a lecture from Mr. Death a while ago. The audience reaction could not easily have been confused with the reaction to a Rolling Stones concert. Waiting in a field for the Mick Jagger to appear is far more fun than a Mr Death lecture. The snappy title of the proposed new course is:

The International Strategic Marketing and Human Resource Management Development of Integrated World -Class Commissioning & Organisational Development Issues in a Strategic Global Best Practice Business Modelling Synergy Generation Change Management & Paradigm Shifting Holistic Envelope Pushing Context via Sustainable Leadership Benchmarking Logistics through the use of Thought Showers in a Blended Learning Environment Going Forward.

After a discussion, the staff's decision is that, whilst such dynamic ideas are very welcome, the rigours of the new course are not sufficient to justify the replacement of international economics. The meeting then turns to the discussion of the open days, including Keith's contribution yesterday. Walter Johnson is not happy. He feels that the money spent on sausage rolls is excessive. He is no fan of Keith's mini-lecture either. Walter has made it clear on numerous occasions that he hates Keith. This had once concerned him. However, after a while, he came to realize that it was nothing personal. Walter hates everybody. Walter could say, with W.C Fields, "I am free of all prejudices. I hate everyone equally".

In a North London Park, there is a bench with a plaque screwed to it. It reads:

In memory of Roger Bucklesby, who hated this park and everyone in it.

Keith thinks that a similar plaque for Walter should be attached to a bench outside of Barmouth's Business School building. Dan is very diplomatic. He suggests that in view of the time, a small sub-committee be appointed to consider options for future open days. Garth Martin is the staff member of the economics department who is on the University wide committee for open days. He agrees to chair the sub-committee. Keith is amazed. Garth is always around at nine-o'clock on the Monday of the first week of term, but his appearances thereafter are as rare as the sight of Angela

Ashton in a bikini. Neither is Keith sure how he came to be elected to the university wide committee. Presumably, no one else could be persuaded to stand. He recalls that it was said of Ronald Regan that he won an election because he stood against Jimmy Carter. If he had stood unopposed, he would have lost.

The next item on the agenda is the extent of mathematics in the economics courses. The proposal is to review this gradually over the coming months. Brenda has been asked to give some preliminary thoughts. The department has relatively few women lecturers, and there is pressure from the directorate to do something about it. Keith thinks this pressure should be resisted. We should appoint the best we can find. What next? Appoint more left-handed people because they are underrepresented? Redheads? Solomon Island footballers? It reminds him of an advert he saw in an Anglican church:

'Curate wanted. Left arm spin bowler preferred'.

Brenda Harcourt is a recently arrived, not-unattractive spinster of indeterminate age with a burgeoning reputation for being a very good mathematician. She presents her thoughts in a clear and helpful way. Although he has hardly spoken to her, Keith is pretty sure that she will prove to be an excellent appointment. Matt Sutherland, a doctoral student in Sociology that Keith has gotten to know, claims to have had a conversation with Brenda soon after she came to Barmouth. Keith doesn't believe the story, but he very much wishes that it were true.

"You know I am hopeless at maths." He tells Keith. "I was negotiating to buy a book from a student who wanted £75 for it. I said that I thought this pretty unreasonable, so he offered to take off twenty percent from the price as a discount. I couldn't work out how much I would then be paying, so I said I would think about it."

"You couldn't work out eighty percent of £75?"

No, I could not. But then I bumped into Brenda in the corridor, so I asked her if I were to offer her £75 less a twenty percent discount, how much would she take off? She thought for a moment and said: "Everything except my earrings."

The first one to comment on Brenda's presentation is David Priest. The problem of being overweight is not confined to students. David has the kind of figure that suggests he could complete a three-month diet programme in two and a quarter hour. He has come from an "old university," maybe to have a quieter life before retirement. David is shocked at the formality of interviews at the new University of Barmouth. He had described to Keith his "interview" for the job at the old university. The three professors had taken him for lunch and discussed the virtues of Australian crabs. On return from lunch, he had been offered the job. At Barmouth, he had filled in an application form a mile in length, which David claimed included a question on the size and colour of his grandfather's bed socks. Keith thinks David was exaggerating. Size, yes, but surely not the colour as well? The directorate hates the connoisseurial approach to anything, including staff appointments. Their idea is to take as much academic judgement from decision making as possible and reduce it to a box ticking exercise. Keith is convinced that the best candidate for a job is usually obvious in five minutes from a CV followed by a ten-minute chat.

Had the connoisseurial approach been taken when appointing Margaret Shawcross, the economics department would be a little more at ease with itself. Margaret was appointed two years ago and is a militant feminist sitting opposite him. Everyone is scared of her tongue. Keith had seen her carrying an enormous pile of books and struggling to open a door. He had made the mistake of offering to help. The outburst on the equal ability of women to open doors had left a mark on Keith he would not quickly forget. He loved the Milton Jones line:

"Militant feminists, I take my hat off to them. They don't like that."

The next item, Keith feels, shows the economists at their best. There is an invitation to give comments upon a proposal from the directorate to reformulate the academic year so as to ease pressure on teaching staff. This is the kind of proposal that happens about every five to seven years. People move on; another group arrives, feeling the need to make their mark. This usually means proposing something that used to happen some years ago and often relates to changing the annual year, usually back to something that happened a while ago. The essence of the discussion that follows is summed up by Dan Billings.

"Since there is absolutely no chance that the directorate will take any notice of anything we think or say, we will discuss at the next staff meeting ways of minimising the damage that the application of the proposal will create."

Keith is in full accord with this. Every change that the directorate has made to benefit academic staff has always led to a marginal worsening of conditions. Any change suggested by the staff is routinely ignored.

A further item on the agenda is a review of the induction week. In its wisdom, the directorate has demanded that the student's introduction to the university should take an entire week, although Keith knows that some had pressed for a fortnight. When Keith had begun his undergraduate degree, the Monday morning lecture at nine o'clock on the first week of term was cancelled so that students could be introduced to the university. The lecture programme began at ten o'clock. Now that it must last a whole week in Barmouth, it has to be filled with fatuous items. Meeting tutees to play icebreaker games of the kind that demonstrated Andy Wilde's brilliance is just one example. Keith wants to say that many people like him are introverts and that such items are only suitable for the relatively small number of extroverts. There is no point in saying something like this; if he says such things, he will be asked what he proposes should take their place. Other ideas to waste time would be no less fatuous. There is zero chance of shortening the induction period. As the staff has already acknowledged today, the directorate has never listened to anything that has ever said by the staff. He puts his head down and waits for the next item.

There is an inevitable item on the agenda from the group of economic historians in the department. Few of them have much knowledge of, or interest in, economics. They give courses in such exciting subjects as French and Italian Relations, 1918-1939, and Farm Labouring between 1550 and 1624. Alas, few students find such courses as these of even minor interest and the economic historians are consequently virtually unemployed. The students are bright enough to know that such information offered in these courses isn't regarded as cutting edge by the firms they hope will eventually employ them. Given their interest and knowledge of economics, the economic historians are themselves not only unemployed but unemployable. They are therefore regularly begging for more courses to be added to the list of options for students to choose. Keith once suggested that they offer a course on post 1945 economic history. The economic historians are still reeling from this mad suggestion. Some of them would be teaching material that happened when they were alive, a ridiculously radical idea. A fruitless discussion takes place again while Keith closes his eyes and drifts off into a brown study.

When he comes out of his reverie, there is only one item left on the agenda, and it is clear that everyone wants to go home. The item involves a proposal to suggest improvements to the staff canteen. Someone proposes that a separate staff meeting be convened to spend an afternoon examining ideas. Keith makes a quick calculation. A four-hour meeting for thirty people at a cost to the University of £150 per hour is £1800. He wonders if the benefits justify the cost. He is happy to forget the whole thing and just eat Joan's sausage rolls when desperate. He says nothing.

As the meeting breaks up, he again finds himself missing Leonard Griffiths, a lovely gentle man, now retired, who had taken Keith under his wing when he had first appeared in Barmouth. Keith had once left a staff meeting early, collecting his things, packing his briefcase and walking out. This had been frowned upon. Leonard had advised him afterwards of a better approach to leaving staff meetings that Keith had used many times.

"Get yourself some paper and pencils out of the stationery cupboard and bring them to the meeting. When you want to go, leave them on the desk and leave. Everyone will assume that you have just gone for a toilet break."

Keith fears that this kind of deep wisdom from the dawn of time will be lost with the passing of Leonard's generation. Despite the lateness of the hour, not everyone is rushing to go home. A group of six or eight colleagues are standing around in earnest discussion. Keith overhears the name of Sam Tomlinson, one of the younger members of the department who was not at the staff meeting. He joins the group, although he does not contribute. The reason for Sam's absence soon becomes clear. News has been spreading fast that he is having an affair with one of the second-year students, a girl known to quite a few staff although Keith has never taught her. No one seems to know where the story began. It could have been that the girl had been bragging to her friends about having made a hit with one of the staff. It may have been Sam boasting of a conquest of an apparently attractive young woman. No one, however, seems to doubt the truth of the story. Opinion in this informal gathering is divided. In general, the younger ones have more sympathy for Sam and the girl than the older staff members.

"They are consenting adults. It is nobody's business but their own."

"How can it be truly consensual? There has to be some kind of power relationship in these matters. The girl may well feel she cannot say no in case she is marked down in some way."

"Oh, come on, she must be about twenty years old. She could have been at work in some office for the last four years. She is hardly a child."

"But she is not in an office. She is in his class. It must affect the other students. What of her exams? Can he really mark her script properly?"

"All the marking is anonymous."

"I bet he knows her handwriting."

Someone asks whether Barmouth has a policy on such matters. It turns out that, in common with many other universities, it does not.

"So, at least he is not in danger of the sack."

Brenda Harcourt insists that this is not so and tells of a case known to her at the university in which she was teaching before coming to Barmouth.

"One of the male lecturers was taking a class of students one morning. He was well known as a man with an eye for the women students. There was one girl he rather fancied. He liked to ask her questions so he could look her up and down. There was one question he asked, and she said she didn't know the answer. In front of the whole class, he said to her: 'I don't know what you're like in bed, but you are not much good at Economics". She was the daughter of the deputy vice chancellor. By the next morning, his office was cleared, and he had gone, never to be seen again. I know the two cases aren't identical, but it shows that if someone in the directorate doesn't like your sexual conduct you may not survive."

It is clear that this particular story will rumble on for some time. Keith moves quietly away and leaves the discussion in full swing. He returns to the office, and within minutes, Martin Anderson knocks his door. Martin is a shrewd economist, and Keith has known him for many years. Martin has contributed nothing in the staff meeting, which is further evidence of his shrewdness. Martin idly picks up a dissertation that Keith has been marking. Keith had awarded a mark of fifty-four. It had been read by a second examiner who had suggested fifty-six. Neither of these marks is shown on the copy that Martin picks up. Martin flicks through it for between five and ten seconds. "Fifty-five." He announces. No wonder the powers that be hate him and others like him. They agree to meet for coffee soon, and Keith checks his email again before leaving for home. Another has arrived from Ellie. As he opens it, he is aware that his stomach is churning, wondering how she has reacted to his offer to cook for her.

Dear Keith,

What a kind offer! I can't remember the last time someone offered to cook me a meal. If it isn't beans on toast, that would be even more wonderful. I am really looking forward to my visit. Hugs,

Ellie x

He is incredibly relieved. It is so difficult to know how bold to be. What on earth will he cook for her? That's a problem for later. The immediate problem is how to respond to her email. He decides to keep it simple.

Dear Ellie,

Believe me, I am looking forward to it too. It won't be beans on toast, but if you are brave enough, you can leave it to me to decide on something. Hugs,

Keith x

There is also an email from Billie, with whom he had been filming earlier in the day.

Dear Keith,

I have had a chance now to look at the shots we took on the astronomy building this morning. They look good. However, I have decided that I like better the pieces you did to camera a few weeks ago. As a result, today's pieces are not necessary for the film, so we won't be using them.

Cheers,

Billie

Yes, Billie, cheers to you and thank you very much indeed, thinks Keith, whose digestive system is recovering more slowly from the rooftop experience than it does even from Joan's sausage rolls. As he is reading this, another email arrives. It is headed "Staff Bonus". He opens it to discover that, due to the success of the University, all staff will this year receive a financial reward. There is a bonus payment of no less than £120. More joy. The University wishes to lavish wealth upon him twice in just a few days. He recalls filming a piece near his home about house prices, which can easily exceed a million pounds. He had interviewed an estate agent and asked about how people could afford such sums. The estate agent had said that the secretaries in London sometimes got a one-million-pound bonus. Keith thinks carefully and decides that, on balance, because the staff bonus from Barmouth is somewhat less than one million pounds, the payment will not cause him to invest in another property, possibly not even in a new Aston Martin.

He heads back home with a light heart. It has little to do with Barmouth's generosity and everything to do with the thought of seeing Ellie again. He makes a trip to the supermarket to buy some things for a meal on Saturday. As usual, he is in despair that many of the things "on offer" are unavailable because they have sold out. The management hasn't yet caught on to that which has always been known by economists: when the price is lowered, people wish to buy more. He thinks about complaining to the manager and suggesting that, before they lower a price, they might like to order more. However, Ellie's emails have put him in a forgiving mood, and he is soon at home with his groceries.

Checking his email, he finds that Ellie has written again.

Dear Keith,

So much has happened to me in the years since I left Barmouth, not all good. I can remember sitting in your office talking about many things. You were always so easy to talk to. I am so glad we will have chance to catch up. I hope you can bear to listen to me sharing my troubles as well as the good things that have happened. If we don't get much chance to do so tomorrow, it will be lovely to do so on Saturday evening. When I emailed you about tomorrow evening, I had no idea how you would react. Thank you for being so positive. I already feel I am getting to know you again. We have left it far too long. Many hugs,

Ellie xxx

He replies.

Dear Ellie,

Yes, far too long. We can at least make a start on catching up.

Hugs,

Keith xx

His dreams that night are not trouble free. For the first time ever, he dreams of Ellie. In the beginning of the dream, she is in his office looking exactly as he remembers her: a very attractive twenty-year-old girl. On the wall behind her is a calendar. As the dream progresses, the dates on the calendar change. As time moves on, Ellie's appearance changes, and she ages with the passing years. She grows ever more beautiful, not less, but Keith is so distressed at the thought of what might happen next that he wakes up in a sweat. Relieved to find that it was just a dream, he gets up and pours himself a large glass of milk. He then sleeps more peacefully until the morning.

CHAPTER FIVE: MOONLIGHT

'Women are never disarmed by compliments. Men always are'.

- Oscar Wilde.

Today promises to be very different from other days recently, and it's not just because he'll be meeting Ellie and his former students at the pub this evening. Today, he is moonlighting, teaching economics to the sixth form of a private school for girls, St. Beatrice's—affectionately known as St. B's. Barmouth knows nothing about this activity. It's close to Keith's home, so getting there will be easy. He can walk there in thirty minutes. He has no teaching commitments in Barmouth today. The economics department has, for some time, had its own honours system. For many years Keith had the DCM. "Doesn't come Mondays". Now, under pressure from the directorate, this happy and wholly sensible arrangement is becoming less common so Keith is privileged to have a non-teaching day. Since the directorate members have yet to find ways to justify a day a week out of their offices for themselves, they are also seeking to take this away from academic staff. The place is full of socialists. The principle, Keith has long understood, is that if we can't have this privilege ourselves, we can at least make others equally miserable. What a contrast St B's makes. It is anything but a socialist paradise. The phrase "socialist paradise" makes him think of a story he was told a while ago. It is the kind of story that academics delight in. There are two people at a nudist colony for intellectuals. They are discussing socialism. One asks the other:

"Have you read Marx?"

The reply comes:

"Yes, I think it must be these metal chairs we are sitting on."

St B's has only one economics teacher and she has been signed off with illness for a while. Keith has therefore agreed to fill in the gap as far as he can until a permanent replacement can be found. There are girls studying for their public exams, so it's a pretty serious business if no one teaches them. The school has acknowledged the severe shortage of economists in the financial compensation that Keith has been offered. He keeps telling the students at Barmouth that the price they will get for their labour services, their wage, is crucially dependent on the subject they study. He keeps reminding them that relatively few students choose economics, so the financial rewards for economists are high. He is not sure how many of his students believe him, but he is quite sure that, if she didn't before, the head of St B's understands the point very well now.

Before he leaves home, he opens his email and finds one that warms his heart and makes the job seem worthwhile. It's from Marina, a delightful, warm Bulgarian girl he got to know when he first went there for Barmouth about fifteen years ago. She had talked to him about the course she was taking, but the conversation led to many other topics. She would be about the same age as the former students he would see this evening. Whereas many were lively, confident types, Marina was a somewhat shy girl. They had managed to stay in touch through visits he had subsequently made, but they had not been in contact for maybe two years. She writes:

Dear Keith,

Please accept my apologies for not writing for a while. Life has been something of a whirlwind in the last year or two. You may remember we had several conversations during your visits about the fact that I have never found a guy that I could fall in love with. There always seemed some good reason for backing away from any potential long-term relationship. You kept advising me to wait, that the right guy would come along and that I would know when he did. How right you were. The relationship between me and the one I met about eighteen months ago seemed so good and after six months I was very sure. His name is Miroslav. We got married a year ago and we very quickly got jobs in Frankfurt. Our first child has just arrived, a lovely little boy. We are so delighted. If ever you are in Germany, I would be delighted to introduce my two men to you.

Love from Marina.

He is thrilled for her and delighted to have been proved right. It seems ironic that her patience has been so richly rewarded that the right one came along in the end, while at his age, there is no sign that the same could be said of him. He immediately responds to her email with warm congratulations, promising to visit if he finds himself in Frankfurt and making it clear how pleased he would be to see the three of them if they come to the UK. Before he leaves, Ben, his carpenter friend, arrives. Keith has hired him for a few days to do some work on his garage.

Ben: "Good morning, Keith. Off to Barmouth now?"

Keith: "No, not today, Ben. I am teaching at St B's."

Ben: "St B's? That's the girls' school, isn't it? What are you doing up there?"

Keith: "Oh, I am going to teach Economics to their sixth form."

Ben: "Sixth form? What are they? Seventeen? Eighteen?"

Keith: "Well, yes, about that age, I suppose."

Ben: "Let me get this right. You are going to spend the day sitting down and chatting to a bunch of eighteen-year-old girls?"

Keith: "Well, something like that, yes."

Ben: "Are they paying you for this?"

Keith: "They most certainly are, yes."

Ben looks awestruck. This is clearly an extreme example of how utterly unfair life can be. He responds:

"Men would kill for a job like that."

The walk from Keith's house to St. B's takes him partly through the local water meadows. He knows how fortunate he is to live in this part of the world and tries to enjoy the scenery as often as possible. He has spent nearly all his life in this area, even during his student days. Across the river, he can see the private boys' school where he worked during summer holidays. Fred, the caretaker, was about to retire and had grown a bit frail, so Keith had been appointed to assist him in his last summer at the school. He recalls his first morning on the job. He and Fred went to the boys' dormitory to replace a lightbulb. Fred, insisting on fair division of labour, had Keith remove the old bulb while he held the ladder, then they switched roles for Fred to put the new bulb in. Afterward, they headed back to Fred's little cubbyhole to make the first cup of tea of the day. That first hour became the pattern for the whole summer, with long lunch breaks when the cricket was on TV. Back then, Keith wasn't an economist—he was just about to start studying economics at university. And lightbulb jokes hadn't yet become popular. He wonders what Fred would have thought of his favourites if he could share them with him now.

Question: How many economists does it take to screw in a light bulb?

Answer: None. If the government would just leave it alone, it would screw itself in.

Question: How many psychiatrists does it take to change a light bulb?

Answer: Only one, but the bulb has got to really WANT to change.

Question: How many academics does it take to change a light bulb?

Answer: None. That's what research students are for.

He is a little earlier than he needs to be and the weather is at its best. He sits on a bench by the river for ten minutes and watches a couple with a dog walk by. They are clearly enjoying each other's company. He has had so many advantages by being single all his life but is becoming progressively conscious of what he has missed. He is bounded in Barmouth by young women to whom he could never relate in anything more than a professional way. How old would a woman need to be before he and she could be attracted to one another? On a whim he takes out his mobile and googles Catherine Zeta Jones. He has always thought of her as a very beautiful woman. Didn't she marry someone much older? She is married to Michael Douglas, who is 25 years older than she is. He tries to find George Clooney. He is seventeen years older than his wife, Amal! OK, he isn't George Clooney but then he isn't longing for a relationship with Amal. He walks on and ten minutes later St B's comes into view.

The school is a magnificent sight, with large expanses of beautifully manicured lawns surrounded by mature trees. The main building is an elegant mix of brick and sandstone, and other buildings are scattered across the grounds, including a drama theatre and a swimming pool. Tennis courts lie behind the main site. The entire place has an unmistakable air of opulence, with money clearly lavished on its upkeep. Given that fees are over £45,000 per girl per year, this isn't surprising. In contrast, most Barmouth students pay around £9,000 per year in tuition, though this is not a strict comparison, as St. B's fees also include boarding and meals. Still, it suggests a level of privilege and class. Not every parent who sends their child here is extremely wealthy, but some certainly are. When the school fees are due, they barely notice how many noughts have to go on the cheque. For others it's a struggle. In some households, mother works full time to help with the fees. Although, when average incomes are around £30,000 before tax, even a second income needs to be comparatively substantial to afford the bills. Keith finds, on talking to parents, teachers, and girls, that the quality of the education is high on the list of parental priorities, but it is not the only consideration. Keeping the offspring in a safe cocoon and away from the hairy kids on the council estates is part of what they are paying for.

Keith has the lower sixth this morning. Unlike Barmouth, there is a total absence of nose piercing and tattoos. He is uncertain to what extent all this represents parental pressure and to what extent it represents school rules. There is also little proof of too much weight so predominant in Barmouth. Looking around the class, but more generally around the school brings to mind the couplet:

"The English woman is so refined

She has no bosom and no behind."

There are just six in each of the two lower sixth classes. There may be three hundred in a lecture and over twenty in each class in Barmouth. St B's has a feel of wanting to maintain the status quo.

The radicalism of a section of Barmouth students is completely absent. There are no songs here along the lines of:

To the rich let's put the boot in,

And wave our bras for Putin.

The revolution's due,

So, wave our red knickers too.

Keith finds it fun to be here. The educational style is quite formal, so Keith's relaxed pedagogic style honed in higher education appeals to these girls. The topic today is forms of economic systems. This is the same topic that he teaches in Barmouth, although here he is very aware that he is discussing markets and market systems with the children of families who have done so very well out of that system. At one point he makes a point about land prices. One of the girls in the group actively supports his argument because that's exactly what daddy discovered when he bought a vineyard in France recently. Keith is an experienced economist. He is familiar with the land price concept but has limited practical experience. He hasn't bought many French vineyards lately. Economists are often accused of being too theoretical, and perhaps there's some truth to that. He really should consider purchasing a few vineyards and maybe a couple of châteaux along with them.

He hopes he has adjusted his teaching method to suit the fact that these girls are a bit younger than his Barmouth students. He's surprised when one of them asks whether he thinks that capitalist greed is leading to the exploitation of the world's natural resources. Keith considers it a highly intelligent question and encourages discussion on two aspects of it. First, is the problem capitalist greed or human greed in general? Would greed be any less in a more socialist or communist society? These girls are only about sixteen, but he's impressed with their level of discussion. He also asks them whether they are sure that the world's resources are disappearing rapidly. They seem very surprised when he tells them about the size of the world's reserves of some key resources. Forty years ago, it was said that the Earth would run out of tin, copper, and other minerals within forty years. Today, it is said that the Earth will run out of these minerals in... forty years. They quickly see how markets adjust prices in a world of scarcity.

One or two of them still feel that capitalism means too much wealth is concentrated in the hands of too few. It's an entirely arguable point but somewhat ironic that some of these girls are the children of people who have done so well, partly due to the market system, that they can be privately and very expensively educated. He is delighted with these girls' willingness to think. It's a privilege to help them do so. At Barmouth it gets harder to see education as helping people to use their brains to reason. Many students seem to view themselves as empty buckets, with knowledge as a vast heap of stuff lying around and lecturers as shovels, filling these buckets until they're full. Once the buckets reach capacity, a degree is awarded. Thankfully, at St. B's, there are some girls who haven't yet started to think in these terms.

The other group of lower sixth girls is a considerable contrast. They are far less fun to teach. He does not know if these two groups have been "streamed" somehow, but they are a very different proposition from the other lower sixth group. One or two of them keep questioning him as to whether what he is talking about is on the syllabus. They make it clear that they have no wish to know about anything that isn't. He finds this attitude disappointing but perhaps not very surprising given their age. However, what he finds difficult to cope with is the arrogance. They feel they know so much more than he does, so that they should be the ones to decide what is relevant and important. He suspects that this arrogance is cultivated in families able to spend over thirty thousand pounds a year on their children's education. "He who pays the piper calls the tune," they say—though some of these patrons might not know the difference between an octave and an octopus. At this age, some students impress with their rapidly maturing thinking, while others disappoint with their lingering childishness.

Keith has no responsibilities at St B's other than to teach economics to the sixth form. Given all the other pressures on him, it has been agreed that he only has time to teach the girls. All the thousand other things that teachers do outside their class, seeing that the girls are holding their knives and forks properly and checking on the state of the third form knickers, must fall on other teachers in the school. However, as a one-off experience, he decides to go to the staff meeting, having never been before. There is normally one per week at St B's, which happens today. It is necessarily short so that it can be fitted in before afternoon school starts. There are at least thirty people teachers there. The head is leading the meeting. She is a product of the private system herself. Keith guesses that she is in her late forties. She is immaculately dressed in an upper-class kind of way. She holds a postgraduate degree in classics and addresses the staff in beautifully modulated tones.

The assembled gathering is overwhelmingly female. The atmosphere is one of great respect, much more respectful than at Barmouth. The meeting is mostly the distribution of information. Little meaningful discussion can take place in such a large group. None of us is as dumb as all of us, Keith thinks.

At one point, he surprises himself by participating in the staff discussion on raising funds for a new running track. The plan involves a dinner dance, and it's clear that staff will be subtly pressured to purchase tickets—even though many have no desire to attend. The question at hand is the ticket price. Sensing the need for an economist's perspective, Keith proposes an innovative solution: set the price at twenty pounds for those attending, and forty pounds for those who prefer not to go. He considers it a stroke of brilliance, imagining that many would gladly pay for an evening of peace and quiet, thus substantially boosting the school's funds. His suggestion is met with a frozen silence. The head decides that this is not a popular suggestion and Keith feels that his genius has been ignored. If the suggestion goes down like the proverbial lead balloon here, it is an idea that many of his students in Barmouth have absorbed. Some of them are willing to pay many thousands of pounds not to attend class, presumably because the University cannot expect both money and work to be awarded a degree. He catches the eye of one of the women teachers who spends most of her time teaching English but has a sideline in despising Keith. In the short time he has been around she has made it clear that she feels her girls should be free only to enjoy the purity of Shakespeare and not have their minds sullied by vulgar thoughts about money. Her look of disdain leaves Keith almost completely unmoved. He has to try to hide a smile. He does not think he will attend another staff meeting here or think his presence will be greatly missed.

As he leaves the staff meeting, he finds Katie waiting to speak to him. She is a fun loving upper sixth girl that Keith will teach in about twenty minutes, after the afternoon bell goes. She wants to ask him something private so they walk around the playing field where they can be on public view while being out of earshot of everyone else. She wants to discuss the hole in the knee of her trousers. She has been told off by the staff and instructed that this is not appropriate dress. The girls in the lower school must wear uniform, while the sixth form are free to wear whatever they like, within reason. It appears that a hole in the knee of her trousers is considered to be outside of that reason. She is seeking wisdom from Keith because he is seen as an outsider; he comes into the school on a piece of elastic. He arrives and is gone. What can he say to her? He is highly sympathetic, coming from an atmosphere in which very large holes in the knee, at least for women, are practically *de rigueur*. He can do no more than encourage her to put her head down. It just isn't worth fighting over. Soon she will be out of the place and free to do what she likes within the law. He thinks, but does not say, "Soon you can be practically naked and no one will care." Glancing at her young figure as they walk, he realises that this would attract a lot of attention from the male population. They walk back to this afternoon's economics class, laughing together at the follies of irrational and pointless rules. He warns her that, although she will soon leave the school and be free to have even larger holes in the knee of her trousers, she will never escape pointless and irrational rules. They are all over the place, inside and outside of St B's, rules made by irrational people in pointless occupations. He likes Katie very much. This is the kind of daughter he would love to have had: beautiful, intelligent, kind and funny. One of the teachers told him recently that Katie had commented on his classes that had amused her.

"She said she often has no idea what you are talking about but she loves your classes."

He thinks Katie was overstating. She understands very well what is going on in the lesson. The average intelligence of the girls is high but there is an occasional exception. One girl is clearly not very bright at all. She struggles to grasp even the most basic ideas. She is warm and lovely, but her warmth and loveliness will not help her pass an exam. Her most common contribution in class is along the lines of:

"Oh, I don't understand any of this stuff. Tell us a story."

If she gets even a bare pass at A level it will represent the pinnacle of Keith's teaching career. Schools look at the results of their students. It would be better if they could look at the value they add in many ways.

At the other extreme is Pippa, who catches on to every idea easily and immediately and is ready to explore its implications. Keith is well aware that many lecturers and teachers are quite nervous about people like Pippa, who are significantly brighter than most, if not all, of their teachers. She makes him think of a story, possibly apocryphal, about Muhammad Ali Jinnah, the founder of Pakistan. He was a law student in London, and his professor asked him if, given the choice, he would choose a bag of wisdom or gold. Jinnah immediately said he would choose the gold. The professor, attempting to demonstrate his superiority, immediately said he would take the wisdom. Jinnah's reply was: "Each one takes what he does not have."

The professor, livid with this remark, gave Jinnah a very low mark on his exam paper and placed on his paper at the end just one word: "idiot." Jinnah is said to have taken the paper to the professor and said "Professor, you have signed the sheet but you haven't given me a grade."

He doesn't tell them this story. Keith hopes he has the humility not to treat any of the young people he teaches like Jinnah's Professor treated him, but he is certainly aware that a student might be brighter than he is.

He is always looking for ways to demonstrate economic ideas using things the students are familiar with. He knows that some of the girls are keen to eat only organic foodstuffs wherever possible, even though organic produce may be fifty to one hundred percent more expensive than the non-organic equivalent. Since they are talking about scarce resource usage, he asks them why they are so keen to eat organic food. They have two different reasons. For one or two of them, it is a question of health. They want to avoid consuming food treated with pesticides. Keith suggests that this may very well make sense. Thus, if they have enough income might well be an excellent choice. One or two others claim that they do so out of altruism. They are contributing to a world problem by buying organic and encouraging fewer pesticides. Keith challenges the wisdom of this. Organic production requires far more resources than non-organic. If the whole world were to be organic, there would be so many scarce resources in food production that there would inevitably be far less food in the world. Far less food means that millions more would starve than currently do. If you all want to eat organic for your health, go ahead. But if you want to save the world, then eat non-organic."

Not all girls are convinced by his argument, but they are not sure why. He ends the class by encouraging them about what they read.

"Check the evidence. Don't believe everything you read. But also, be open to change your mind when evidence presents itself. In other words, don't believe everything you read but don't believe everything you think either."

As he walks back home through the meadows, he realises yet again how much he enjoys teaching, how very lucky he is to spend time with younger minds and have the opportunity to help them think their way through to an understanding of so many issues. He also thinks, however, that this is not enough for him. He sometimes wishes for the company of people older than the students at St B's and Barmouth, with whom he can discuss so much more. The age gap between himself and his students seems too great to meet this deeper need within him. The St B's girls will sometimes flirt with him, albeit in a quite innocent way. They see few men and so an occasional man allows flirting in an entirely safe environment. He smiles permissively at this behaviour.

He has plenty of time to shower, change and be ready to leave the house more or less on time for the short trip to the pub. He is perfectly happy to drive and not drink. Maybe he will have a glass of wine when he gets home to celebrate a good evening, or an extra glass of milk if it goes really well. By the time he gets out of the car he is quite nervous. Is this all a mistake? It's too late to back out, and he heads for the pub front door. They have taken over a private function room upstairs, and he can already hear the sound of laughter before he is halfway there. One of the things he has been dreading most is the background music. The student 'wow, wow, yeah baby' stuff distracts him. So, it's a pleasant surprise to hear quieter light classical music coming from the room. Their musical taste has improved with the years. He opens the door and immediately sees that the room is laid out in a buffet style arrangement. This will make it easier to mingle and catch up with lots of his former students.

Ellie gets up out of her chair and is the first to come and say hello. He had remembered her as attractive in much the same way as he remembered dozens of other female students he had taught over the years, but it was immediately obvious that she had matured. He remembered her as attractive, now she is beautiful. She still has dusky blonde shoulder-length hair, but now there are perhaps a few streaks of silver. The eyes are still blue but less startlingly so. He presumes the contact lenses are now clear. She wears a plain royal blue blouse and close-fitting white trousers. She is no longer the young girl he once knew; she is now a beautiful, mature woman. They embrace briefly, followed by the inevitable kisses on the cheek. In the UK, the standard seems to be one kiss, while in some European countries, it's two, and in others, three. Keith now wants a Southern English standard of at least four. She wears no perfume that he can notice but she smells delightful. Ellie is the first to speak.

"It's so good to see you. We can talk a bit later. There is so much to catch up, but now let me introduce you to the others and see who you remember."

"That sounds good, but yes, it's so very good to see you and thank you for inviting me."

Ellie takes him across to meet the others. It's a relief to Keith that there is no sign of tattoos or holes in the knees. Nor is there, at first glance, anyone like the piggy-wig with a ring at the end of the nose. The thought of Edward Lear's piggy-wig reminds him of how the owl and the pussy cat purchase the ring and marry. Then later:

"Hand in hand, on the edge of the sand, they danced by the light of the moon."

Oh wow, what he would give to dance hand in hand with Ellie, even though he has two left feet. There is a general hello from everyone and Keith begins his attempt to spend a little time with as many different people as possible over the next couple of hours. He starts with a group of four and inevitably cannot recall the names or faces of all of them. He would hardly forget Gary, however. He is built like an outside toilet and when playing rugby for Barmouth must have scared the life out of some opposing sides. For all his size, he is quite a gentle guy. Keith's failure to recall names is not the problem he feared. Ellie has organized for everyone to have a name badge. He isn't sure whether this is entirely for his benefit or whether she feared that with the passing of the years, some people might not recognise one another.

The group of them recall about the last time they had spent some time together with Keith. After the graduation ceremony they had all had a meal together. Keith had then gone home, leaving at about 11 p.m. They had attempted to persuade him to come with them to a nightclub. He was tempted by their kind offer, but in the end, their efforts to coax him were unsuccessful. Julie had organised for a party of them to go and the entrance was just around the corner from where Keith had parked his car. He had said goodnight, accompanied by the usual meaningless promises to keep in touch. They had all sworn they would write twice a day for the rest of their lives and then he had not heard from any of them again until now. For the first time he hears what happened immediately after leaving them. They had walked around to the nightclub entrance and Julie had presented the tickets to the bouncer. For some reason they never knew, he was aggressive and unhelpful, refusing to allow them entrance. Julie explained that the tickets had already been paid for and that they would now like to go in. To the astonishment of the whole group the bouncer took this as aggressive behaviour on Julie's part and hit her. Julie explains to Keith that this was a big mistake. Keith guesses the next bit of the story. Gareth, the gentle giant who has learned how to handle himself in many a scrum, was enraged at this behaviour and quickly compressed the bouncer with a couple of well-aimed punches. Within minutes the police were called. Keith laughs at the tale and realises that he was minutes from appearing in the headlines of the local newspaper:

"Barmouth University Lecturer in Nightclub brawl"

Gareth, of course, enjoys Julie's recounting of the story even more than Keith. Julie is the only one of Keith's former students wearing a very short skirt this evening. He glances across at two other people whose faces he has forgotten. He does, however, vaguely recall that they were an item when he was teaching them and he is interested to discover that they are still together. It appears that they may not be so for very much longer. The guy is looking Julie up and down with obvious relish and in the most obvious manner. He is making no effort to be English and look surreptitiously. His girl is looking at him pretty blatantly too and is obviously extremely irritated. It's clear, though, that she thinks it is mostly Julie's fault. Keith lip reads just enough to catch a couple of her words: "little minx." So, women approaching their forties can be very attractive. Guys approaching their forties clearly notice attractive women. Women approaching their 40s can still be very annoyed with male behaviour.

He chats to several others and then moves around the room to chat briefly with Ellie. On his way he hears one of the guys tell Julie how great she looks in the short skirt. She says to him:

"I was wondering if it made me appear a bit overweight...."

Keith hopes that the guy can translate correctly:

"This is your opportunity to tell me how fabulous you think I look."

He doesn't wait to hear the response.

When he finds Ellie, he is again struck by how beautiful she is. She doesn't flaunt her beauty, but she makes no effort to hide it either. He has a momentary picture of some of his Barmouth students—women nowhere near as beautiful—who flaunt their looks and carry an air of those who think the world revolves around them. But Ellie, even in a crowded room, stands out, at least to Keith. He finds himself a little surprised that not everyone is staring at her. In the few minutes he gets to spend with her, they swap a few brief stories about life in the last fifteen years, and he discovers that since she left Barmouth, she has done several jobs but currently runs her own online business. He decides to wait until tomorrow to ask for more details. He wants to see if she has a ring indicating she is married. He then realizes he has no idea which finger to look at. He decides to look that up online before they meet tomorrow evening. Somewhere in the recesses of his mind he senses that, although she is smiling, there is some sadness about her. Perhaps it is there in her eyes. Keith is not greatly skilled in the art of reading women but he had years of experience in talking to people and listening for what is not said and what is being said. Behind her smile he is pretty sure there is this sadness but he has little idea why it is there. How could he know what is in the mind of one he hardly knows but is desperate to know better? He recalls a phrase from her recent email about things that have happened to her: "not all good." He thinks this is no time to try to find out but would love to know if he is right. Maybe tomorrow there will be a chance to ask about that phrase, if he isn't too scared to say the wrong thing.

Most of the group is staying at the pub overnight but the alcohol consumption is still quite modest. They really have grown up. The Barmouth students go out each evening with the intention of getting smashed. He hopes that they may grow up one day as well. In the meantime, Keith sticks to soft drinks, given that he has to drive home, but he hopes to open a bottle of wine or two with Ellie tomorrow.

There is some discussion with others in the group about job prospects. One or two thank Keith for his help setting them on the road to their first job, but fifteen years into their careers, there is nervousness about the future. Will AI and robots make them jobless before they reach retirement? Keith encourages them to think like the economists he tried to train them to be. "More capital doesn't create unemployment. It just causes people to do different things," he explains. Some of them had once worked as bank tellers. Automated banking came along, and now there are more people than ever working in the banking sector.

It takes a while for him to work out what is different about Julie. She has had her hair cut shorter. He loves long hair on a woman, but he has to acknowledge that the style does suit Julie. He compliments her on it. She says it is a recent innovation. She laughs and tells him of a recent reaction from a friend. When she saw it, she said "Julie, your lovely hair...... what have you done with it?

In the early days of teaching in Barmouth, the vast majority of students were English. Now, it is a much more multicultural mix. Julie was one of the first foreign students he taught. She came from the Ukraine where she was known as Yulia. She recalls how uneasy she was when she first met Keith. He remembers it.

"Why were you so nervous? Did I seem so unapproachable?"

"Not at all but although I had studied English since I was six it was the first academic English chat that I had with a real live Englishman. Did the English language work in England or only in the classroom in the Ukraine? I was relieved when I discovered the answer."

How uncertain of herself an eighteen-year-old can be. How confident and at ease with herself she seems now. He recalls with another group about the last lecture course he gave them. They don't remember very much of the analysis but remember the fun it all was. Someone reminds him:

"At the end of your last lecture we all applauded and I remember your response."

"I probably said not to applaud but to throw money. I am still saying this to some groups but nobody hears me. They just go off into commerce and make their millions."

There are more memories with Gary and some others about the cricket match Keith remembers so well. In their final year, and after their last exams, the business studies students had challenged the staff to a game of cricket. The students then struggled to raise a team and asked Keith to play in their team as a guest. In a momentary lapse, he agreed.

"We asked you whether you were a batsman or a bowler and you said you were a batsman."

Keith explains the background to his reply.

"When I first came to Barmouth, it was my first lecturing job. I was asked what my teaching specialism was and I said microeconomics. The main reason for saying this was to avoid being given too wide a teaching remit. At least that way there was only one area of economics in which I could make a mess of lecturing. I used the same principle answering your question. I might mess up in batting but not batting and bowling."

"I recall that we got you to open the batting but that was after the staff had their innings and scored a few thousand runs."

"Yes, the cads had practiced beforehand. It was so unfair. Had they no sense of fair play?"

Keith can still clearly see what happened as he began the student team's reply. The classic way to open the batting is to defend the first few deliveries and get a feel for things before trying to score runs. In most things Keith finds himself to be one of the old schools and doesn't think there are many of us left. In cricket, however, a game he hadn't played for years he chose to be somewhat different. The opening bowler for the staff team was none other than Dan Billings. Dan bowled with evangelical zeal and at a speed just shy of a bullet from 007's gun. To Dan's opening delivery, Keith's plan of action was far from what would be recommended for someone hoping to play cricket for England. He closed his eyes and swung at it wildly. Amazingly, his bat made some small contact with the ball. When Keith opened his eyes, he saw that it had flown to the boundary for four runs. The key now was not to reveal his amazement at this outcome. He looked nonchalant, surprised and disappointed that it hadn't gone straight over the boundary rope for six. The second delivery was an exact repeat of the first. By now Keith started to believe that he could play cricket. He could play only one shot to the next Billings delivery. He duly heaved at the ball with the exact same outcome as before with just one difference. This time he made no contact whatever with the ball. As a result of this minor difference the middle stump when cart wheeling out of the ground. If he had made only four it still proved to be close to the top score for the students as the staff team thrashed them. He recounts the story and looks up to find Ellie has joined their group and is sitting next to him. She is laughing at him in a way that melts his heart. She leans over and squeezes his hand.

Once she lets go, he thinks it's time to leave. He has an early start to his day tomorrow. He offers his thanks for a delightful evening and says goodbye, with all-around promises to stay in touch. Ellie escorts him to the door. As they get up together, she leans forward and he catches a glimpse of the top of her bra. Why can he see yards of some female student's legs, be unmoved, and then find himself excited by this minor and unintentional display? They make arrangements to meet tomorrow evening. He gives her his address.

"Please leave your car here and come by taxi. That way we can both avoid using a car so we can open some wine and feel relaxed about it."

They have a final hug, with a few more kisses on the cheek. The hug lasts a little longer than when he arrived a few hours earlier. Going home he thinks how easy it has been to spend time with these people. It has been so much more relaxing than being around Barmouth students. However, he thinks this comparison to be rather unfair because the people he has been with this evening were a great group even at twenty-one. And Ellie is now quite something. Wow, he gets to have her all to himself tomorrow evening.

At home he relaxes with a glass of milk before sleeping. He dreams of Ellie again. She is smiling that fabulous smile and it is for him, but then, as the dream ends, she turns and walks away from him. He hates that.

CHAPTER SIX:
IN AND OUT OF PRISON

"What I don't understand is how women can pour hot wax on their bodies, let it dry, then rip out every single hair by its root and still be scared of spiders."

- Jerry Seinfeld

The early start to the day is necessary because Keith has to travel to the Isle of Wight. He works in a part time capacity, just a few hours each month, for the Open University looking after several students studying from a prison there on a course in business and management. The students read books, study materials online, write essays, and have occasional visits from people like Keith, who act as tutors. He has to go in to meet them because, unsurprisingly, the prison authorities won't allow them to come out. He had begun acting as an OU tutor many years ago and had been incredibly fortunate to be regarded as an ideal person for the job. He had earlier been appointed to tutor a group of about twenty people from across the South of England. Since none of them was a prisoner, they would travel to Southampton each month to discuss some study material. The particular unit of study had drawn upon a range of disciplines, including geography and economics. Keith had very little idea about the geography material and had been dreading the tutorial meeting, which was arranged to go over it. Sure, as little green apples, the students wanted to discuss something in the geography material that Keith hadn't understood, and they had looked to him for guidance.

"Can I explain something that might help?" said one of the students in the group.

"Be my guest," says Keith, who doesn't say:

"Because I have no idea how to answer the question."

Ken Heather

The offer had come from a man in his forties who had proceeded to explain the issues clearly and succinctly. There were lots of follow up issues. The same man dealt with them all while Keith smiled and acted as a kind of referee. The class was regarded by all as a great success, and Keith had been thrilled at the way the man had dealt with the whole thing. Keith had needed to say virtually nothing throughout the two-hour tutorial and had merely collected the payment for his profound input. After the class Keith had approached the man who understood the material.

Keith: "That was very impressive. You seem to have grasped the substance of the unit and showed some remarkable insight. You were also very good at explaining the issues to the group."

Student: "Thank you, but it was not difficult. I am a geography teacher who never obtained a degree. This was the very easy bit of the course for me."

Keith had sighed with relief that this man had been there. The next tutorial, a month later, was on economics, and Keith was able this time to demonstrate a total facility with the material and to convey his knowledge clearly to the group. It was to this particular tutorial that Tony Davis, the senior tutor, a full-time employee of the OU, had turned up to check him out and to see how things were going. Afterwards he and Keith had enjoyed lunch together.

Tony: "Keith, that was great. If you want to do summer school or prison tutoring, just ask. We need people like you."

Keith decided not to say that it would have seemed a very different occasion if the senior tutor had turned up to the previous tutorial in Geography. He now drives to Portsmouth and takes the hovercraft across to the Isle of Wight. From there, he gets a taxi to the prison. The prison building is, inevitably a pretty depressing and forbidding looking place. The weather is cloudy this morning, and a low mist hangs all around. What a contrast this makes to the beautiful buildings and atmosphere at St B's. Given the tight prison security, the entrance is claustrophobic, and Keith wonders if he will ever be allowed out at the end of the session. As with all prisons, mobile phones are forbidden. He is required to provide a photo ID and proof of address. There is a fairly cursory search before being admitted, presumably to check that he is not bringing in drugs or a hacksaw. Since the authorities are now confident that he has concealed neither item inside his textbooks, he is then allowed to enter.

Before he meets his tutees, he is taken into the small room where the lesson would be held and the prison offer sets him down by a buzzer.

"If there is any problem, just hit this buzzer, and the resulting alarm will send someone running."

Keith feels somewhat reassured. He feels that the Open University is a great idea and that making it possible for prisoners to study with them is something of which he wholly approves. It doesn't stop him feeling nervous about being trapped in here, especially with people, some of whom have committed crimes of violence. What it must be like to be incarcerated here for years is beyond his imagination. It must surely affect the character of the inmates.

He then greets his tutees, and the warder leaves the room. Keith decides to get straight to the subject matter in hand. He has no wish to know what the reason is that has brought these men here. He is pretty confident that it isn't for murdering economics lecturers, but beyond that he doesn't wish to know anything else.

They spend some time discussing how economic crises affect businesses. He is surprised at how normal the conversation is. Indeed, the atmosphere, aside from the surroundings, isn't much different from the sessions with the Barmouth students. Does this mean that Barmouth students might be here in large numbers in future? He pushes the thought out of his mind.

As Keith introduces another topic for discussion, his arm accidentally knocks the buzzer. He is not reassured that it takes twenty minutes before someone puts a head around the door and asks if all is well. He could have been dead in those twenty minutes. The other topic to be covered is ethical challenges in business and management. It is ironic, though he does not say so, that some of his tutees are here because their own ethical behaviour was less than the highest possible.

The session ends. Keith has warmed to these characters. Parts of the material they have covered are similar to that which he covers in Barmouth. The questions and comments from his three tutees are very different from those of the comparatively innocent students back in the university. He hopes that that these students are successful in completing their studies and that the qualification will in due course, help with life outside. He is escorted back through security by a warder. How do these guys willingly come here daily and live in this stultifying atmosphere? The prisoners have no choice. Presumably, the warders do. For himself, he is relieved to escape the place and breathe some outside air. The trip back across the water to Southampton passes quickly, and he manages not to spend the whole time thinking about his evening with Ellie. On the drive back home, he gets to do his good deed for the day. He pulls into a petrol station to fill up the car. He is approached by a lady in her mid to late thirties. She is probably very close to Ellie's age.

"Excuse me, but I don't know how to use these pumps to fill up the car. Would you kindly show me?"

Keith duly obliges, fills her car with petrol, giving a running commentary on what he is doing. She nods in understanding and thanks him when the job is done. It is clear that she has no interest in learning how to work the pump. Obviously, she does this every time the car needs petrol. Politeness forbids him to say so. He suspects that she knows he knows, but why would he embarrass her? He wonders if she will suggest that she watch him pay for her petrol with his credit card so she will know how to do that next time as well. She doesn't.

On a whim, he decides to make a small detour in the hope of seeing an ex-student, Jenny, who is now a deputy manager at a small hotel. He has half an hour to spare for a cup of coffee if she is free. He enters the hotel lobby and passes a prominently displayed notice which catches his eye. It is clear that the hotel is being used today by some delegates of a conference and the programme is available for anyone to read.

Southern Area Business Conference: Programme
•   10.30 Arrive
•   11.00 Coffee
•   11.30 Introduction
•   12.00 Guest Speaker
•   12.30 Lunch
•   2.30 Open Discussion
•   3.30 Coffee
•   4.00 Closing Remarks
•   8.00 Evening Meal

Wow! These people in the private sector work so hard, even if the only thing at which they work is complaining about the idle teachers in the state sector. He quickly finds Jenny. She seems very pleased to see him. They sit in the lobby, and she orders coffee. The coffee is on the house. Keith thinks but does not say: the vice chancellor gets around half a million pounds salary a year, the use of an executive car, and first-class travel perks, but, fair enough, Keith gets a free cup of coffee when visiting an ex-student. She seems to feel the job is going very well and especially likes the days the manager is off duty and she is in charge. As they talk, a couple arrive to register for the night. They have no bags. He is dressed in a moderately smart business suit and appears to be about sixty. The girl is in her early twenties, she has big boobs, and blonde hair that even Keith can tell is out of a bottle. The man signs the register with his right hand and squeezes his companion's buttocks with his left. They disappear up the stairs. Jenny goes across to check the register and comes back, grinning.

Jenny: "Mr and Mrs Smith. No luggage. How original."

Keith: "I expect they want to get straight on with doing the *Times* crossword."

Jenny: "Yes, there seems to be a buoyant demand for that crossword in this hotel."

They say goodbye and he reaches home in plenty of time to prepare for Ellie's visit.

He is a tidy person by nature so there is little to do to make the house look acceptable for a guest. The meal will take a while to prepare. He is a little too wise and a lot too nervous to try anything new, so he decides to cook a favourite and familiar recipe based on duck, peaches, and honey. He has all the necessary ingredients from his trip to the supermarket yesterday. He will assemble the food, put in the oven, and leave it for some time. He is the son of his mother. He likes his food very well cooked. In this respect, he is not quite as bad as she was; bless her. If she could count the sprouts in the saucepan, then in her view, they needed longer to cook. Keith is fond of combining meat and fruit. Pork goes well with apricots, but he had already decided upon the duck combined with peaches. This would have appalled his mother, who didn't like "mucked up" food. It goes in the oven with a few vegetables that will roast nicely. He has several bottles of wine that will work well and will decide which one to suggest at the time they eat.

He plans a simple pudding of sweetened cherries with yoghurt. What can go wrong with that?

He does not think of himself as a man easily given to panic. As far as he has been aware, the only exception has been the effect upon his equilibrium of changes in technology. When teaching with a blackboard and a stick of white chalk had given way to the new technological miracle of coloured chalk, he felt that he had coped well. With the introduction of all modern technology thereafter it had proved a struggle to remain calm. He is about to find another area of his life that creates panic, or, more accurately, borderline hysteria. It is the presence of a beautiful woman.

He cooks the cherries and adds the sugar. He then tastes the concoction to make sure that it has the right degree of sweetness. It is ghastly. It is the work of but a moment to see why. Salted caramel has become popular in recent years. He now knows why salted cherries have not. He decides that he really should not keep the sugar and the salt in similar bowls. He tries to remove the salt with a spoon. He tries straining the cherries. He tries shouting at the bowl. All these procedures meet with the same result. Total failure. Finally, he calms down sufficiently to tell himself that he should not panic about the thought of someone coming for a meal.

"This is ridiculous. I am a mature man simply entertaining a friend to a meal. Be still my beating heart", he says to himself, "panic will not help."

He throws the ruined cherries away and decides that yoghurt alone will appeal to Ellie. A chef must always retain the upper hand.

With deliberate calm he sets out the table in the small dining room. Later, he will light a fire in the lounge as the temperature drops. He now needs only to prepare himself. He has time for a bath which he so much prefers to a shower. It's impossible to read a book in the shower. He has discovered that the pages get wet and stick together. Later, he chooses a royal blue needle cord shirt, which he feels will work well, and set off his deep blue eyes.

He tries to read a few emails, but they are all crushingly dull, and he finds himself unable to concentrate. He does, however, google some information about wedding ring fingers. He discovers that it is traditional for the ring be on the third finger of the left hand. He shocks himself by realising that he has never known this or noticed what married women do in this regard. Maybe now he can take a surreptitious look at Ellie's hands. Finally, the doorbell rings, so he closes his laptop. He looks at his watch. She is only ten minutes late. Someone arriving ten minutes late is an occurrence well known to any lecturer.

He opens the door, and this picture of loveliness is smiling at him. He welcomes her. She wears only a short light coat, and he takes it from her. She wears a plain red dress cut well above the knee. It clings to her curves, curves that are very definitely in the right place in Keith's view. She looks very relaxed in the dress. He is surprised. He had imagined that she would be somewhat dressed down, maybe in jeans and a loose-fitting jumper. The shoes, though, are fairly informal, quite flat and comfortable, and easy for walking in. She wears a touch of makeup, but not more. Some of the women in Barmouth wear so much he has no idea what they look like underneath it all. He is no doubt what Ellie looks like. She looks gorgeous. He knows little about popular music but he recalls a song that he has heard and indeed it is one of which he has a copy, although he has almost never played it. It has the line:

"Lady in red, is dancing with me...." Just now, that's a dream.

He looks into her eyes. "The years have been kind to you. You look lovely." he says. She accepts the compliment with the ease of one who is well used to receiving them.

"Thank you". She has a voice that he just wants to hear and hopes he will not make the mistake that he fears, talking too much himself.

"Come through to the lounge. Can I get you a drink?" She settles herself on the settee, and Keith sits opposite her in an armchair. They settle on some red wine. When he hands her a glass, he looks at her hands and discovers that she is not wearing any ring at all. They discuss the events of last evening, and Keith discovers that all the others have returned home, so she is the only one left at the hotel. He had not spent much time last night discovering what people are doing now. Conversation about the members of the group follows. Ellie explains that one or two of them have taken jobs in finance in London and are working incredibly long hours, making a fortune.

Keith: "Well, at least when the inevitable heart attack comes shortly, they can afford the private medical care that may help them to survive it. Let's eat, and you can tell me what you are doing now."

Together, they put the meal on the dining room table. Ellie declares the wine and the food very acceptable and they begin to eat. Neither seems in a hurry.

Ellie: "The duck is very tender."

Keith: "Did I ever tell you what economists say about ducks?"

Ellie: "I don't recall."

Keith: "There is a saying that if something looks like a duck, swims like a duck, and quacks like a duck, then it is a duck."

Ellie looks intrigued.

"Yes, I have that expression before, but what has it got to do with economists?"

Keith: "Sometimes economists get tired of explaining things to people and producing clear evidence to support that what they are saying is true, only to hear abstruse and absurd arguments to avoid the force of their reasoning. In exasperation, they might use this expression to show that if it appears to be something and it can be shown to have all the characteristics of that something, then it is surely what it appears to be."

Ellie: "I get it."

"My mother liked her food cooked really well. She was not an economist, but her variation on the theme would have been that if it looks like a duck and quacks like a duck, it needs longer in the microwave. I like even duck to be well cooked, although culinary fashions dictate otherwise. I remember someone saying about a chicken when it was served that it was so underdone that a skilled vet could have saved it."

She smiles that wonderful smile again, and he asks her about her life after she left Barmouth. She describes her employment after leaving Barmouth before taking him by surprise.

Ellie: "After I left, I had several different jobs, but in recent years, I have developed my own business. It's early days yet, but so far, I am rather pleased with the way it's going."

Keith: "What's the business?"

Ellie: "I was dreading you asking me that." For the first time since he has seen her again, she looks a little uncomfortable. "I sell women's underwear online."

Keith is unable to resist a broad smile. He hopes that she will not mind this and says: "Is that so? How did you get into that?"

She leans across the table and touches his hand. She does not mind.

Ellie: "Well, I came into a fair bit of money – I will tell you how a bit later – so I could afford to give up my job and buy a modest house in the suburbs. Then I spent time starting up a business in a small way. I did some research and discovered that women's underwear was a profitable opportunity. I developed contacts with suppliers and created some online content to promote the products. I was surprised that I was able to get to see senior managers of firms making the underwear I thought would sell. They were very supportive, and it all developed from there. I had no idea that a few years later I would be sitting with you, blushing because of what I chose to sell."

Keith: "You shouldn't have been surprised by getting to see senior managers. I suspect they were mostly, if not entirely, male. These people won't do deals with someone just because she is beautiful, but they will give her twenty minutes of their time that you may be able to use – and you, Ellie, are beautiful.

She blushes, but only slightly.

Keith: "Looking back on it, do you think that it was a good decision to come to Barmouth to do a degree?"

Ellie: "I do, although it took me a while to settle down. I was put up a year in my junior school, so through most of my education, I was a year older than the people around me. I was only seventeen when I arrived at the university. I was reminded of those times today since I spent most of it wandering around down there while you were in prison. It reminded me of how I had made a lot of friends, how I got a good degree, and then jobs that set me up so that I could pursue a successful career. And I was so lucky that I didn't need to acquire the fifty thousand pounds of debts of today's students. To be honest, though, I thought the teaching was mixed. We had some great teaching, but there was some dross too."

Ellie recalls one lecturer who was so bad that the students had got together and insisted on meeting him so they could tell him frankly what they thought. Keith is aware of the story because he had been asked by the students to attend the meeting as an independent witness.

Keith: "I was amazed at your bluntness. What you don't know is the follow up to that occasion. The guy wrote me a letter accusing me of several things that were blatantly untrue. I went straight to his office and waved the letter at him. He claimed that I had misunderstood and that he didn't mean any such thing. But his letter making the accusations stayed on the file."

Ellie: "What happened to him? Is he still in Barmouth?"

"Oh, no, he isn't. He was so bad that a year or two after you left, he got a professorship abroad." She laughs, and the laughter reaches to her eyes.

They have finished their main course so Keith asks to see her website.

Ellie smiles that heartbreaking smile: "Do you like looking at women's underwear, then?"

Keith: "It depends on who is in them".

They use the laptop, and she shows Keith a few of the electronic pages to give him an idea of how the site works. He is very impressed. Their heads are close together. He feels a spark like an electric current passing between them. He has never felt anything like this before and wonders if Ellie feels it too. Whatever is going on, it has nothing to do with the sight of women's underwear.

Keith: Do you wear any of these items yourself?"

She blushes again, rather more deeply this time.

Ellie: "Yes, I like this set in particular."

She shows him a picture of it. He allows himself a moment to imagine this beautiful lady wearing it.

"Fortunately, so do enough women to keep the business profitable", she adds.

He is a strictly Marks and Spencer man himself. They finish their duck, and he tells her the story of the salted cherries. There is more laughter, and she says she would love a little yoghurt. They go into the kitchen together with the plates and the dishes. She looks out of the window. The meadows are there, but the light has faded too much for it to be much of a view. He comes and stands behind her, looking out of the window with her.

"You are very lucky. This is a lovely house and a great spot." She says.

Keith: "I know it's dark, but a little later, we could walk across to the meadows and take some air, if you like."

Ellie: "I would like that very much."

The back of her dress is cut even lower than her hair. As he stands behind her, he almost involuntarily, touches her neck with his fingers. He has shocked himself with his temerity and waits for her to pull away. She stands absolutely still. He plays his fingers up and down her neck area. She still remains motionless. There is complete stillness between them. Finally, reluctantly, he moves away, and they take the yoghurt back to the table.

Ellie: "We loved your teaching. I only remember one occasion, early on, when you got irritated with us."

Keith: "Remind me."

Ellie: "You asked us to read an article to be discussed in the seminar. We usually did whatever you asked of us, but there was a birthday party celebration the night before the class. When we turned up, you asked if someone would summarise the contents, and no one said anything. You picked on someone; I forget who it was. He said sorry, but he hadn't read it. You picked on someone else who said the same thing. In the end, it turned out that none of us had read it. I will never forget your reaction. You said that if we couldn't be bothered to do the work beforehand, you couldn't be bothered to stay and discuss it. You walked out."

Keith finds himself laughing.

Ellie: "What is so funny?"

Keith: "I have never admitted this to anyone in all these years, but I will tell you the rest of the story. I was rather busy at that time. I hadn't read it either. It was a huge relief to me that no one had done the work."

Ellie: "Are you serious?"

Keith: "Yes, I am absolutely serious."

Ellie: "After that, we all got down to it and did the work, so I guess it was a lesson to all of us."

She throws her arms around him. They smile at one another, and Keith is thrilled, and not a little amazed, that she is clearly enjoying his company.

The yoghurt is a definite improvement on the combination of yoghurt and salted cherries. They decide against coffee and go back to the lounge. Ellie looks across at the piano.

"Do you play it?" she asks.

Keith: "Alas, I do not. It's a good piano, but I can't play a note. I am keeping it for a friend who is abroad for a couple of years. He even sends someone around regularly to tune it."

She runs her fingers over the keyboard as lightly as he had run his fingers across her neck.

"How about you? Do you play?" he asks.

She doesn't reply for a long time but sits and looks at the keyboard. Finally, she begins to play. He recognises it at once, Chopin's Nocturne Number one in B flat minor, a quiet and lyrical piece evoking the intimate atmosphere of the evening. He stands watching her hands, listening to the music. He has not heard this piece live since he was a teenager. He finds that his tears are beginning to fall.

"That was beautiful," he says. "How did you learn to play like that?"

She turns, and he sees that her eyes are glistening with tears also.

"Mother was a piano teacher. I grew up with the sound of the piano all around me."

Keith: "Maybe you will play something else for me later?"

She smiles through the tears. "I will. But I would need another glass of wine first."

They both move to the settee, and Keith is delighted that Ellie feels relaxed enough to put her feet up. He decides to adopt a similar position.

"How did you get on in prison today?" she asks.

Keith: "Well, the most important thing is that they let me out after I did my teaching. It was quite depressing. I spent yesterday in a strange environment, a very expensive private girls' school. Today, I was teaching similar stuff in a forbidding looking prison to guys who have been incarcerated for years. I was glad to have gone but relieved to get out."

Ellie: "I remember you telling us about the story of the prisoner's dilemma. As I remember it, two people are arrested for robbing a bank, but the police don't have enough evidence to convict them, so they need to get one of them to confess. They put the two men in separate cells and offer each a reduction in the sentence if they sign a confession. I recall that we discussed whether it would pay each of them to keep quiet when they are uncertain what to do because they don't know choice the other one might make. You then showed us some economic problems based on uncertainty illustrated by this prisoner's dilemma. I learned a lot from that."

Keith finds himself reverting to a teaching mode, which is not something he wanted, but the story he wishes to tell her he has always appreciated.

"Since you remember that so well, I will tell you a story from a few years ago. A friend of a friend lectures in economics in Greece. He had taught a course, which included stuff on the prisoner's dilemma, and he set an exam one morning. The night before the exam, four of his students got together to revise. They decided to start with a few beers. It got out of hand, and they got drunk. As a result, the students turned up too late to sit the exam. The claimed to the professor that they were late because they had had a puncture. They asked if they could sit a different exam. They were very surprised when the professor said that would be okay if they came back the next day. When they turned up, they were put in four separate rooms with their exam paper. On the paper was just one question. Part A was for ten percent of the marks. It said, 'Briefly outline the prisoner's dilemma'. Part B was for ninety percent of the marks. It said, 'Which tyre burst?' I suspect those four men learned more about the prisoner's dilemma in those moments than you learned from me in that class all those years ago.

Ellie: "That's a great story. I remember that your lectures were always full of such stories. We were never sure which ones were real and which ones were made up."

Keith: "Neither was I. Time for that coffee?"

They bring the coffee into the lounge, and Keith lights the fire. They sit on the floor enjoying the flames, and Ellie comments on the horse brasses that are there.

She moves in very close to him.

"This evening is the first time in years I have felt truly happy."

Keith: "Will you tell me about the things you hinted at in an email, the things that have happened that are not all good?"

Ellie: I will, but it's hard to start. Tell me first about the horse brasses. One is just the plain shape of a horseshoe. Are you superstitious?"

Keith: "I am absolutely not superstitious. It's just a horseshoe brass. But you may have heard about the economist who had a horseshoe prominently displayed above the front door of his house. A reporter came to interview him and asked what it was for. He told her that it was for good luck. The reporter expressed great surprise that he believed such a thing. He assured her that he did not. So, she pressed him and asked him why he kept it there. He replied, 'Ah, it works whether you believe in it or not.'"

He looks at her mouth as she laughs again. He longs to kiss it.

Ellie: "You are so very easy to be with." She leans forward and, as if she can read his thoughts, her lips find his. The kiss is gentle but unhurried. To Keith, it is the taste of ambrosia. She gets up and goes over to his old-fashioned music centre.

"Will you play something for me?" she asks.

Keith: "Of course I will. I don't play the piano, but I got a solid upper second at CD playing."

His choice of song is inevitable. Soon, the sounds of the Chris de Burgh track 'Lady in Red' fills the room, but quietly.

"The lady in red is dancing with me, cheek to cheek. There's nobody here; it's just you and me. It's where I want to be..."

He invites her into his arms, and they dance. Keith is quite remarkably bad at dancing and does little more than shuffle his feet. Fortunately, Ellie appears not to care. They both move closer to each other, and her cheek rests on his.

"But I hardly know this beauty by my side. I'll never forget the way you look tonight."

He wraps his arms around her and holds her tightly as they dance.

"And when you turned to me and smiled, it took my breath away."

The song comes to an end. The fire is still warm, but the coffee has gone cold. Without waiting to be pressed further, she sits down and begins to speak of the days after she left Barmouth.

"Life in Barmouth was very good. I had done well in my degree studies – thank you for all you did, I am sorry I never said that to you - and I was falling in love with a young lecturer from the foreign languages department. He was very good at German, but then, although his mother was English, his father was a German, so he was bi-lingual. He was in the process of leaving Barmouth for another post. We married the summer after we left Barmouth, and very quickly, I became pregnant. It wasn't planned. We had planned to have a few years together before we thought about a family, but neither of us minded. Within a short time of knowing for certain that I was pregnant, my husband went out in the car on business one morning. I said goodbye to him, and he never came back.... ".

She shudders and throws herself in Keith's arms. She weeps for some time, and he says nothing. He just holds her tightly. Eventually, there are no more tears left, and she stops.

Ellie: "I have made your shirt wet with my tears. "

Keith: "It doesn't matter. Do you want to tell me why he didn't return?"

She doesn't speak for a long time. Keith gets an impression of one whose mind is miles away. Eventually, she takes up her story again.

"There was a multiple crash in fog on the M6. Many were injured, but there were three fatalities. He was one of them. I had to go to view the body. He was badly disfigured. It wasn't easy. I loved him. I have never felt close to a man since - until tonight."

She shudders again, clings so tightly to Keith that his ribs begin to hurt.

Keith: "What happened about your pregnancy?"

Ellie: "Are you not bored listening to my tale of woe?

Keith: "Certainly not, my dear Ellie. Sad though it is, I want very much to hear it all."

Ellie: "Thank you. I get to spend quite a bit of time on my own because of the online business. I don't get to hear the sound of my own voice very much, although talking about these things isn't easy, even with you."

It is no problem to Keith. She has a voice that makes him feel he could listen all night.

Ellie continues: "I had a baby boy. It was a straightforward birth, but it was difficult raising him. He wasn't an easy child at all. My husband had been reasonably wealthy, so we never lacked for money. It was his money that made it possible to start my own business a few years ago without having to be in debt to the banks. As my son got older, it became ever more difficult to be close to him. Recently, he got a place to study business at Barmouth. I asked him to go and say hello to you when he got there, but I didn't think he would. I saw him today. That was partly why I stayed around an extra night. Although we are not close, he is my son, and I do love him. I got an impression that he was very unhappy at the university, but he wouldn't talk about it. He is very bright. He too was put up a year at junior school. He is still only seventeen now. Can we go for that walk you mentioned? I fear otherwise; I may just sit in your arms all night and cry."

The thought of this beautiful lady in red in his arms all night is not one that gives Keith any pain at all, but he willingly accedes to her request.

Keith: "When we return, I will make you one of my hot, milky drinks. It's compulsory." She looks up at him, and although the sadness is still in her eyes, for the first time in a while this evening she smiles. The evening is warm, and there is no forecast of rain, so Keith sets the burglar alarm, and they leave the house, each wearing just a thin coat. The plan is for a twenty-minute walk so that he can show Ellie the meadows. It's dark, but there is sufficient light from a gibbous moon to make it a pleasant stroll. A water vole is disturbed by their approach, and it splashes noisily into the water. Ellie jumps and grabs his hand.

Keith: "It's okay. It's only a water vole. I guess you are not used to such noises where you live."

Ellie: "No, there aren't too many water voles in Croydon."

Her heartbeat returns to normal, but she doesn't let go of his hand. Soon, seemingly out of nowhere, it suddenly begins to rain heavily. In a few seconds, it feels like a cloudburst and in moments they are both soaking wet. The rain is coming down in sheets out of the dark sky. They can not only feel it but see it by the lights from the boys' school on the other side of the river. They look at each other, and as the water drips from their faces, Keith decides to complain about weather forecasters:

"What amazing people they are. Have you noticed how they come on TV and tell you it won't rain tomorrow? Then, when it pours the next day, they never admit their mistake. They just carry on as though they had been entirely accurate."

She looks up with water dripping from her hair, her nose, and her chin.

"Keith, does your rational, economist mind tell you that this is the best place to discuss the accuracy of weather forecasting?"

She laughs, this time loudly and from deep within. It is a wonderful sound to Keith. Holding hands, they run back to the house, where they arrive totally drenched. He turns off the alarm and they remove their shoes, sodden from the rain. He shows her up to the bathroom.

"You can take off all those wet things and have a shower. There is a bathrobe on the back of the door. I hope that gorgeous dress isn't spoiled. Come down when you are ready, and I will make you that hot drink of milk."

He turns to go.

Ellie: "Keith, thank you, the dress will be fine when it's dried out. I am having a wonderful evening."

Keith: "Ellie, you are soaking wet."

Ellie: "Yes, that's certainly part of it, but I am enjoying everything else as well."

Keith: "Me too. Take your time; I will sort myself out in the other bathroom."

Within ten minutes, he has showered, dried, and changed and is back in the kitchen preparing things for a milk drink. Suddenly, there is a piercing scream from the bathroom. He leaps up the stairs. How can there possibly be a burglar? The alarm had been on all the time they were out. The bathroom door is ajar. He pushes it open. Ellie is standing there with her back half turned, completely naked. He can see the outline of one of her breasts. She looks magnificent, beautifully proportioned, perfectly shaped. He files the picture in his memory for later contemplation. She turns to him, sobbing, pointing to the bath. She grabs hold of him, clings to him, oblivious of her nakedness. In that moment, he tries very hard not to laugh. He is holding in his arms a beautiful woman who is clearly genuinely terrified. She is leaning as far away from the bath, consistent with holding on the Keith for her very life. She is pointing at an ordinary, common, or garden sized spider. He fears that he is not being entirely successful in keeping a straight face.

He gently eases her away from him, reluctant though he is to do so. He quickly gathers up the spider in one hand, opens the window, throws the spider out, and closes the window again. It is the work of but seconds. She turns back to him, holds him close, and then begins to smile herself. He can still feel her heart racing. Then she playfully punches him on the chest:

"I saw your laugh, you beast. I was really scared. I always have been of spiders."

"And I am so very glad you are." Keith thinks but does not say.

As her fear subsides, she becomes conscious that she is wearing absolutely nothing. Keith is quick to reassure her:

"Please don't be embarrassed. You look and feel absolutely gorgeous."

He doesn't often blush, but he is aware that he is doing so now. If all women, when naked, looked as magnificent as this, she would never sell enough bras for her business to survive.

"You really are very beautiful," he says gently.

It is her turn to blush. She opens her mouth, closes it again, and says nothing.

He catches a glimpse of her wet underwear, the very same that she had shown him on her website. Reluctantly, he detaches himself from her.

"I will be in the kitchen. I would like to say that I hope there are no more spiders, but I am not sure that I can."

"Go, you terrible man." She grins, robbing her words of any possible offence.

A while later, Ellie comes into the kitchen. Her hair is wet, Keith's bathrobe fits her badly, and, thanks to the weather forecaster's incompetence, she has a generally dishevelled appearance. Keith thinks she looks sensational. There is no doubt that apart from his bathrobe, she is wearing nothing. They make hot chocolate and go back to the settee in the lounge. She tucks her feet up under his thighs. It feels like an intimate gesture. He loves it. He is already playing a CD of the Chopin nocturnes but set at a low volume.

Ellie continues her story:

"So many things have happened since I saw you last. Some of them have been sad. Mother caught some dreadful disease and was so poorly that my father could stand it no longer. He left ten years ago and I have not seen or heard from him since. Then a few years ago Mother died so I have no close relatives other than my son. But I haven't been totally unhappy since I last saw you. My career and the business have both gone very well. But it hasn't worked out with any of the few men who have come into my life. When my husband died, Gary was very kind and supportive. He and I tried to make a go of it, but we both knew that we were not suited to each other. After that, a few others have come and gone over the years. Maybe I am very fussy."

There is a peaceful, wholly agreeable silence between them for a while before she continues:

"Keith, I haven't felt so close to a guy for more years than I can remember."

He goes to the kitchen for more hot chocolate. On his return she has removed a book from one of his bookshelves. It is a copy of J.R. Tolkien's magnificent 'Lord of the Rings' the story of how Frodo, a hobbit from The Shire carries a ring into Mordor, the evil empire ruled by Sauron. She is reading it with a faraway look in her eyes. She looks up, sees him as if for the first time that evening, and says:

"When my son was about ten, I started reading this to him for maybe half an hour at night before bedtime. It took a year and a half but those times were very special. It seems such a long time ago now."

She closes her eyes, and this gives him opportunity to look at her, which he does with great delight. As the nocturnes finish, he realizes that she doesn't just have her eyes closed; she is asleep. The wine and the emotions of the evening have clearly exhausted her. He doesn't mind at all that she is sleeping. He is delighted that she feels sufficiently relaxed with him that she can allow herself to do so. He gets off the settee. He strokes her forehead gently, but it produces no response. He gets a blanket to cover her. The fire has gone out. He turns off the CD player. After a few more minutes, he makes a decision. She is not heavy, so he will try to move her. He goes up to his bedroom and pulls back the covers. Then he comes back to her and lifts her up. She stirs but does not wake. He carries her up to his room, lays her on the bed, and pulls a duvet over her. Still, she doesn't stir. Then he kisses her gently on the forehead. Now she smiles but doesn't open her eyes. He creeps out of the room and turns off the light. Ten minutes later, he is asleep in the spare room.

In the morning, he makes her breakfast. For him, breakfast is usually a banana and a glass of milk. This morning, he finds eggs, toast, and coffee. He carefully checks the marmalade. No, he hasn't added any salt. He puts it all on a tray and takes it up to Ellie. His timing is excellent, for she is just beginning to stir. In a sleepy haze she says:

"Did I really fall asleep on the settee? Did you really carry me up here? Did I really sleep all night? Did you really cook me breakfast in bed? "

Keith: "Yes, yes, yes and yes."

Ellie: "No one has made me breakfast in bed for as long as I can remember. You didn't get into bed with me."

Keith: "I certainly did not. You will never know just how much I wanted to, but I was not about to take advantage of a defenceless lady. Enjoy your breakfast. "

Ellie: "I will. Let me kiss you first."

The taste of ambrosia is still there. Keith feels that he could easily get used to this.

Ellie: "Did you arrange for that rain last night?"

Keith: "No. Would you mind very much if I had?"

Ellie: "I would not have minded very much at all. How else would I have got such nice marmalade for my breakfast?"

The breakfast is unhurried, as breakfast should always be.

Keith: "There's a spare toothbrush, toothpaste, soap, etc in the bathroom, but no lipstick. I have never found the colour that suits me. I also checked this morning. I am sorry to say there are no spiders either. Your clothes are just about dry enough to wear back to the hotel.

Forty-five minutes later, they have loaded the dishwasher, tidied the place up a little are both dressed and ready to leave. Ellie has to go to the hotel to check out. Keith has a taxi coming to take him to Gatwick. This week, he is to be in Bulgaria on a job for Barmouth. He loves travelling, but this time, he is going to carry an Ellie shaped hole in his heart. A little later Ellie's taxi arrives. They hug each other but say nothing for a long time. Finally:

Keith: "Thank you, Ellie, that was a very special evening for me."

Ellie: "I loved it. How will we see each other again? We both have commitments."

Keith: "I hope as soon as possible. I have no wish to lose you now I have found you. I let you go for fifteen years. That was a mistake I do not wish to repeat."

He hugs her. Again, it is for a long time. She doesn't object. One final tender kiss, and she is gone.

Keith has only a limited acquaintance with the works of the *Austrian-Czech novelist* Franz Kafka. However, he recalls a quote from his book, The Hunger Artist:

"Anyone who keeps the ability to see beauty never grows old."

Since meeting Ellie again, he sees this quote in a different way. Maybe Keith has found a way to limit the aging process.

CHAPTER SEVEN:
BULGARIAN INTERLUDE

'I don't hold with abroad and think that foreigners speak English when our backs are turned.'

- Quentin Crisp

During the next few days Keith will be in Bulgaria. Many universities, including Barmouth, have arrangements with foreign institutions. Barmouth has a link to University College Sofia, UCS. The students at UCS study the same subjects as the Barmouth students, sit the same exam papers and are awarded the same degrees. Keith's job is to facilitate the link and this involves going there several times a year. It's a private business school. This makes it expensive so some families struggle with the fees but it's a country with a long tradition of placing a high priority on education and there is some kudos in having an English degree and also a chance to come to Barmouth for higher degree study.

He teaches students there, liaises with the staff and, on this occasion, at the end of the week he will attend the degree ceremony for the UCS students who are graduating. Several other members of the Barmouth Business School will be flying in later to attend the ceremony and in a few cases to do a little teaching. He has always enjoyed his visits. He is looked after even at the weekends by friendly warm-hearted staff and students who take him around to see the sights. This time, though, he is already missing Ellie even before the plane has left the runway. Clearly the University pays his costs but Barmouth has to cover those costs from the fees the Bulgarian students pay so he tries to find relatively cheap flights. Some years ago, the airlines tried to charge more to business travellers than to leisure travellers. They did this by assuming that if someone planned to stay away on a Saturday night that person was a leisure traveller, if not it suggested that person was on business. The price difference for the fare was enormous, approximately £200 for a return flight with a Saturday night stay and approximately £1200 without it. He has always been willing to stay on a Saturday night. There are those in the university administration who resent staff being able to travel at university expense. Some of the staff will go to places like the Bahamas and the Seychelles where Barmouth has links. The administration tends to mind less when Keith goes because Sofia has no beach and so they presume he doesn't enjoy it very much. He has no intention of disillusioning them.

Keith speaks no Bulgarian even though he has been there often. Knowing the language isn't necessary. The language is very difficult to learn and he is too lazy. But it isn't important. The students speak very good English, at least as good as the English students in Barmouth and frequently better. They have learned formal rules of English grammar and many of his UK students haven't. They may speak with an accent, but they do know an adverb from an adjective. In some cases, the Barmouth students can't tell the difference between an adverb and an aardvark.

Their knowledge of mathematics is also far superior. Last time he was there he brought some material on maths and statistics for the students. One student looked at what he had brought and said:

"Keith, we did this stuff when we were eleven. "

Sometimes when he arrives at Sofia airport, he gets a taxi to the hotel, at other times a member of the UCS staff is there to greet him. This time he is greeted by the director of the school. When he had first travelled there the roads were in a very poor state. Drivers would use one of two techniques to deal with the large potholes in the road. One technique was to swerve around them. Keith would look up and find himself on the wrong side of the road with vehicles heading straight at him. Somehow the driver had always avoided an accident. The other technique involved the driver ignoring the potholes entirely and simply hitting them, often at some speed. In some ways this was safer but the jarring tended to loosen the teeth somewhat. Things have improved markedly in recent years. There are still holes but at least they are no longer as bad as those in the UK.

The weather is pleasantly warm for March, although he has been here in the depth of the winter when it has been cold and there has been a considerable amount of snow. There is still a lot of snow on the surrounding Vitosha Mountain, visible as the aircraft comes in to land. He recalls that the coldest he has experienced is the middle of Finland. He visited a university in the town of Joensuu during one December when it reached -19 degrees centigrade. When he had asked about this, he was told that he had hit a warm patch. Cold would be -45 degrees centigrade. He recalls being disappointed that it had not reached -20 degrees because at that level there is the charming custom that anyone can knock the door, even if a complete stranger, and come inside for a short while to warm up. Bulgarians are very friendly but they do not seem to have any such custom.

The journey from the airport to the centre is a short one. It is difficult to miss the many ugly apartment blocks of brutalist 1960's Soviet construction, but in the centre are some delightful buildings from a period before the communist era. Keith prefers to stay in the Hilton or the beautifully appointed Hotel Sofia but he, and the others arriving later in the week, has been allocated a rather lower grade, but still adequate hotel this time. At the reception desk the director is having trouble checking him in but after a while things seem to be sorted. He promises to find the director at the university tomorrow, thanks him for his help with the transport and heads for his room. He has stayed here before but never in a room so enormous. It is not very modern or elegant but it is huge and at least it has a minibar. The standard of service from the hotel staff is okay. The standard generally in hotels and restaurants when he first came was often very poor but under pressure from international chains like the Hilton it has improved considerably. He recalls what a delight it was when he first stayed at the Sofia Hilton. The staff had been superbly trained. They had been told that it was not the boss that paid their salary but the customers. He was made to feel that the only reason the staff had got out of bed was to take the opportunity to serve him. This is not often how he is made to feel in the UK.

The problem of staff attitudes has not yet disappeared entirely. One of the students from UCS is now the deputy manager of another hotel. When she suggested some possible improvements to the running of the place the response from the manager was unequivocal:

"I have been working in this industry for forty years. Don't tell me how to do my job."

Keith checks his email, hoping for something from Ellie. He is not disappointed.

Dear Keith,

Thank u so much for a lovely evening. I hope I didn't outstay my welcome. It's a very long time since I felt so looked after and cared for. Let me know when you would like to meet up again. Many hugs.

Ellie.

He responds straight away.

Dear Ellie,

Greetings from Bulgaria. I can't remember the last time I had such a delightful evening. U certainly didn't outstay your welcome. I wish it had been longer. The evening did take a lot of preparation, though. Finding the spider was difficult and training it not to move from the bath was particularly difficult. It was worth it though. I would love to see u again as soon as possible. Tell me your plans in the next few weeks. Maybe you can find me on Facebook that we can chat.

Love from Keith xxx

He takes a taxi to the house of friends who are expecting him for a meal. As so often before there are other friends there too. Everyone speaks great English, although this applies somewhat less to the cat and the dog. At the end of the evening, he gets a lift back to within a few hundred yards of the hotel and walks the last bit of the way. As he nears the hotel he hears footsteps behind him. He turns to see a lady, who, he guesses, is in her late thirties. She speaks to him.

"Seeee-garrrr –ett?"

"I beg your pardon?"

She says it again in the voice of one repeating an instruction to one who is a few cents short of a Euro.

"Matches for my seeee-garrrr –ett?"

"Oh, very sorry, I don't smoke"

"Yes, matches for my seeee-garrrr –ett?"

"No, no, I am very sorry, I don't smoke. No smoke."

She pauses and looks very frustrated before developing the conversational gambit.

"Sex? Sex?"

"Oh, thank you very much, that's very kind of you but not just now".

He runs quickly into the hotel lobby. It was twenty years ago, outside of one of the Barmouth university buildings when he had last been approached in this kind of way. His response had been much the same then, a polite middle-class Englishman running as fast as decently possible. As an economist he finds it interesting that she had not got as far as suggesting a price. Maybe this is usual in this industry. Keith is not very familiar with it. This limited contact with it does nothing to make him feel that he has lost out. Before he sleeps, he makes a note to share the incident with Ellie, so he decides to send her another email. He hopes that she finds it as amusing as he does.

To get from the hotel to UCS he can either take a taxi, a tram or just walk. This morning, he walks. He is greeted on arrival by Polina, the superb administrator whose work makes his life so much easier. She is one of the old school who sees her job as making it possible for academics to do their job. Barmouth could usefully do with a few more like her.

Soon he is teaching a group of students. Some of these people really impress him. One guy comes from a low-income family. He is doing so very well even though he has had to borrow heavily to fund his investment in the degree. He also works for a company to help support himself, although doing paid work as well as studying is common here as it is in the UK. The topic of the lecture is the causes of unemployment. At the end of the hour a group of six male students stay behind and ask to speak to him so that they can share their frustrations.

"Life for males in Bulgaria is so unfair. We work just as hard as the women, we get just as good degree results as they do, but they are the ones who get the jobs. The people in the firms who do the hiring are older guys who like having beautiful women wandering around the office, so we don't get appointed and they do."

Keith has no evidence either to support their view or to deny it but it is his job to make them think.

"If this really is the case, it seems to me to be eminently reasonable. Inevitably, you will earn a wage well above the average for Bulgaria because you were lucky enough to be born with above average intelligence. You expect to use this accident of birth. It gives you an advantage relative to others. Why shouldn't some of the women students here, who by an accident of birth have been given an advantage of good looks, exploit this advantage in the same way that you will exploit your intelligence?"

"But that's not a fair comparison. Our above average intelligence contributes to the company and the nation's prosperity. We get paid according to what we are worth. A woman's good looks will add nothing to the company's profitability."

"I disagree. Their beauty is a not a direct gain for the company. It is a non-pecuniary benefit but it is still a benefit. If what you are saying is correct then it raises morale among senior male staff and therefore, indirectly, leads to greater productivity and profitability. "

"We don't believe this. They are more likely to be a distraction, lowering the productivity of employees and therefore reducing company profitability. "

Keith is enjoying this.

"Actually, the evidence is that I am right and you are wrong at this point. If these women, because of the distraction they create, lower productivity and therefore profitability, the firm would not survive. Other companies in those industries, those firms with more enlightened views, would appoint you men. This would make these companies more efficient. They will produce their goods and services more cheaply and take the market away from the firms employing the beautiful women. According to you this is not happening. We must therefore infer that the managers are making wise, profit maximizing decisions."

A stunned silence follows.

He suggests that in other countries he is aware of the young women are the ones discriminated against because they might go off and have a family. Therefore, what they are suggesting may well not be so. He encourages them to do two things. First, they should ask themselves whether they have any evidence for their assertion or whether they are generalizing on one or two particular occasions when they have been beaten to a job by a girl. Second, they should look for some statistics on unemployment of male and female graduates in Bulgaria so that there is some evidence to reflect upon. Then they all go off for coffee. There is a café around the corner that a lot of students use and there are already a number of others there. Sitting with fifteen or more students at coffee is not unusual for him and the discussion ranges across a huge range of topics, although rarely economics related ones. Many of the women are very attractive. He sits next to a girl he has not seen before. He asks her about what she does apart from study. With a little embarrassment she says that she enters beauty contests and was Miss Bulgaria a few years ago. Keith is amazed. He looks around and decides that, if all the women students had entered the competition and he had been the judge, he would have placed her fourth.

As he leaves, he finds two other students wanting to speak with him. Things aren't much different here than in Barmouth. One of them is a girl who looks quite happy and one is a guy who looks sad and distressed. He decides that the guy will need more of his time so he asks him to wait a few minutes while he talks to the girl. He has met her before when he has been here and knows that she is into extreme sports. Last year she had asked him to take part in something like bungee jumping, caving or rock climbing. Keith had suggested chess. In the end they had compromised and a group of them had spent a day last spring whitewater rafting seventy kilometres south of Sofia. The weather had been good, the river valley was beautiful with the trees just breaking into leaf and Keith had admitted that it was a much better idea than chess, although rather wetter. Now she is back pressing him on taking part in other life-threatening exercises. He promises to think about it. He is right about the guy. He has failed a lot of his exams and Barmouth has told him that there are too many failed papers for him to resit. He will have to repeat the year. The guy comes from a low-income family. He simply cannot afford to take an extra year to complete his degree. He also claims to have a medical problem that could account for one or two failed exam papers. Keith has heard stories that medical certificates can be bought but he cannot argue with a doctor's certificate. He has no power to waive the Barmouth rules about failed exams but says that he will ring the authorities in Barmouth to see what can be done. He is not hopeful but he will try and he rings Barmouth from Polina's office.

He fears that what passes for the thought processes of the members of the directorate will mean a blanket refusal to offer any assistance. He is pleasantly surprised. Sanity prevails. He finds someone at the end of a phone who suggests that Keith write a letter explaining the circumstances. The student will then be given a special exemption from the rule and will be allowed to resit all his failed papers without having to wait another year. Keith then explains this to the student. It will be a big task for him to re-take so many exams but the guy is delighted with the outcome. Keith wishes him well in his resit exams.

Later that day the Board of Studies meets. An occasional board gives opportunity for staff and students to discuss issues and share information. Keith acts as chair. He will report any issues that have arisen in the course of the year and he tries to do this with a light touch. The minutes of the previous meeting are circulated and are often assumed to reflect what was said last time. Keith thinks it preferable if they reflect what should have been said. One of the first items is a mind numbingly dull presentation from the assistant director at UCS. The guy is a lecturer in statistics. This becomes clear every year when his entire report is taken up regurgitating statistics of student numbers, proportions of people obtaining different degree categories and expected future student numbers.

Keith's mind wanders and he begins to consider whether he should present his own report in the same style....

"Thank you for that fascinating insight, contributing zero-point nought, nought one percent of enlightenment to the meeting. Today's meeting is attended by thirteen people of whom 65.9 percent are male. Of these only 14.2 percent have beards. Less than ten percent of the women have a beard. The director's speech took 17 minutes longer than last year. If this trend continues, then the 2075 meeting will begin before the 2074 session has ended. One of the women students has a skirt estimated at 7.5 inches above the knee which is 24 percent shorter than...."

He looks up and wonders why there is total silence and everyone is looking at him. Ah, the director's report has finished. Mercifully the students have no wish to discuss any issues. This is not because they don't care but because they prefer to raise matters of concern with Keith in private.

After the meeting one of the students comes over to say hello. She was very kind to him last summer but almost created trouble for him. He and Billie were filming on Bulgaria's Black Sea coast. Her father owned a business there, close to the Turkish coast. He had agreed to let Keith take some footage of the business. At the end of the shooting Keith and Billie had been invited to their home for a meal. They had then gone down to the beach and changed into wetsuits. Then she and Keith had taken the family jet ski out in the darkness. Keith had found it enormous fun. After a while there were frantic signals from her father to get back to the shore. They had quickly gone back and hastily changed into day clothes. Within minutes the border police had turned up to find them sitting around drinking coffee. After a few minutes of desultory chat, the police left.

Then and only then the family had explained that it was illegal to be out on the Jet Ski in the dark. Keith then discovered that the father was a friend of the chief of the border police who had rung his mobile to warn him that the police were on their way. Having many years ago just missed seeing a headline to the effect that he was involved in a nightclub brawl in Barmouth, he had now just missed being in a headline about being arrested by the Bulgarian border police authorities.

This morning Keith has no responsibilities at UCS so he plans to go to a Children's orphanage to meet some children there. Some years ago, he had met an amazing lady, Ana, who runs a foundation to support a number of orphanages around Bulgaria. She had invited him to take an interest in the work. She is picking him up from the hotel and will drive him the hour or so to the home and he can be back for the late afternoon to teach at UCS. The particular home they will visit today was in a very poor condition when Keith had first gone there. It has been transformed, largely as a result of a bunch of twenty or thirty Dutch Christians who come every summer to work on improving the homes. The work they are doing is transforming lives. The visit is a mixture of pleasure and sadness for Keith. It's so good to see what is being done and so sad to hear stories about some of the children. They all wish to be adopted into a family. Sometimes foreigners offer to adopt. These people visit a number of the children and when one is chosen there is great joy. However, there is great sadness in the eyes of the ones who are not chosen because they feel rejected. Keith fights back the tears himself. There is time for the ritual humiliation of being beaten by a seven-year-old at chess before they leave. There are more tears as he visits a day centre for disabled children, some so disabled they can barely move and certainly not speak.

On the way back they stop off at a day centre for old folks, a place also built and run as a result of the foundation's work. Keith spends an hour chatting to six or seven of them with Ana acting as the translator. These people remember the days when Bulgaria was under communist rule and they talk freely about what life was like then. They recall how guarded they had to be in what they could say and how delightful it is that they can now say whatever they like without fear of reprisals. Keith loves such conversations. It gives such an insight into a different culture that can never be obtained by a few days as a tourist on some arranged city break. He shares the lunch a few of the ladies have kindly prepared and then it is back to Sofia to teach.

He gives a few classes in the late afternoon and early evening. Some students work with a firm during the day and UCS arranges their classes in the evening after work. He then has a meal with the director and is back to the hotel to see if there is any more email from Ellie. There is. It is very brief.

HI Keith,

I found you on Facebook. When you get back to your hotel, if it's possible please look for me and we can say goodnight.

Love Ellie.

It is now quite late but he looks on Facebook and finds her immediately.

Hello Ellie, so good to be able to chat. In due course I might even be brave enough to work out how to speak. I am told it's even possible to see one another as we speak but that sounds like something for people with a PhD in technology.

A reply comes almost immediately.

Hello Keith, it isn't that difficult. We can work it out together soon. I have some news I want to share with you. I have been invited to expand the business by co-operating with a small company that is doing similar things to me but in Spain. It could be a really exciting joint venture.

He responds.

Congratulations! It sounds very good. Ellie, I have been thinking of you a great deal. Can I now think of you in Spanish underwear?

He response comes quickly.

Oh no, I don't think you would look very good in Spanish women's' underwear at all.

He loves her sense of humour.

Ho ho. How about I think of Ellie when Ellie is wearing Spanish underwear?

How easy it is to chat with her.

Well, you have seen me in rather less than that, although having looked at a few examples of what they are selling, the difference would not be very great. That reminds me, I didn't congratulate you on your spider training skills. I must have been so red faced with embarrassment.

He replies:

Ummm, I am not sure. I wasn't just looking at your face.

Ellie:

Now you are making me go red again. One problem about the Spanish underwear venture is that it may make it more difficult to meet up soon. I have agreed to fly to Algeciras soon for a week or so to discuss it further and work out some details of how it might work.

Keith:

I am so very keen to see you as soon as possible but when I get back, I have to go away for a few days visiting students working in industry and then be on jury service for ten days or so. However, that takes me up to the end of term so life should have a few more breathing spaces then.

Ellie:

Well, it might be tricky to make things work for a while but it sounds like we won't be short of things to talk about when we do meet. Let's compare notes about dates soon and see what is possible.

Keith:

Ellie, we have spent very little time together but I am missing you greatly.

Ellie:

Me too.

Keith:

Goodnight gorgeous. Speak soon. Please stay in touch. xxxxxx

When he has finished chatting to Ellie, he finds an email from Derek regarding the two students who have been caught cheating in exams.

Hello Ken,

I hope you are enjoying the time in Sofia. I want to let you know about the two students we discussed who were involved in cheating. Carrie will do the exam again with a mark capped at 40 percent and has been warned that a second offence will almost certainly lead to her removal from the course. A note has been placed on her file to this effect. As for Peter Fischer, I have now been told by the directorate that, because this was a second offence, there is nothing I can do for him. He must be removed from the course. He has been told of this decision and that there is no possibility of a successful appeal.

Regards,

Derek.

Such decisions are always painful for the student but also for the university, not least because they will lose the student's fees for the next couple of years. Keith, however, has no doubt that the right decisions have been taken and he emails Derek his thanks for letting him know.

This morning Keith takes a taxi to one of the state universities in Sofia. He has been asked to give a paper at a conference there. He has been informed that everyone presenting is restricted to twenty minutes each. He has explained to the organizers that he has other commitments today so it has been agreed that he will give his paper first, at nine am, but then stay only until the morning coffee break. He will be the only one speaking in English, but he has been assured by the conference organizers that it is fine that he addresses the conference in English since everyone has good enough English to follow his paper. He walks into the room at fifteen minutes to nine. The room is already laid out. There is a desk with a lectern at one end. On each of the two sides he sees a number of desks, about sixteen in all. At the back there are about thirty chairs but these have no desk. It's immediately clear that the desks are for important people, presumably staff, and the chairs without desks are for the peasants, the students. He assumes that he is an important person and chooses a desk. By nine the room is full and a member of staff stands at the lectern and introduces the conference. Although Keith can't understand a word it's obvious, given the context, that he is welcoming everyone to his little show. He then looks at Keith who presumes he means that it is time for him to perform. He presents in the same style that he uses to teach in Barmouth. He focuses on the students at the back who seem far more interested than the staff. With great discipline he stops after his allocated twenty minutes.

The next presenter is a sight to behold. He is about sixty, is somewhat overweight, and moves to the lectern at the speed of a tortoise with a wooden leg. He has a huge pile of papers in his hand the thickness of a house brick. He places them on the lectern, leans forward and with his nose hovering over his notes begins to do something that approximates to speaking. Although Keith can understand nothing, he suspects that none of the Bulgarians can either. After eleven minutes the presenter looks at his watch. He takes half his wad of notes and turns them over. He then proceeds exactly as before for a further eight minutes. After nineteen minutes he looks at his watch again, turns over all the other pages except the last, resumes his impersonation of a stone gargoyle and reads the last page, stopping after exactly twenty minutes. The next few presenters are little better. By now some people are feeling the need for a toilet break. Indeed, well before coffee the room is virtually empty. It is clear that many people have enormous bladders that must be emptied. Thankfully, the coffee break arrives and Keith can escape. Keith has been deeply bored and yet he has found this a fascinating experience. It is clear that these presenters have no interest in communicating knowledge. They simply need a line on their CV to say they have given a paper at a conference. He finds it vaguely comforting that the same lunacy that is higher education in the UK is alive and well in Bulgaria too.

Back at the hotel He waits for Dan Billings to arrive. Others are coming tomorrow but by getting Dan here a day earlier he can get his own personal delivery of the *Times* for an extra day. If he is unable to see the *Times* for more than a few days he gets withdrawal symptoms and his hands tremor. Dan arrives and unpacks and they decide it would be interesting to go to UCS on a tram. They buy the tickets and, as with much of Europe, they must validate the tickets with a machine on the tram. Failure to do so results in a large fine. In talking to one another they forget to do this. Alas an inspector gets on. The tram is crowded, mostly with old folks and Dan and Keith are standing. The inspector approaches so Keith hands over his unvalidated ticket. The inspector looks decidedly unimpressed. He says something which sounds to Keith's untrained ear like:

"Gobble de gobble de gook."

Keith responds with a Gallic shrug although the meaning of what the inspector is saying is perfectly clear. So, the inspector does to Keith exactly what English people do to foreigners who don't understand them. He says exactly the same thing, but louder.

"Gobble de gobble de gook."

Keith and Dan know that it is not a good idea to laugh and both try very hard to keep a straight face. Keith thinks that he can keep up this charade as long as the inspector can so he repeats his Gallic shrug. Now the inspector is shouting at him:

"GOBBLE DE GOBBLE DE GOOK."

There is an old guy who looks about ninety years' old sitting down listening to this one-sided exchange. He now addresses the inspector in a clearly irritated voice:

"Dumble de dumble de doo."

It is quite obvious that the old guy is saying that Keith is a foreigner who doesn't understand the system and to leave him alone. Now the inspector rounds on the old guy and addresses him with more incomprehensible language. The response comes from another guy on the tram. It's clear that he also is telling the inspector to leave Keith alone. By now the inspector is feeling very isolated with no friends at all. The tram comes to a halt and the inspector crossly gets off the tram. Keith turns to the people on the tram:

"Thank you everybody, thank you."

There follows a chorus of approval, which Keith interprets as:

"He is our enemy too so you and we are firm friends."

At last, they are able to laugh with their new friends. As they arrive at UCS Dan tells Keith that something similar had happened to him and his wife in Budapest when they had failed to validate their metro ticket. A man with a large medal on his chest had approached them. He had spoken to them in Hungarian, which proved about as incomprehensible to them as the tram inspector's Bulgarian. Dan had urged his wife away from the man saying that he had no wish to purchase his war medals. It had taken a while to realize that the medal was his authority to check tickets and fine passengers accordingly and they had then paid a large sum of money as a fine. Keith commiserates and says that it always helps to have a few dozen Bulgarian friends around. More teaching for both Keith and Dan is followed by a restaurant meal, and it is time to see if Ellie is available for a chat. He finds a Facebook message apologizing that it won't be possible to chat this evening because she has had to go and see her mother who is unwell.

By the next morning everyone coming from the UK (plus Keith's *Times*) has arrived for the graduation ceremony in the afternoon. They have all agreed to do some teaching in the morning, except the dean of the Business School, Brenda Collins who will present the degrees to the students, but who is far too important to engage in such trivial matters as teaching. They all agree to meet up for coffee after their respective classes. Keith has a group that is enthusiastic and interested. Like anywhere else in the world there are always exceptions. One of the students reminds him of Ellie. Her demeanour suggests that she regards herself as very beautiful. She may even be right. There is no way of knowing for she has such heavy makeup which seems to have been plastered on with a trowel. Keith had once done a summer holiday job as a bricklayer's labourer which involved knocking up cement, putting it into a wheelbarrow and carting it around to the bricklayers. The material on this girl's face looks eerily similar to the cement he remembers producing. The quantities used look similar also. Underneath this cement could be a face that launches a thousand ships, though Keith suspects that if she were on board one of them it would probably sink under the weight of her makeup.

Presumably, she finds that some guys here are drawn to this kind of appearance. None of this remotely reminds him of Ellie but the girl has one other outstanding feature. She has applied the most ludicrously long false eyelashes. One end of them finishes above her plucked and pencilled eyelashes. The other end rests on the cement on her cheeks. Her eyes seem to be peering out between spiders. He immediately christens her "Spider Eyes" and recalls Ellie's reaction to the spider in his bathroom. Would Ellie look at this student and scream? Keith looks at her and tries not to laugh. When he arrives back from his class, he finds all the others sitting around.

"Everyone else finished already?"

"We had to stop because of the power cut. We couldn't show our PowerPoint presentations."

"What power cut?"

"The one that started twenty minutes ago."

Keith had no idea that there had been one. Chalk on a blackboard works just as well even without electricity.

The afternoon degree ceremony is a joyful occasion. The dean presents the degree certificate and makes her inevitable "onwards and upwards" speech. It's a pity she can't or won't teach while in Sofia but she has to give an impression that time is too valuable for such a minor activity. As it is, she will only be in town for about twenty-four hours. Keith wonders if they can arrange next year for the ceremony to be held at Sofia airport. The plane would come into land, the students would file up one set of aircraft steps to receive their degree certificates and down the other set. The dean would then give her speech and her regal wave and never have to leave the aircraft. That way she could keep her time in Sofia to about forty-five minutes.

Inevitably, parts of the ceremony must be conducted in Bulgarian for the benefit of parents who do not know English. The English are each assigned a student to whisper a translation for these parts. Keith has a very attractive female student to translate for him so this causes him little pain.

All the students and their parents, all the Bulgarian and English staff smile and have photographs taken by the thousand. There is a short forty-minute session of drinks and nibbles to complete things. However, the rest of the day will still be hectic. In the early evening the English visitors and one or two Bulgarian staff go off for a meal to a restaurant. To please those who are here for the first time they choose a restaurant that caters for the tourists and has some traditional Bulgarian music and dancing. Keith confesses to Dan his incompetence with the Bulgarian language. When he was first in Bulgaria he had seen a word over a number of buildings. It was PECTOPAHT. He had thought that he had learned his first Bulgarian word. You simply have to say PECK TOE PAT and you have the Bulgarian for restaurant. He subsequently felt red faced to discover that PECTOPAHT is the word "restaurant" written in Cyrillic letters. Cyril has much to answer for.

The meal is a relaxing one. A lamb is being cooked over an open spit. Keith finds it the tenderest meat he has ever eaten. It just melts in the mouth. The music is fun although this time someone is playing an instrument like the Scottish bagpipes that one person describes as a dead goat. Customers are invited to join the dancing. The dances chosen have very simple steps. It has to be. It isn't too embarrassing for those with more than one left foot. The students are celebrating in a place very nearby so they walk. Keith recalls to the others an occasion when he and a few others had gone by taxi to a restaurant one evening without any Bulgarian staff. One of them had suggested they walk back to the hotel afterwards. Keith was not keen. The danger of getting lost was too great. He was overruled by a democratic vote. Democratic decisions can sometimes produce rotten outcomes. After walking for some while Keith had persuaded them to acknowledge that they were hopelessly lost and the only solution was to hail a taxi, not difficult in the centre of Sofia. Finally, the others had agreed. Keith had approached a taxi and given the name of the hotel. The taxi driver looked baffled. Keith had repeated the name of the hotel. Surely one would expect a taxi driver to know the location of one of the largest hotels in Central Sofia? In the end the taxi driver had said OK and they all piled in. They drove fifteen yards round the corner.......and stopped outside their hotel.

The graduating students have gone to a nightclub to celebrate and all the English staff are invited to join them. Keith would rather be boiled in oil but it is part of the job so they all go. The music is very loud but at least this discourages conversation. The women are dressed to kill. Keith doesn't think any of them have the allure of Ellie. The dean looks quite incredibly uncomfortable, so after an hour Keith suggests that they have fulfilled their obligations and they could go back to the hotel if she would like. She reacts like someone in a desert who has just been told that there is an oasis over the next sand hill. Dan offers to leave as well so the three of them depart while the others remain to boogey the night away. Amazingly the dean doesn't wish to retire for a while and suggests they have a drink. Keith suggests that they could open the minibar in his room.

"Minibar? I want to see this minibar."

It had not occurred to Keith that she would have a room without one. As the three of them open the door of his room it suddenly dawns upon him what is going on. The mix up at reception earlier in the week is now explained. He has been allocated the room meant for the dean. She is in a room the size of a dwarf's toilet where he is supposed to have been put. He has a minibar and she does not. He tries to press her to swap rooms but she is very gracious about it and insists on staying where she is. An hour of conversation follows, most of it rather desultory, although they appreciate one of Keith's stories from last year. A group of Barmouth lecturers had been staying at the Hilton hotel in Sofia and one evening they all watched a football match being shown in the lobby area. During the match the waiter was wandering around taking orders for drinks. One of the Barmouth team there was Dave Parton. He is rather fond of Baileys and asked the waiter to bring him one. Not long after the waiter reappeared and Dave ordered a second Baileys. A third order followed before half time. Keith then pointed out the Barmouth rules about alcohol consumption. If alcohol is taken with a meal it is regarded as a legitimate expense that can be claimed. If it is taken on its own, it is a private expenditure and Barmouth will not pay. In reply Dave said nothing to Keith. He just turned to the waiter and said:

"Could I have a salad and twelve Baileys please?"

Soon they all agree that it is time to retire to bed.

There is an email from Ellie.

Dear Keith,

I am so sorry it's difficult to chat just now. I think my mother is getting better but only slowly. It's pretty time consuming. When you are back in the UK tomorrow let's try to find some time to share a few things and work out how to meet up. I miss you.

Ellie xxxx

He replies.

Dear Ellie,

I miss you more than I would have thought possible. I hope mother continues to improve.

Love Keith xxx

The next morning all the team are on the flight back to the UK. Across the gangway sits a girl of student age who reminds him of Daphne, a Greek student whose dissertation he had supervised. In Greek mythology, Daphne has a melodic and peaceful quality to it which is how he remembered her. When she returned to Athens they had stayed in touch, so when the university asked him to visit Athens, he had suggested to Daphne that they meet up while he was there.

She took him to the Acropolis and they had arrived there at seven in the morning before the crowds had come. It was so peaceful and awe inspiring. He also remembers their meeting in a hotel lobby in the centre of town that evening. The long legs and the short skirt were a combination that was not easy to forget. They had gone to a Greek restaurant, eaten well and danced together. As the plane landed on British soil, he found himself daydreaming about the touch of Ellie.

CHAPTER EIGHT: MORDOR

*'So much of what we call management consists in making it
difficult for people to work.'*

- Peter Drucker

It's nearly the end of term. Keith has a last bit of teaching this
morning and then a meeting this afternoon in the University
directorate's building commonly known among teaching and
research staff as Mordor. When Keith first began his academic
career there would be a small group of administrators who saw
their task as offering assistance to the lecturing and research staff.
This group had a very useful function. Some support in areas of
admissions procedures and perhaps exam arrangements, was very
welcome. How things change. The administrators now *control* the
faculty members and do this with a whole army. In Barmouth it
has now reached the point where there are considerably more
administrators than faculty staff. This is not unique to Barmouth.
It is depressingly true of most UK universities.

Keith has often wondered what all this army of people actually
does. It is clearly no longer one of support for teaching and
research. Rather their role seems to be to urge it, organise it,
arrange it, manage it, control it and profit from it as opposed to
supporting those who actually do it. They also see themselves as
providing "visionary leadership". Thus a few years ago the staff
began to refer to the huge building where the management
structure is housed as "The Starship *Enterprise*", a reference to a
TV series where a fictional spacecraft would go "boldly where no
man has gone before". When it became clear that such a
description was ludicrously beyond parody, the staff developed a
new name. One might almost say that there was a "rebranding
exercise" that took place. Its new name became "Mordor". Mordor
plays a key role in the story of The Lord of the Rings, a book and
subsequently a film by J.R. Tolkien. It is the name given to the
place where the Lord Sauron and his host hold sway over a vast
empire and seek to extend that control over all. To enter Mordor

149

is to feel a pall of gloom descending and a sense of foreboding closing in on those who must venture there. It seemed an apt name for the directorate building. Mordor, unsurprisingly, is not popular with academic staff. Indeed, there is a story, full of black humour, circulating that illustrates this well. A member of staff in the Economics department is approached by a secretary.

"The senior members of the directorate have been taken captive by terrorists. They say that unless a ransom of £10,000 is paid they will pour petrol over them and set fire to them. I am collecting donations."

"I see. What offers have you had so far?"

"The offers so far amount to twenty-seven litres of unleaded."

Keith, then, approaches the thought of time spent in Mordor with little enthusiasm. Before he goes to Barmouth he checks his email. Buried in the endless drivel is one which warms his heart. It is from Lilia, a student who graduated with first class honours about ten years ago from UCS.

Dear Ken,

I wanted to let you know that I have just finished my first term in Uxworth University as a lecturer in Business. It has been very enjoyable and how I went about teaching I modelled on how you taught me on the occasions you came to Bulgaria. Many thanks. I hope we can meet up at some conference or other in the next year or so. If, however you are in the area I would be delighted to see you and introduce you to my husband and family.

Take care,

Lilia

He realises that indeed he will be in that area soon. He has to be in Nottingham shortly and will be driving from there to Maidstone. He will be passing very close. He will reply and set up a meeting with her. There is also one email emanating from a senior member of staff in Mordor. Usually, he would at this point be looking for the delete button on his laptop but because the meeting this afternoon is on his mind he decides to open it. The main part of it reads as follows:

It has come to the attention of the directorate that in a number of faculties staff have failed to turn up to lectures. This is an unacceptable practice. It will not be tolerated and must cease forthwith. The putting of personal considerations before their professional responsibilities will result in disciplinary action.

June Whitely,

Vice President of Academic Affairs (Faculty Liaison)

Goodness, can the woman not even spell while she is insulting staff? Given the spelling errors he decides not to delete this stuff in case it comes in useful on some future occasion. He smiles inwardly as he recalls Boromir, one of the characters from Lord of the Rings:

"One does not simply walk into Mordor.... The Great Eye is ever watchful.... the very air you breathe is a poisonous fume."

Just at that moment an email arrives from Ellie.

My dear Keith,

Mother is a lot better. Can we chat on fb this evening? I would love to hear about your time in Bulgaria. I can be here by nine o'clock.

Much love,

Ellie xxx

He dashes off a quick reply, expressing his delight that her mother is better and assuring her he will be able to chat this evening. Then he rushes off to the station in time to catch his train to Barmouth. He almost misses it and this reminds him of a notice he once read on a website from Transport Direct. It said:

"Warning. Certain combinations of outward and return journeys will result in your needing to leave your destination before arriving at it".

Well, nothing could be clearer than that.

The lift situation has changed today. The notice that once suggested that repairs might one day be possible has been removed. Now there are yards of sticky tape placed haphazardly across the entrance. Presumably it is thought that staff cannot cope with reading a notice. Perhaps it is felt that they are more at home with art. The placement of the sticky tape makes the lift look like an exhibition from the Tate Modern. He finds a student waiting outside his door. It is one of his first-year tutees. Keith sits him down in his office and asks him what he has come for.

"I am thinking of switching from the economics degree to the Sociology degree. I am told that it's much less demanding and the sociology department has said they will accept me. I just wanted to hear your thoughts first."

Keith wants to find some way to explain to him that he is right. The sociology degree will be much easier, but that's why more people will choose it, then subsequently find it harder to get a job and when they do find employment the pay is much worse. Perhaps an indirect approach will be best.

"OK here is a multiple-choice question for you. Which of the following is the odd one out?"

A degree in Economics.

A degree in Economics and Business.

A degree in Sociology.

A large pizza.

The student says he presumes it's the pizza.

"No, the answer is the degree in Sociology. All the others are capable of feeding a family of four. Of course you can switch degrees. It's a free country. But please think about it first."

Now it's time to teach. It's ironic that he has been thinking about the sheer waste of resources represented by the armies of Mordor just as he has to deliver a class on aspects of efficiency. He tells the group a true story that he read about some years ago.

A time and motion expert had been appointed by a county in California to look at how efficiently their administration was. After some time, he realised that everything he was doing was already being done by other people. He handed in his report to this effect, pointing out that that his own job was entirely unnecessary and he was therefore resigning. The county accepted his resignation. They then appointed two people to take his place.

The irony in the last sentence is lost on the students. Keith loves this story and tells it not only because it says something about the efficiency of organisations but because he thinks it is funny. The students have no idea why he has bothered to tell it to them. As a piece of humour, the story is a flop. Keith reflects how individual humour can be. He had given a lecture two years ago during which he had made what he thought of as a mildly amusing remark that might produce a few smiles. He was amazed when the whole audience had burst into laughter. Twelve months later he was giving the same lecture to a new bunch of students. He had been so surprised and impressed with last year's reaction that he wanted to repeat the remark. He was careful to set the scene and delivered the punch line exactly as before. He then paused for the outbreak of laughter. This time there was absolutely no reaction.

These students have already heard his story about driving British cars and how he had to buy a Japanese car to be able to get from A to B reliably. Now he develops the story. At one stage he had a Japanese car made in Japan because he feared that a Japanese car made in the UK would be less reliable. It turned out that this was wrong. All the evidence suggests that Japanese cars produced in the UK using Japanese management methods are just as reliable as the models made in Japan. Maybe, then, the problem is not with British workers but with British management? He thinks, but he does not say, that more confirmation of this argument will almost certainly be found in Mordor this afternoon.

In thinking about inefficiency in management one of the students has come across the "Peter Principle" and asks Keith about it. Aware that he is to spend an afternoon in Mordor, where he believes that the principle can be seen in action, he gives a brief explanation.

"The Peter Principle is an idea from management theory. It says that the way someone is chosen for a job is based largely on how the candidate has performed in their present position, not how they are likely to perform in the new position. Therefore, the people who are performing well in their current roles will be promoted, possibly again and again, until at some point they get promoted to positions which they cannot handle. They are now doing a job at which they are incompetent. Since they will then not be able to demonstrate further competence, they will remain in those positions. According to this principle, then, everyone will finish up in a position in which they are incompetent. In a large organisation one can expect everyone to be promoted out of their sphere of competence into their sphere of incompetence. Management is inherently inefficient. What makes this principle even more frightening is the tendency of the second rate to appoint underling's dimmer than they are in order to avoid feeling inferior. Thus, A managers appoint A people but B managers appoint C people. When the C person is promoted, there is a tendency to appoint D people. In time the organisation is not only riddled with incompetent people but people committed to appointing the ever more incompetent."

What Keith thinks, but does not say, is that when he came to Barmouth he thought it an interesting and amusing idea in theory. The Barmouth directorate has convinced him that it has wider validity than he had realised.

He has promised to meet with Marin Anderson for coffee but Martin wants to go to a tailor's just a few minutes' walk away and asks Keith to accompany him. Martin's son is getting married soon and a month ago he was measured for a new suit that should be ready to try on. They enter the shop and the tailor assures him everything is ready for a fitting. When Martin tries on the trousers they simply do not fit. They are two inches too small around the waist. The tailor looks embarrassed.

"It does seem that sir has put on rather a lot of weight since we measured you a few weeks ago."

This is clearly a ridiculous comment. It is obvious to Keith that Martin has not put on weight but that the tailor's measurements were faulty. He has known Martin for a long time and so he is not surprised at Martin's response.

"Are you seriously suggesting that I have increased my stomach size by two inches, an increase of about seven percent in a month? If we extrapolate that trend, you are telling me that my stomach will cover the entire surface area of the south of England within fifteen years."

Keith finds this response to be hilarious. The tailor, however, looks completely blank. The image that Martin has painted seems lost on him, but he does agree that some adjustment is necessary. They leave the shop with a smile. There is just time for Keith to attend a short meeting of the resit exam board if he skips lunch and eschews Joan's sausage rolls. This is a meeting to determine whether students who failed an exam and have now attempted it for a second time have done sufficiently well to be given a pass and be allowed to progress to other areas of study. The meeting is chaired by Brenda Harcourt and Garth insists on calling her "chair" over and over. Keith finds it hard to focus on the discussion and as a result of Garth's form of address to Brenda he starts to think about an advert he saw some while back in his local newspaper. It read:

"Antique chair by lady with fine carved legs".

There are only a few students to be considered but the last two cause some interest. One student has made a complete hash of the paper and has been marked at a very low level. It is a clear failure.

Garth Martin has nursed this student through the course to this point and is desperate to persuade the meeting to be generous. The key person present is the external examiner, a member of another university appointed to check that the standard of assessment is broadly comparable with his own institution. Garth has no chance of persuading the meeting to be absurdly generous to this student unless he can gain the external examiner's support.

Garth: "Chair, I am trying not to be difficult here....

Keith: (sotto voce): "Well I wish he would try a bit harder"

Garth: "Is there no way we can help this student?"

Chair (with fine carved legs): "Perhaps the external would like to comment...."

External examiner: "I think we have reached an accommodation with this student. He didn't understand our questions and we didn't understand his answers."

Chair (with fine carved legs): "I think perhaps that brings to an end the discussion on this student."

The last student has passed comfortably and has written a huge amount, although not all of it relevant.

External examiner: "I agree it's a pass but could you please tell this student that we read the work, we don't weigh it."

Chair: "Thank you, everyone. That concludes the meeting."

The leading lights in Mordor prefer to be known as "The Senior Management Team". However, many members of the teaching staff decline to call them by this title. It is felt that the proximity of the word "management" to this particular collection of individuals might subject the word to greater epistemological strain than it can reasonably be expected to bear. Instead, they are often referred to as the "Senior Post Holders," or SPH. This group is quite at ease with their huge salaries, reminding the staff that it would be hard to find people that are of their calibre. Some unkindly, though accurately, concur with this judgement. Keith feels that it is unfair to criticise their remuneration. After all, it is carefully considered and approved the Board of Governors, which consists of the Chief Executive, his friends, relatives and odd chaps he knows from the golf club. Keith rushes off to Mordor with a heavy heart and an empty stomach. Being an academic institution committed to freedom of expression, all staff members know that they are free to question decisions made by SPH, preferably in written form. Unlike some institutions where such questions are ignored, all questions at Barmouth receive an answer. These answers have the merit of following a standard procedure. The member of SPH will begin with a phrase such as: "Thank you for your question. I want to be clear, open and frank here and to reply in detail." This will then be followed by a few paragraphs which will not be clear, open, frank or detailed.

Indeed, they can be guaranteed not to address the question in any way whatsoever. Should people wish to come personally to make their representations, it is a simple matter to do so. The doors are all locked and barred but entry is simpler than to the original Mordor. The application of a small hand grenade or medium sized battering ram will be sufficient to gain access.

Like Frodo Baggins and Sam Underhill approaching the gates of Mordor, Keith enters the directorate building weighed down with gloom. The meeting is on the third floor. Mordor's lifts work perfectly of course. As he enters the lift one of the directorate staff is coming out of it. Keith has met her quite a few times. She has been in Bulgaria several times to present degree certificates to the UCS students. She either doesn't recognise Keith or, more likely, does not wish to acknowledge him. She probably sees him as just a lowly worm crawling out from under a rock. He steps out of the lift and walks along the corridor to the meeting room. Hordes of people are in heavily carpeted offices with seemingly little to do. If someone were to ask him how many people work in this place he would be tempted to say:

"Oh, rather less than half of them."

It's as well that Keith's vertigo is not too serious today. The thickness of the carpet here would create problems if he stepped off of it into the lift on the way out of the building. He passes two administrative staff talking and slows to listen because he hears the name June Whitely, the woman from whom the staff had received the unpleasant and illiterate email this morning.

"People have been complaining about the mistakes in the email she sent out this morning."

"I am not surprised. Is she dyslexic?"

"No, her cousin Deirdre's little girl has a birthday party today and she had promised to bring some chocolate buttons to put on the cake, so she had to rush off to get them."

Keith is impressed with himself. He manages not to be sick all over the directorate's carpet. The irony is as lost on the administrative staff as were his students concerning the Californian time and motion expert. When Keith was teaching his students this morning using the car industry as an example, he didn't quote a story that used to be told some years ago at a time when the Japanese economy was the envy of the world. He thinks of it now because being in Mordor reminds him of it.

An American car company and a Japanese car firm decided to have a competitive boat race on the Detroit River. Both the teams practiced hard and long in order to reach their peak performance. On the big day, they were as ready as they could be.

The Japanese team won by a mile.

As a result, the American team became discouraged by the loss and their morale sagged. Corporate management decided that the reason for the crushing defeat had to be found. A Continuous Measurable Improvement Team of "Executives" was set up to investigate the problem and to recommend appropriate action to improve matters.

Their conclusion: The problem was that the Japanese team had 8 people rowing and 1 person steering, whereas the American team had 1 person rowing and 8 people steering. The American Corporate Steering Committee immediately hired a consulting firm to do a study on the management structure.

After some time and billions of dollars, the consulting firm concluded that "too many people were steering and not enough rowing." To prevent losing to the Japanese again next year, the management structure was changed to "4 Steering Managers, 3 Area Steering Managers, and 1 Staff Steering Manager" and a new performance system for the person rowing the boat to give more incentive to work harder and become a better performer. "We must give him empowerment and enrichment." That should do it.

The next year the Japanese team won by two miles.

The American Corporation laid off the rower for poor performance, sold all of the paddles, cancelled all capital investments for new equipment, halted development of a new canoe, awarded high performance awards to the consulting firm, and distributed the money saved as bonuses to the senior executives.

He does not know if anyone in Mordor has heard the story. If they have, the irony of the story is almost certainly lost on the management in Mordor but it is certainly not lost upon the academic staff. Mordor likes to exercise total control. Keith has run the programme at UCS successfully for many years but Mordor needs something to keep its minions happy so they "review" the programme every few years. This involves sending these minions out to Sofia to look at the library and their other facilities and also Asking Keith to fill in an enormous questionnaire including information about the size of the bed socks of all UCS staff. They then spend three to four hours questioning him about his answers. Key to all of this is establishing a committee that knows nothing about it to whom Keith will this afternoon be accountable. It is not enough that these people know nothing about UCS. Mordor has also chosen people who, with one exception, know nothing about economics and business. Most are academics drawn from different parts of the university. These people are now assembled before him. Keith thinks yet again: What is the point of all this? Is there nothing that is so successful that administrators can't foul it up?

When Keith is at his most paranoid, he believes that there is a man employed by his local supermarket whose job is to observe what Keith buys and then to remove those items before he returns to get more. Just as he gets to know what is best for him, the supermarket decides to change what it sells. Now Keith has come to think that perhaps this supermarket employee has a brother who works in Mordor. Both the brothers seem to have been to the same training course. The morning agenda appears to centre upon finding out how people go about their lives efficiently. The afternoon agenda seems to focus on finding ways of stopping them. Certainly, his past experience here suggests that this committee will be working on the same basic principles.

Administrators simply don't know how to keep things streamlined. Keith was appalled to discover a while ago that if another University like UCS applied for a link with Barmouth it would take a year and a half to make a decision upon their suitability whilst it went through a three-stage process of approval by various committees. The directorate vowed to simplify things.

After reviewing the process, it became a five-stage process. Perhaps the need for scrutiny is particularly important in this area. Barmouth seems to feel that there are only three worthy Universities in the country. There is Oxford, Cambridge and Barmouth, and they still entertain serious doubts about Oxford and Cambridge. The need to protect the Barmouth academic integrity is clearly paramount.

Keith knows the chairman of this afternoon's committee, although not very well. The man is highly intelligent. He has a reputation among the students of being a hopeless teacher. He is far too intelligent to be otherwise. He is utterly unable to understand that students are not as bright as he is. Keith has a theory that the best teachers are bright enough to understand what they are trying to communicate but not so bright that they can't understand why people find some ideas difficult. The highly intelligent so often lack sympathy with ordinary mortals. He hopes that this will not apply to today's chairman. Another person Keith knows is from the English department. He is as dim as the chairman is bright. How did he get elected to this review committee? Keith can only assume that no one else was willing to do it. It reminds him of something he once heard about President Ronald Regan. It was said that Regan won an election because he stood against Jimmy Carter. If he had stood unopposed, he would have lost.

As he casts his eye over the committee, he sees that a variant on the Peter Principle is at work here today. Some people were incompetent teachers and have now been promoted to management where they are equally incompetent. It appears that some do get promoted out of their sphere of incompetence after all. They get promoted into a different sphere of incompetence.

He recalls a conversation with his head of department in which he pointed out that a member of staff had a very light timetable and his time was filled with minor administrative tasks. When he asked why the guy couldn't be given a more equitable teaching load he was told:

"I can't put him in a classroom to teach. He is so hopeless that the students would riot. Besides he has a list of publications that not all staff here can match."

Keith had looked up his publications. The head of department was right. The riveting list included:

The Poetry of Tudor Drainage Systems

Fourteenth Century Agricultural Implement Prices: A Self Teaching manual

The Philosophy of Nineteenth Century Latin American Birth Control Costs

And

Trade Patterns in Welsh Mythology – a Practical Guide

The problem of the inequitable load was solved when he was moved into Mordor.

There is also a woman on the committee that Keith has come across before. A year or two ago Barmouth decided to create "Champions of University Teaching, or CUTs." This would simply be a title to be conferred upon those so honoured but there would be no extra pay involved. It was open to all teaching Staff. Keith had no interest in the title but at the time he was actively seeking funding for a film project and thought the title might be useful as part of his filming application. Maybe he would be seen as a CUT above the rest. He had filled in the inevitable form and been offered an interview before a panel of Barmouth's great and good. The lady sitting opposite him was on the panel. The interview did not go well. Keith was asked by her if he would be willing to go around to other departments giving seminars on how to teach. He said he would not. He would not tell people how to teach subjects in which they were experts when he himself knew little about them. This, he thought, would be arrogant. This answer had clearly not been very diplomatic. He should have found some weasel words along the lines of yes of course, whilst always being subject to the individual's subject expertise. The next morning the lady opposite had rung him and told him that he was not going to be a CUT above the others because of the answer he had given. He hopes he can be suitably diplomatic this afternoon.

The cross questioning begins with this motley crew plus one or two representatives from Mordor. Keith expects a lot of what

Donald Baverstock, once controller of BBC1 called in a slightly different context, "cross-sterilisation".

The first major area of consideration is the financial control of the link. The link is supposed to cover costs and make a profit. There is concern that the profit is not sufficient. Keith remembers how he submitted expenses from a trip last year and was called in to explain his behaviour. He had submitted a claim for two cups of coffee during the same afternoon. Such profligacy cost the University the best part of a pound. This time Keith has honed his diplomatic skills and so he apologises. He doesn't point out that the time spent checking and questioning such wild extravagance costs the University several hundred pounds in staff time. Neither does he point out that on his next trip he had enjoyed a massage at the hotel. No one queried the expenditure. He had enjoyed it but had been hoping for it to be done by a beautiful Bulgarian girl. The huge muscle-bound hulk of a guy that had done it was very good at his job but it was not quite what Keith had anticipated. However, the university paid so all in all it wasn't a bad deal.

When the committee continues to press the point that the profit on the venture is insufficient, he responds by pointing out that the University receives many thousands of pounds when UCS students transfer to Barmouth and pay fees, either to complete their undergraduate study or to register for a higher degree. This does not show up in the accounts so the profitability is considerably greater than apparent from the accounts. He really struggles to keep a straight face at the reply.

"We can't count that income because there is nowhere to put this in the business plan."

The University is very careful to have a suitable, modern employment policy in place. It guarantees that there will be no discrimination on grounds of race, religion, colour or gender. It seems that Barmouth is really modern. It doesn't appear to discriminate on the basis of ability either. Keith considers three responses to this lunacy. The first is to scream. The second is to suggest that they must have a lousy business plan. The third is to say "Oh right." He chooses the third option. The financial arrangements are beyond parody. By custom a group of six outstanding students spend two weeks each year studying in Barmouth. Three years ago, the head of department at the time was Dan Billings who took the students out for a meal. In order to claim the cost, he had to submit the expenses. This had to include the names of all the six students. Dan had rung Keith to ask for their names. Keith could only remember five and said he would look up the sixth name.

Dan: "That's okay, I've got Stoichkov".

Keith: "No, no that wasn't his name."

Dan: "It doesn't matter, I always have Stoichkov. What a footballer he was. I always take him out for a meal."

No one in Mordor ever raised an eyebrow so a great Bulgarian footballer appears to have had a free meal at Barmouth's expense every year.

The questioning then turns to the maintenance of standards in awarding degrees. How does Keith make sure that the same standards are applied to UCS students as to students studying in Barmouth? It is not difficult to demonstrate that all the checks that are in place. What is much more difficult is not to raise the standards of assessment in Barmouth. The proportion of eighteen-year-olds attending University has increased hugely over the years so that the average ability has sharply declined. This is particularly true for Barmouth. When the need for more students became financially apparent, the decision was made to drop to an absolute minimum the requirement to obtain a place in the University. Barmouth raced to the bottom faster than most universities. Ludicrously, given this considerable fall in the average intelligence of the students, the proportion of top marks awarded has risen inexorably. As with many other Universities, over twenty five percent of students now receive a first-class honours degree. Keith says nothing about this. He is playing a diplomatic blinder. At this point the great minds surrounding Keith begin to talk among themselves and Keith's mind is soon wandering. It finishes up on a few more relevant light bulb jokes.

Q: How many administrative assistants does it take to change a light bulb?

A: None. It is not possible unless a complete lightbulb design change request form is completed in quadruplicate and considered by at least three appropriate committees.

Q: How many bureaucrats does it take to screw in a light bulb?

A: Two. One to ensure that everything possible is being done while the other screws the bulb into the water faucet.

Q: How many members of the management team do they think it take to screw in a lightbulb?

A: Just one. He holds the lightbulb and he thinks the universe revolves around him.

The other area of discussion that takes up time is Barmouth's new approach to recording the minutes of meetings. One of Barmouth's senior management team has decided to replace the outmoded business meeting structure of minutes used all over the world. This old, outmoded system is simply not good enough for a forward thinking, dynamic, thrusting University like Barmouth. Barmouth is now introducing "Leapfrog". Leapfrog is the Learning, Evidence and Action Plan for Reaching Our Goals. Keith has studied this new procedure for at least forty-five seconds. This is more than sufficient to establish that it is pointless, administratively unnecessarily complex and time consuming. This will become so obvious to everyone within two years that the whole thing will be quietly forgotten. Keith has no intention of wasting time on this nonsense.

It is not long before the inevitable question is asked.

"How do you propose to introduce Leapfrog into UCS?"

Most academics love to hear the sound of their own voice which leaves Keith an obvious way to respond:

"This is a new approach and I think we will need to introduce this carefully. I have a feeling that an overseas collaboration like the one with UCS may raise extra issues from those raised within Barmouth. Given that we are in the early days of utilising this new approach, I would be very interested to hear the committee's thoughts on that."

The committee proceeds, exactly as Keith hoped, and indeed expected, to discuss the issue among each other. For some time, they ignore Keith who is clearly a poor benighted guy who can't tell a minute from a matter arising. By the time they have finished sharing their distilled wisdom it only remains for Keith to mutter a few phrases of thanks and to assure the committee of his best intentions to ensure the success of Leapfrog. He has just come up with his own alternative name for leapfrog, which he regards as brilliant. He wants to suggest that it be called "Capability Resource Action Planning" because the acronym is so appropriate. He says nothing.

The other few issues go very much faster. They all want to get out of here and go home. The atmosphere is similar to the annual exam review board in the economics department. The economists gather at two pm and discuss all the proposed exam papers of all the staff. The first paper takes forty-five minutes.

"Chair, should there be a comma at the end of the line in Question three?"

"Perhaps question four would be more challenging if we replace "what" with "how".

"Or even "why".

"Or even fish and chips" mutters Keith sotto voce.

By five o'clock the discussion has always changed somewhat.

"Everyone ok with year two Trade Relationships with Europe... Welsh Economic history..."

And the last fifteen papers are dealt with in twenty seconds. Since the decision to take the papers in alphabetical order Keith has wanted to revise his own exam paper titles to "AAA Economics" and AAA Business Economics".

The same dynamic is now taking place here. The meeting will be over shortly. First the committee will retire for fifteen minutes and then summarise its conclusions and present them to Keith. Out of boredom Keith wanders along the corridor. Some have gone home. Others sit around avidly discussing he knows not what. So, he imagines what is happening in the discussion between the various committee members:

"Come on everyone. I need some suggestions on how to persecute this guy and stop him from helping UCS students."

"But surely we have been making his life harder for years."

"Well of course, but we are dynamic thrusting organisation. We must be ever moving onwards and upwards."

"Couldn't we make him go to Sofia by train and tell him we need him to do this to save money?

"Good idea Darren. However, we will need more like that if I am to complete my task of preparing the case for another 25 percent pay increase for the Vice Chancellor."

"We could make him stay in really poor-quality hotels so that he is too tired to do his job".

"Good grief, I thought we were doing that already."

"How about giving him a positive, encouraging review and telling him what a great job he is doing."

"Why? How will that help?

"Well, he will be so shocked after the treatment we have given him all these years he will be really worried and wonder what on earth is going on."

"That's a truly lousy idea. Now are there any more ideas...."

Keith's fifteen minutes are up and he returns to hear the wisdom of the mighty. He tries to look interested. The group graciously gives him permission to continue the work but also gives him the benefit of several recommendations. He would like to respond along the following lines:

"Oh, these are such excellent suggestions. Why didn't I think of these things myself?

He would then like to thank them profusely, go away and forget their ideas entirely. However, there is a problem with this approach. They will ring the UCS director in three months' time and check whether their ideas have been acted upon. Thus, Keith will need to write to the director shortly and get him to make appropriate meaningless noises when the call comes. It is at that point that everyone can, and will, forget all about the recommendations.

What he actually thinks of the meeting's recommendations is summed up by a colleague at a gathering Keith attended last year. The economics department had assembled in its entirety to listen to a member of Mordor make some proposals for improving staff morale. His basic tenet was that people should be more touchy feely. They should not be separate individuals but should be encouraging one another. He claimed that the department organised itself to get tasks done and then simply left people to get on with it. He had finished his speech and invited a response. No one had said anything until finally after a very long pause one brave economist had said:

"Yes, we are all very proud of that."

This was not what Mister Mordor had hoped for. There followed a desultory discussion before one economist summed up the feeling of the department.

"This is all bollocks".

Just so, both then and now. On the way out of the building, as the gloom begins to dispel, he is joined by the one other person present who was from the economics department.

"I was very impressed by the way you handled that discussion on LEAPFROG."

"I don't even know what LEAPFROG is."

"I know you don't. That's why I was so impressed."

Keith laughs and finds himself almost running out of the place. He gets home with great relief to find a card sticking out of the front door. He recognises it immediately. It's from a delivery firm that wanted to leave a parcel but found that he was out. He anticipates what it will say:

Sorry you were not in to receive your parcel. We have left it:

☐ Under your gooseberry bush where the packaging will have completely disintegrated in a thunderstorm

☑ By the dustbin where it has been shredded by your neighbour's Alsatian

☐ By the potting shed where the rats have had a fine meal from the cardboard

☐ With a neighbour who is losing his marbles and will have forgotten he took it in for you.

He looks for and finds the parcel immediately. It is by the dustbin in perfect condition. Oh dear, the time in Mordor has made him a little cynical.

He opens the parcel to find a small booklet. He looks at it with some curiosity because he hasn't ordered a book recently. He reads it quickly. There is no indication as to who has sent it. It is called "Love's Opportunities". Its main thesis seems to be that people miss their chance of love by being too shy and introverted. It is essential to be brave in love. He doesn't know whether to agree with the author or wish that the book had been shredded by the neighbour's Alsatian.

By nine o'clock he is ready to look for Ellie on Facebook.

"Ellie, I am missing you."

"I am missing you too."

"How is mother? "

"She is just about recovered. How was Bulgaria?"

"It is always interesting. I want to see you as soon as possible and will tell you more then. In fact, I would love to take you there to see it for yourself and introduce you to some delightful people. Oh, when I was entering the hotel, a lady offered me a cigarette and when I indicated that I didn't smoke, (I used my very best sign language) she suggested maybe we could have sex. I think I must be more beautiful than I realised.

"Well, that's one interpretation of her suggestion."

"I received a book this evening saying I should take every opportunity to find love. There was no indication of who the sender was."

Pause.

"How interesting, I wonder who could have sent it. But it's always worth considering new ideas...."

"Yes, thank you. I will. Have u tried on yet the Spanish underwear samples they sent you?"

"Ummm yes, I have. It seems like excellent quality stuff. I think I am keen to try to do business with these people."

"Would you value my opinion, although I confess that I have never seen myself as an expert on women's Spanish underwear?

"Of course I would value it."

"Well, purely in the interests of helping you with your business opportunity, may I suggest that you try a few things on and send me some pics?"

"Are you serious? I am almost forty years old."

"Ellie, thanks to the thoughtfulness of my pet spider I have had opportunity to judge what a nearly forty-year-old Ellie looks like. Let me tell you, you are gorgeous."

There is a pause in the conversation. The pause is so long he thinks she has gone away. Maybe he has upset her. It's that stupid book. Bravery is not the best option after all. Bravery is just a nothing name for foolhardy stupidity. He drowns his sorrows in a large glass of milk.

Fifteen minutes later he gets an email from her. He opens it and finds that it has several picture attachments. The attachments are stunning. The combination of Ellie and Spanish underwear is sensational. He recalls the sight he was afforded by his friend the spider. He knows that she has no need of a bra but she looks wonderful in it. He opens Facebook again.

"Oh Ellie, absolutely gorgeous."

"Really? I am going bright red here."

I think you should forget the idea of selling with these people. You can just model for them. I am very willing to do the photography."

"Keith, thank you for making me feel so good. Do you recall a TV advert for cream cakes? I saw it in the marketing course in Barmouth. You reminded me of it. The line was 'Naughty but nice'."

"I am old enough to remember watching it at the time it was on!"

"Let's meet up as soon as we possibly can."

He says goodnight, goes to his printer, prints off the pictures and takes them to bed with another large glass of milk.

CHAPTER NINE: STUDENT VISITS

'No matter how politely or distinctly you ask a Parisian a question he will persist in answering you in French.'

- Fran Lebowitz

As with any job there is an element of repetition and therefore potential boredom. However, Keith has been very fortunate to travel in the course of his work, relieving any long-term tedium in the Barmouth environment. Today he is travelling in the UK and then to France to visit some students. If they wish, students can spend a part of their degree course by doing a job for a period of six months or a year in order to get valuable experience of work in the real world. They can expect a visit from someone In Barmouth during that period to check that everything is satisfactory. Keith is soon to visit four such students to see how they are progressing and to sort out any problems that have arisen. This will involve meeting each student but also meeting at least one line manager to discuss what tasks they have been given and how well the student is performing.

Before going visiting, however, he is spending the morning in Barmouth in order to attend a rather unusual event. Dan Billings has recently accused one group of his students of being boring. They have not responded with much enthusiasm in his classes recently. Today Dan is giving this group a lecture. The students have responded to Dan's criticism in an unusual way and have planned an event to demonstrate that they are not always as dull and uninspiring as Dan claims. This is an event of which Dan knows nothing. Keith has discovered what is going on from one of his tutees and plans to be in Dan's lecture to observe what is to take place. It is not very common for lecturers to attend the lectures of colleagues but he has made up an excuse to be there, claiming that he wants to hear how Dan explains a tricky concept to the students.

It is now twenty minutes into the lecture. Everything is proceeding as one might expect. Dan is an interesting and entertaining lecturer. Suddenly the door of the lecture theatre opens and Dan looks around in surprise. Keith well understands the surprise. A lecturer is accustomed to regarding a lecture room as his own personal fiefdom. Dan would not expect any disturbance during this time unless there is something quite unusual going on. A lady in her late twenties enters. She is wearing a long mackintosh.

"Doctor Billings?"

Dan looks pretty bewildered. She is quite an attractive lady but there is nothing remarkable about her appearance except that the mackintosh looks rather out of place.

"I am, yes, can I help you?"

"I have a greeting for you."

She slips off her mackintosh to reveal that underneath she is wearing only a bra, knickers, suspenders, fishnet stockings and a garter with a flower attached to it. The reaction of the students is mixed. The girls are finding this highly amusing. The men are also finding it amusing but there is a level of interest and enjoyment in the look of the young lady that is absent from the female students. Keith is finding the whole thing hilarious but making comparisons in his mind with how he imagines that Ellie would look in this outfit. He decides that even if this girl was wearing Spanish underwear, he would still much prefer that it was Ellie. Maybe he can see a new job opportunity for her.

"Please sit in the chair" the young lady says firmly.

Keith has known Dan a long time. It is clear that Dan has two options. Either he walks out and refuses to take any part in this kissogram lady's performance or he just goes along with it. He makes what Keith thinks is the right decision. He sits on the chair as he is told. She then sits on his lap and gives him a long slow kiss. The students applaud. Dan glances across at Keith to make it clear that he understands perfectly well now why Keith is in his lecture. Keith grins back, making it clear that he knows Dan knows.

The half-dressed lady then takes out of a briefcase an enormous card in order to read from it a short poem that the students have obviously written especially for Dan. In her best well-rehearsed, sexy voice she begins to read:

By your students I hear you've been bored,

Yet by them you were widely adored.

Now here is a task,

Please do as I ask

And your reputation's restored.

Now that I'm sat on your knee

It's very easy to see

That I'm such a cutie,

So now do your duty

And take the flower from me.

You want to; it's easy to tell,

It's something at which you'll excel.

Now, at your leisure,

For me it's a pleasure,

I know that you'll do the job well.

> *Despite his embarrassment Dan starts to remove the flower from her garter with his hand, but she stops him.*

"Wait, there's one more verse I need to read first."

Oh Dan, you are such a tease.

Remove it now for me, please.

With your <u>teeth</u>, if you will,

It will give me a thrill

And make me go weak at the knees.

Dan is now less clear that he will do as she asks. There is a pause. Finally, he lowers his head onto her thigh and does as she asks. The room is filled with students pointing their cameras and cheering. One more kiss and she has slipped on her mackintosh and disappeared out of the door leaving him with the flower between his teeth. Dan stands up, looks at the students, removes the flower from his mouth and laughs.

"You have just guaranteed that your exam paper will be virtually impossible."

He cannot bring himself to finish the lecture after all that and he leaves the lecture room to even more applause. The students know him well enough to be sure that he is joking.

Since he has arranged to visit a student in Nottingham Keith wants to be on the road quickly after the kissogram show but first he checks his email. There is one from Lilia inviting him to a meal this evening with her family. She has enclosed her address and suggested he might like to stay overnight. The house is easily big enough to accommodate him. He responds by saying how pleased he would be to accept and hopes to arrive around Six o'clock. There is also one from Ellie that leaves him stunned.

Hello Keith,

I think perhaps I do not want to continue our correspondence. I wish you well in your future career at Barmouth.

Ellie

He wants immediately to respond and to try to discover what is going on, but decides that he needs a while to reflect upon what this may be about. The drive to Nottingham may help him do this. As he sets out on his drive North his mind is filled with what could possibly have caused such a change in Ellie's tone. Of course, she has a right not to continue what has become so precious to him, but surely, he must attempt to discover what it is. He finds himself feeling that he has come rather quickly down to earth. He has fallen hard for such a gorgeous lady. How could he ever have expected that such a relationship could continue? What should he do with the pictures she sent him? Maybe he should destroy them but he knows that this would prove very difficult for him. He decides to take his mind off her and to play a CD. One of his favourite collections is of Nat King Cole, whose silky voice he has enjoyed whenever he has found time to listen. He is soon listening to the track of "When I fall in love".

> *In a restless world like this is*
> *Love is ended before it's begun,*
> *and too many moonlight kisses*
> *Seem to cool in the warmth of the sun.*

So sad. When he stops for a break at a service station, he can stand it no longer and sends Ellie an email from his mobile.

Dear Ellie,

It is clear that you are very upset. I have no idea why. You must know that I found your email extremely painful. Of course, I accept your right not to continue what was growing between us but for the sake of a fantastic evening at my home please tell me what it is that has so suddenly happened to explain your email. Please. I imagine that whatever it is, you find it painful also.

Keith

He drives on to his appointment in Nottingham. Sad though he is, he decides that he should feel very thankful that he got to spend one wonderful evening with someone so lovely.

The student he is meeting is working for an estate agent in Nottingham. It is probably not going to prove to be a great training place but the student wished to find a job near his home and this was the only such possibility. He wants to live at home for a period to keep his student debt down. Sometimes the biggest benefit of a training place is learning how to handle difficult people in the workplace. It is possible to learn this in almost any organisation. He locates the estate agent, has a quick check of his email but finds nothing from Ellie. Come on, Keith, focus on the job. It is time to put aside these foolish thoughts about a younger beautiful woman. How could he have kidded himself that it had a chance of working? Oh, dear, he finds a parking place in a cul-de-sac just around the corner from the estate agent and discovers that it is called St Peters Close. He is very sad about Ellie but he hopes this is not true for him. He isn't suicidal yet. He has a few minutes before he is due to meet the student so he checks his email yet again and this time he finds an email.

Keith,

I find this very difficult to write. It was indeed a fantastic evening but something has changed. I did not know then that you had treated my son badly. I know I have had problems relating to him but he is still my son and I love him. It hurt when he told me how you treated him and it hurt when you did not even mention it to me.

E

Since he has never met her son, he is now even more baffled and sad, but the job has to be done so he enters the offices of the estate agent and finds his student. In the three months the lad has been working he has been given a variety of tasks, including accompanying potential purchasers to view property. Currently he is preparing details of properties to put online. He is finding it quite a challenge to describe properties accurately but attractively. Keith makes a few suggestions.

"A tatty back yard could be a bijou suntrap patio. A slum that ought to be demolished could be a place with potential for modernisation."

His creative juices are really flowing now.

"A broom cupboard could be described as a utility room. How about describing a large broom cupboard as potential for a small additional bedroom?"

Keith decides that this really isn't helping much. The look on the student's face seems to indicate that they are in agreement about this. After checking that there are no major issues at work, he goes into the office of the senior partner to ask how things are going with his Barmouth protégé. He is offered the inevitable cup of coffee. The rather unique taste seems to have been produced by mixing furniture polish and windscreen washer. Keith takes an immediate dislike to the man. His hair and moustache seem to be modelled on Josef Stalin. It soon becomes clear that this is true of his character but without the warmth. He has pictures on his office wall showing him shaking hands with the mayor and other dignitaries of no significance. He is clearly an important person, at least in his own eyes. It seems, however, that there are no great problems that need to be sorted out and Keith is soon able to go back to the student to say goodbye and wish him well for the rest of his training period. He asks the student whether he is interested in a career in estate management. It appears not so Keith feels able to share with him a story to illustrate that estate agents have a reputation for greed, even though he has no idea whether the reputation is justified. The story goes like this.

An estate agent takes possession of his new Porsche and parks it at the office in order to show it to his admiring colleagues. As he gets out of the car a lorry comes by and takes the door completely off. The estate agent is distraught, screaming with frustration at the lorry as it disappears into the distance. He summons a policeman demanding that action be taken against the lorry driver:

"Look at my new Porsche! It's ruined. It will never be the same again."

When the estate agent finally pauses for breath, the policeman says:

"Sir," – he is very polite so it's clearly an English policeman – "Sir, you do seem to be a very materialistic person."

Estate agent: "What on earth makes you say that?"

"Well, I notice that when the lorry hit your car, it not only removed its door but it also took your arm off and yet you don't even seem to have noticed that."

The estate agent looks down where his arm should have been and says:

"Aaarrgh, my Rolex!"

Keith leaves the office musing on the difference between American and British perceptions of displayed wealth. To an American an estate agent, or perhaps a lawyer, driving an expensive flashy car like a Porsche suggests a successful businessperson. It suggests that such a person is so good at their job that they have acquired a substantial income. To many British people the same thing suggests someone who must have been involved in shady dealing to acquire such wealth and is therefore someone to avoid. He returns to his little Lexus and sits in St Peters Close, and from there he sends an email to Ellie.

My dear Ellie,

I have not even met your son. At least, if I have, I am unaware of it. Help me here.

Keith

It takes him some time to find his way through the traffic, out of town and south down the motorway to where Lilia lives. Although he is driving fast, he only has a small Lexus so when he comes to the part of the motorway with chevrons painted on the motorway surface he is in difficulties. The sign tells him to keep two chevrons from the car in front. However, it is a Porsche, possibly driven by an estate agent for all he knows. It is travelling at around 125 miles per hour so staying within two chevrons is asking a lot of his Lexus. He decides not to try. He has not seen Lilia for some years and looks forward to meeting up again. Before he gets out of the car to ring her bell he finds an email from Ellie.

Keith,

How could you possibly forget that you had met him? Does what I thought we had between us mean so little to you after all? Peter came to you to talk to you about his foolish decision to cheat in an exam. I did not think that you could ignore this or make the problem go away. What hurt me so very much is that he knows about a girl called Carrie, who also came to see you, and you treated her in a very different manner. Peter has had to leave; Carrie continues her studies. He says that Carrie is very attractive. It seems that you treat women, especially if they are attractive, differently from men. I find this had to forgive.

Ellie

The penny drops. Peter Fischer has to be her son. Others would have known immediately by looking at his face and recognizing the similarities. Such an ability is wholly absent from Keith. He marvels at how some people, particularly women it seems, can look at a three-day old baby and pronounce that it has ears that are just like its Uncle Fred's. To Keith one baby is much like another. Even with adults it requires something close to identical twins to recognize a family likeness. He responds immediately.

Dear Ellie,

I presume now that Peter Fischer is your son. I had no idea that this was your married name and that you had reverted to using your single name. When he came to see me, he gave me no indication that he was your son. But I did not treat him in any way differently from Carrie.

With each of them I went to the relevant head of department and explained what they had told me. In each case he spoke to them. The reason they were treated differently from one another is that in Carrie's case it was her first offence, in Peter's case it was his second offence and he therefore could not be treated in the same way. The head of department was doing the only thing he possibly could – following Barmouth's rules. I am so very sorry this has happened but it is hard to see how I, or indeed Barmouth, could have acted any differently.

You still have my deep affection.

Keith

He tries to dismiss from his mind these sad problems with Ellie and rings the bell of Lilia's house. It's lovely to see her again. He supported her when she did her degree in Bulgaria, including help with her thesis. He had also helped her with her first tentative steps into teaching. Now she has done higher degrees, she is married with two children and he is seeing her for the first time in years. He soon discovers that she has a delightful family, friendly husband and welcoming children. It isn't long before the two children, a five-year-old boy and a four-year-old girl, are showing him their toys. After tea he gets to read to them. It feels delightful. He didn't know how exciting the story of Cinderella is. It hasn't been on his reading list for a while. It saddens him to think that he has missed out somewhere. Some colleagues go home to read to their children every night. He goes home to an empty house. They finish with some nursery rhymes including:

Little Miss Muffet

Sat on a tuffet

Eating her curds and whey.

Along came a spider

Who sat down beside her

And frightened Miss Muffet away.

Keith decides that whilst he understands Miss Muffet's behaviour, he much prefers Ellie's reactions to the appearance of a spider. Just before bedtime the five-year-old favours Keith by rendering to him his favourite new joke.

"What's the difference between a duck?"

Keith is already highly amused and he hasn't heard the punch line yet.

"I don't know. What's the difference between a duck?"

"One of his legs is the same".

Unrestrained laughter follows. Oh, this lad surely on his way to a degree in philosophy in Cambridge. Later, after the children are in bed, the three adults sit and eat a meal together, a meal that Lilia has cooked. It's the first time Keith has had a Bulgarian meal in England, including Chicken Kvarma, something he has enjoyed many times in Bulgaria. She explains to her husband something of how she came to know Keith:

"He supported me in my first nervous attempts at teaching. We shared the presentation of a paper at a conference on the black Sea. I wasn't very good but he helped me through it."

Keith explains something of his motive in helping her along:

"As a young teacher I had to take the economics lectures for a course in Russian studies. I needed support and encouragement from the course leader and all I got was veiled nastiness. The external examiner was the great PJD Wiles who criticised one or two things about my exam paper. We discussed them. PJD Wiles was right and I, of course, immediately agreed to change the paper in the light of his remarks. The course leader tried to use Wiles' comments during a meeting, making it clear that he didn't think I was very good. I never forgot Wiles' response to this veiled attack on me. I recall his exact words: "My colleague and I are in complete agreement." I was a colleague of the great man! And he and I were of one mind. In response to this one line of the great man the course leader shut up and never opened his mouth to me again. That was a lesson in supporting colleagues I still remember, Lilia."

Lilia: "I hope I can show support one day soon for younger colleagues. Keith, I am sorry we lost touch for so long. I regret that. "

Keith: "So do I and I will not easily forget your kindness to me when I was in America." Keith explains to Lilia's husband that he had spent six weeks at a summer school in the Carolinas:

"The people there were superficially friendly. They would shake me warmly by the hand and tell me how they were going to invite me for a meal or go on a hike with me. None of it ever happened and I came to hate the place and wanted to shake some of these people warmly by the throat. Lilia and I knew one another a bit by then and we were emailing one another every two months or so. She knew I was in the USA and when I was in my first week there, she emailed me to ask how it was going so I replied and told her how fed up I was. After that she emailed me almost every day for the next five or six weeks. I looked forward to her emails every morning. You don't easily forget such kindness."

Lilia has to give a class at nine tomorrow morning and suggests Keith come along and give a guest lecture. They decide that he has just enough time to do this before heading to Maidstone and that he will show her students a business game to teach them some ideas about business behaviour. They put the washing up in the dishwasher, says goodnight and retires exhausted. Before he sleeps, he checks to see if Ellie has responded. She has.

Keith,

I can well understand the different treatment given those circumstances but this is not what Peter told me. He never mentioned that he had committed a previous offence. Do you think the head of department would be willing to speak to me about all this?

Ellie.

Keith feels he has no option but to reply with some not very good news.

Dear Ellie,

I fear that he cannot speak to you about this. Peter is now eighteen. He must therefore be treated in his own right and not as your son. He would not be allowed to discuss Peter's performance with you. You can only resolve this through Peter. I am so very sorry for him and this is hard for me to say to you, but he has behaved very stupidly. I am very sorry for us too. Given the circumstances, would you have expected me to behave differently?

Keith x

Despite feeling sad at what has happened with Ellie, his exhaustion causes him to sleep well. By the time he is up and breakfasted with Lilia's family he is ready to check his email correspondence before going with Lilia to the university. Ellie's email is pretty brief.

Keith,

You are telling me that my son has effectively lied to me. I find this hard to take.

Ellie.

He feels he has no option but to back off.

Dear Ellie,

I have no wish to come between you and Peter. You told me things were difficult between the two of you. I do not want to do or say anything to make things worse for you. I hope you are able to be on good terms with your son.

Keith

This feels like the end of what had promised so much between them. He hopes he can now focus on the business game with Lilia. The game goes well. The students appreciate a different form of learning. He has the chance now of a quick coffee with her in her office.

Lilia: "You go to Maidstone and then over to Northern France to see a student? Will you use the Channel Tunnel? I have never been through it."

Keith: "Indeed, I will, as I have several times before, although I sometimes feel a little guilty about it. I was once involved in making a film about it saying that whilst it would be a fantastic engineering achievement it would be a financial disaster for investors. They even showed bits of that film on the BBC news."

Lilia: "So, you were famous?"

Keith: "I had an auntie, Auntie Rose, who saw the news bulletins and spoke to my mother, who was still alive at that time. From what my mother told me she said my cogent reasoning proved to be very powerful and persuasive."

Lilia: "Really? What did Auntie Rose say?"

Keith: "She said I looked handsome in my suit. Such is fame".

Lilia is not very tall and has to reach up to kiss him goodbye. The kiss reminds her of a previous occasion they had been together:

"I have not forgotten the walk we did with you when a group of us came to Barmouth to study there for a short while."

Keith: "Remind me...."

Lilia: "It was a lovely afternoon and there were about twelve of us. You and a couple of other lecturers took us on a favourite walk of yours through some countryside about thirty minutes' drive out of Barmouth. It was huge fun and we all got to chat to you and to each other as we went along. When we came towards the end of the walk, we came to a kind of gate I had never seen in Bulgaria and you said it was called a kissing gate."

Keith: "I remember now. That was true. The kind of gate at the end of that walk is called just that. It is designed to allow people to pass, but not sheep or cattle. Perhaps I didn't tell you, we get that name because the gate is just "kissing", or touching the enclosure and it does not need to be latched in any way."

She grins at him:

"Yes, I found this out later but it isn't what you told us at the time. You claimed that at this kind of gate there is an English tradition. The guy has to go through first and then he has to hold the gate open and kiss each of the girls as they come through. You then proceeded to demonstrate."

Keith laughs at the memory:

"Oh, you must have been mistaken. It was probably another day with another lecturer."

They both know full well that this was not so.

With a warm hug and a promise to keep in touch he is gone and on his way to Maidstone. As he drives south, he knows how hard it will be to put Ellie out of his mind. Nat King Cole is by now on the second of the two CDs that form the set. The song he is listening to is "These foolish things".

The ties that bound us
are still around us.
There's no escape that I can see
and still those little things remain
that bring me happiness or pain....
Those stumbling words that told you what my heart meant....
These foolish things remind me of you.

In such a short time everything around him has come to serve as a reminder of Ellie. It now looks like it's going to be a long slow process forgetting her. She had changed him. Will the change she had brought about survive her going? Time will tell. The place in Maidstone is a large accountancy firm and he has arranged to see one of the senior managers first and then to see the student afterwards. He is immediately surprised by how young the manager is to be holding a quite senior position. She is warm, friendly and clearly very intelligent. She is impressed by the work that his student has been doing. She says that he has learned many concepts in Barmouth that he is now able to use. This is exactly what a good placement can do. Unfortunately, there is a delicate problem that she wants to raise with Keith. He has fallen in love with another placement student from another University and the open displays of affection are creating a problem in the work environment. She has told him that this relationship has to stop or, regrettably, the firm will insist that he leaves.

Keith: "Isn't it hard to tell a couple of young people that they can't fall in love? Most of our waking hours are spent in the workplace. It's difficult enough to find someone that we can truly love. Do we want to reduce this opportunity much further?"

Manager: "We have rules in place banning hugging and so on. In today's environment even giving compliments is frowned upon. He was told the rules when he came. It seems the only way we can prevent problems escalating."

Keith: "If I tell him that he is not forbidden to have any contact with the girl, just no contact in the workplace, is that an acceptable compromise?"

Manager: "Given that he only has another couple of months to be here, I will accept that. I can also move him to a different floor but they will both have to accept that they cannot visit one another's floor at all."

Keith goes off to find the student and explains the position. He tells him that in every way except his relationship with the other placement student everything is going really well. The guy is not very happy to hear about the discussion Keith has had about the new girlfriend:

"It's all very well for you to say it's a reasonable request but we fell in love. I don't want to cut down on my chances of spending time with her."

Keith thinks, but doesn't say, that he has probably lost permanently the one with whom he has fallen in love so he doesn't see a couple of months as such a big deal:

"You really have no choice. You are not being asked to give her up, just give up seeing her on the work premises. It's that or you fail an otherwise successful placement and cause her to fail hers too. Don't you love her enough for that?"

Reluctantly the student agrees and Keith returns to confirm this with the senior manager. They part with an agreement that if there is any breaking of the agreement she will contact him immediately. He now travels on towards Folkestone to find the place he has booked for the night. The CD player has now moved on to one by the Kings Singers and he hears the haunting melody of Billy Joel's "And so it goes".

"And every time I've held a rose
It seems I only felt the thorns
And so it goes, and so it goes
And so will you soon I suppose."

Why does every song seem to remind him of a woman with whom he has fallen in love but now seems destined to lose?

"So, I would choose to be with you
That's if the choice were mine to make
But you can make decisions too
And you can have this heart to break."

He has loved listening to this remarkable group for years and has found this song so moving, but just now he can't stand to hear any more.

The place he has booked is called the "WESSEX HOTEL". By the time he finds it darkness is already falling and the letters of the sign are picked out boldly in the failing light. He can't quite believe what he sees as he parks and looks up. The lighting has failed in the first three, and only the first three letters. Does this mean that the clientele will be somewhat different from what he had imagined? Will there be someone hovering by the door asking him if he has a Seeee-garrrr –ett? Mercifully, there is not. He checks in, walks to a nearby supermarket to get a large bottle of milk, has a meal and before sleeping looks yet again at his email. He is surprised to find another from Ellie.

Dear Keith,

I had a long conversation with Peter over the phone last night. It was obvious to him that I was deeply distressed. He was aware that part of my unhappiness was caused by his removal from his course. But he was quite unaware that part of it was my distress that through his being at Barmouth and all that has happened since I have lost you. In the end he admitted that he had cheated before and that Carrie had not done so. I am sorry I was hasty. I treated you unfairly.

Love Ellie x

He tries to get his mind around a sensible reply.

Dear Ellie,

I know these things have been so difficult for you. Maybe we could chat on Facebook tomorrow evening when I am in France.

Love Keith. x

He is so delighted that maybe all is not lost. He celebrates by drinking all of the milk from the large bottle bought from the supermarket earlier. The next morning, as he exits the tunnel on the French side for a short drive to meet his student, he feels more cheerful about Ellie and decides to play an old recording of the anarchic radio programme "I'm sorry I haven't a clue". The one he is playing is from the days when Humphrey Littleton, Humph, was the chairman and one of the panellists was Willie Rushton and the EU was known as the" Common Market". It's a round where Humph plays a piece of music and the panellist must sing along to it. When the music fades out the panellist must keep singing. When the music comes back after a minute or so the panellist must try to be still in step with the recording. Willie has to sing along to Edith Piaf's recording of Non, je ne regrette rien. He is making a dreadful fist of it. At one point he stops singing and says "Bloody Common Market". He then continues to sing. When the music fades back in Willie is somehow in time with

Edith to the millisecond. The audience erupts with laughter and applause and Humph says:

"Amazing, I think Edith Piaf must have said 'bloody Common Market' too. Keith still laughs at this having heard it a number of times before but it seems just a little bit funnier still that he is in Europe listening to it.

He arrives at the Tourist information Office in Normandy where Helen is on placement. She is unusual in being able to speak very good French and her placement is designed to develop her language skills further. He finds her in the offices above the part where the tourists come for information. He greets her with a "bon jour" and in doing so practically exhausts his knowledge of the French language. He can also say "Marseille" but only in an English accent. He has not met her before and is struck by how very attractive she is. She has a lovely face and the way she is dressed is quite striking. The low-cut top and the very short skirt do little to hide her excellent figure. The male tourists must be queuing up to ask her anything they can think of. She tells him that she loves the job but is not getting on at all well with the lady who is the boss. Helen regards her as a frump who is jealous of her youth, though she is too modest to say that she thinks she is also jealous of her looks.

Keith says he will try to raise tactfully their relationship when he meets her shortly. He has no need to find a tactful way to raise the matter. The boss makes it very clear that Helen speaks excellent French and has a great knowledge of the area so that she can deal efficiently with tourist questions. However, she is clearly appalled by Helen's dress sense, regarding it as inappropriately immodest. She claims that it upsets the tourists. Keith thinks, but does not say, that it is unlikely to upset about fifty percent of them. He ventures to suggest that in France many women dress in a very "feminine way". It is the wrong thing to say. The manager responds frostily.

"What do <u>you</u> think is an appropriate length of skirt?"

He thinks, but he doesn't say:

"I think it depends upon how good the legs are."

The boss: "And what do <u>you</u> think is an appropriate cut for a top?"

The bosom opposite him seems to consist of a horizontally placed bag of cement. He thinks ... but then decides not to even think it. Instead, he replies by saying that he thinks Helen should dress in keeping with the requirements of the Tourist Office and that he will tell her so. He returns to find Helen. She is not terribly happy to be told what she can and can't wear. Keith begs her to keep the boss happy for the remaining few months of the replacement and then to wear whatever she pleases after she has left:

"For just a few weeks think of the long term and say yes miss."

Helen agrees to be diplomatic and he feels able to leave.

His Facebook chat with Ellie raises mixed emotions. He is delighted to be back in touch but it is clear that they have lost something of the ease which they have previously felt in communicating with each other. He is also delighted that Ellie seems very keen to meet as soon as is at all possible. She is travelling to Spain on Saturday week and Keith is about to start jury service. It seems improbable that he will be on a jury on a Saturday so they arrange to have coffee together at the airport before she boards for her flight. He wonders whether they will we ever be easy again in one another's company.

For his evening meal he makes the mistake of ordering a steak. He prefers it to be medium to well done. When it comes, it is brought to his table it is virtually raw. It looks as if it has been cooked over a lighted matchstick. He asks if they will take it back and at least warm the blood up a bit. The steak is brought back and looks as unappetising as ever. In the end he goes to bed hungry. At least he likes cold French milk. After a comfortable night's sleep in a Logis de France he makes an early morning start to his return journey. He decides that it will be pleasanter to use the minor roads and so early in the morning all is very quiet. He passes a tiny village with about twelve houses. Oh, how very French. There is no shop, no boulangerie, but it has two hairdressers. On this minor road early in the morning there is just one vehicle coming towards him and the idiot driving it is on the wrong side of the road. The gap between the two vehicles is reducing rapidly. When they are about fifty metres apart Keith realises that he is the idiot. He has time to stop being English and return to the right side of the road before an accident takes place. He is delighted to get back to the UK without further incident.

He drives along the coast to Brighton for his final meeting before returning home. He has never liked Brighton very much. It reminds him of Keith Waterhouse's comment:

"Brighton has the perennial air of being in a position to help the police with their inquiries."

Nevertheless, he is so glad to find his student, Andrew, in a large firm where there is a careful plan of how to give him every opportunity to learn from his experience. The line manager is thoughtful and positive and the student is happy to be there. He does say that there is one manager to whom it is hard to relate, a man who, he believes, is incompetent and has been there for only a short while. Again, Keith suggests that being diplomatic and quietly coping with the problem is the way forward since it is a short placement. He does also suggest that if this particular manager is indeed incompetent, he may not last very long in the job. He tells the student a story which is sometimes related to students on management courses. The story goes like this.

A new manager has been appointed to replace the outgoing one who has been fired for incompetence. As he is leaving, the sacked manager tells the newcomer that he has placed three envelopes in his desk. He suggests that when things get difficult that would be a good time to think about the envelopes.

After about six months the new manager finds that things are starting to go wrong. Then he remembers the three envelopes and so he decides to open his drawer and read the contents of the first one. It reads: "Blame the problems on your predecessor." This seems like excellent advice. He follows it, people accept this as reasonable and the crisis passes.

Another six months go by and things get tough again. The manager goes to the drawer, takes out the contents of the second envelope and reads: "Reorganize everything. In the ensuing chaos people will forget what the original problem was." Again, he follows the advice. It works well and he is absolved from blame.

After a further six months more problems are occurring and so he goes eagerly to the final envelope for more wisdom. He is already inclined to accept whatever advice he finds. After all, the contents of the previous two envelopes proved to be a great success. He opens the last one and the piece of paper inside reads: "Prepare three envelopes."

The student smiles and Keith leaves asking him to make contact if the problem gets worse. He returns to his office in Barmouth to sort out the paperwork from his placement visits. He bumps into Martin Anderson who wants to share something with him.

"I have just been with a bunch of students and we talked about teaching as a career. Twenty years ago, when I first came here, I asked a group if they would consider teaching or lecturing as a career. They thought about it and then said no. I asked the same question of today's group and they just laughed."

Keith goes home feeling very sad. To him showing young minds how to think, stimulating them and challenging them to understand the world around them, is a most noble occupation. Now, it seems, the world's inclination is to despise teaching as a career. He recalls Terry Pratchett's book "Mort". He probably thinks about it because mort is a play on words, being the French for death. He remembers the line well:

"It would seem that you have no useful skill or talent whatsoever. Have you thought of going into teaching?"

He wonders if it would have been a better line if it had said:

"It would seem that you have no useful skill or talent whatsoever. Have you thought of going into Mordor to manage the teachers?"

Hmmmm, probably not.

CHAPTER TEN:
THE JURY IS OUT

"When you go into court, you are putting your fate into the hands of twelve people who weren't smart enough to get out of jury duty."

- Norm Crosby

As the term ends, Keith is about to spend time doing jury service at the local magistrates court. With a few exceptions anyone between eighteen and seventy-six years old can be called to serve as a juror in the UK. He was summoned a while ago but wrote to ask if he could be excused because of the impact that his absence would have on his students. It's a form of national service in the UK, a requirement of the law that you must serve, unless there is a good reason for being excused. At the time he was given permission to skip jury service until a later date, but now the teaching term has finished and his time for service has become due. Like many people, he has read a few novels based on a courtroom and watched a few films based upon the law. However, he has never sat on a jury before and he is rather looking forward to it. He thinks about his mother who was never called to jury service. The idea would have terrified her. Economists are trained in logical reasoning. For Keith this is surely an opportunity to put his training into practice in a different area of life.

For him it will be fun to see whether what is portrayed in the novels and the films bears any resemblance to what actually happens. On this first day, he has been told that he doesn't have to be there until late morning, so he has time for a swim first. He goes a bit later than is his custom, and it is inevitably somewhat more crowded and more difficult to swim without getting in the way of others. Keeping two chevrons apart from the swimmer in front is problematic. As he relaxes in the pool, he reflects upon his relationship to legal matters.

In an entirely amateur way, he has always had an interest in the law. He recalls how many years ago he read a book by A.P.

Herbert called "Misleading Cases," which revolves around a character called Albert Haddock, who raises and argues about obscure points of arcane English Law. Keith found these fanciful stories fascinating. He loved the one where someone had taken a plane up into the sky and produced smoke from the rear, forming rude words for someone he didn't like. It was then argued that this could not be libel because libel must be written in a permanent form. However, it could not be slander because slander must be spoken, and nothing had been said. What amusing stuff! Utterly devoid, of course, from the reality he expects to find in the magistrate's court.

He might have liked to study law at university, except that no one at home or school had told him that this was possible. His parents would never have known and so could not have advised him. The school just didn't bother to inform him of possibilities. He had been left to find out things for himself, something he had not done well. He only found out about the possibility of a law degree when he was at university studying economics, by which time he felt that it was too late to change. Now he has a chance to see the process of law from the inside. He does not expect to be on a jury with a trial anything as interesting as A.P. Herbert's cases but hopes for something stimulating. At the same time, he dreads being involved in anything like a rape case. He would be thinking of Ellie, and he would be appalled, not only by the treatment of the victim in the case but by the very thought of Ellie being treated in that way. The legal system means that he has no way of knowing in advance what case he might be involved in.

After his swim, he arrives at the court to find the other potential jurists. It seems that it is necessary to sit around in a large room for some time before being called. He discovers that it is possible to come each weekday for two weeks and never be called to be on a jury at all. He must just hope that this is not his fate. He sits next to a guy who does not appear very happy. Keith engages him in conversation. It soon becomes clear that the man is there under sufferance. He feels that he has more important things to do. When he had received a letter summoning him, he had responded by telling them so. The man is just beginning to realise what a mistake it was. It was made clear to him that he had no choice but to attend and that the consequences of absenting himself could include a fine of £1000. Some people cannot understand that politeness is the only option. Keith maintains a diplomatic silence. Sometimes it makes sense to tell a person he is behaving stupidly, but not very often.

He goes to the loo and bumps into a man on his way out who has put on his coat and is clearly leaving. Keith asks him how it is that he is allowed to leave. The man responds:

"I was asked to be a juror on a trial that might go on for weeks. I have a small business that I own and run. There is no one to replace me. The consequences of my absence for a long period would be severe. I asked politely if I might be excused, and I was so pleased that they agreed."

Keith is delighted for him. Financial compensation for jury service exists but its value is quite unrealistic. As an economist, he knows how hard it can be to survive as a small business person. So much is loaded against these people. Health and safety laws are such that large firms can afford a person to make sure such laws are kept, but a small firm cannot do so. Tax regulations are complex so that, while larger firms employ accounting specialists, small businesses struggle to afford them. The agreement of the court to excuse him will have saved his business and the jobs of the people he employs. Keith recalls a story he has used before in his teaching. It is about a small businessman in trouble with the law over the payment of wages. Trading Standards decided that a small carpentry shop owner is not paying wages in accordance with the minimum wage laws, so a representative is sent to interview him.

Trading Standards Officer: "You have to supply me with a list of all your employees, and I also need to know how much you pay each of them."

Carpentry Shop Owner: "Well, I have an experienced full-time worker. He has been with me for five years now, and I pay him a salary of £35,000 a year."

Trading Standards Officer: "Is there anyone else that you employ?

Carpentry Shop Owner: "Well, I have an apprentice, but he has only been here for about six months. I pay him £1,500 a month."

Trading Standards Officer: "Is there no one else who works for you?"

Carpentry Shop Owner: "There is no one else except the half-wit that works here about eighteen hours a day. He makes about £10,000 a year, and I buy him a case of beer every Friday,"

Trading Standards Officer: "This is the person I need to talk to."

Carpentry Shop Owner: "That would be me."

After some period of waiting, he and a number of others are called to go to a courtroom. Keith is surprised to find that it is more than just twelve of them. Soon, he discovers why. The trial is to take place of a young junior petty officer who is accused of stealing a power screwdriver from Beagles, the only large department store in Barmouth's high street. The price of the screwdriver is about six pounds. The defence lawyer has the right to challenge and object to a number of potential jurors without giving a reason. It becomes clear that he thinks his client has a better chance with a younger and therefore possibly more sympathetic jury. When he has run out of his permitted challenges, Keith gets to become a part of the jury. He wonders if the defence lawyer would have challenged him. He will never know. The completed jury has a mix of ages, rather more men than women, and everyone is white Caucasian. The defence lawyer is about forty and exudes confidence in himself. He looks and sounds like someone from the private sector. The prosecuting counsel is older, less sure of himself, and gives every impression of being nowhere near as bright. Is that typical of someone from the state sector, Keith wonders?

The defendant looks scared but rather supercilious at the same time. Keith thinks that if he were in that position, he would try to look humbler, even though, at this stage, he has no idea of the strength of the case against him. The combination of the apparently super-confident defence counsel and the supercilious defendant reminds Keith of a story, possibly apocryphal, that was said to have taken place in a murder trial in the USA.

The story is told of a noted criminal defence lawyer who was making his closing argument for his client who was on trial for murder. The body of the victim had never been found. The lawyer dramatically turned to the courtroom clock. Pointing to it, he said:

"Ladies and gentlemen of the jury, I have some astounding news. I have found the supposed victim of this murder to be alive! In just ten seconds, she will walk through the door of this courtroom and you will see her for yourself."

A hush settled over the courtroom as everyone waited for the dramatic entry. Nothing happened.

The smirking lawyer continued:

"The mere fact that you were watching the door, expecting the victim to walk into this courtroom, is clear proof that you have far more than a reasonable doubt as to whether a murder was actually committed."

Tickled with the impact of his cleverness, the cocky lawyer confidently sat down to await acquittal. The jury was instructed by the judge. They all filed out to consider what had happened and filed back in just ten minutes with a guilty verdict.

When the judge brought the proceedings to an end, the dismayed lawyer chased after the jury foreman:

"Guilty? How could you convict? You were all watching the door!"

"Well," the foreman explained, "Most of us were watching the door. But one of us was watching the defendant, and he wasn't watching the door."

Keith knows little about the law but he finds himself pondering why this young petty officer has opted for a trial? He could have pleaded guilty and received a fairly small fine in the magistrate's court. Either the man is more confident than he looks, or there is something else going on of which Keith is, as yet, unaware. Maybe he will find out later.

The judge arrives. He is also a white Caucasian male. Keith thinks that he looks to be about one hundred and twenty-five. He gets the trial underway. Over the next two days the case unfolds. The prosecution case is that the petty officer was on duty at the naval base and falsified a document to say that he was not on duty at all at the time. Furthermore, the case goes, he falsified another document claiming that he was using a navy vehicle for official business but then used it for his own personal use. He drove it into town before parking it and then entering the store. He went to the upper level, the prosecution claims, stole the power screwdriver, came back down the stairs and left the building. At this point two store detectives challenged him and took him to their office to search him. When they found no sign of a screwdriver on the defendant, one of them retraced his steps and found it on the downstairs level, thrown in among the gardening tools. The prosecution claims that on the way back into the store the petty officer had managed to extract the screwdriver from his pocket and had thrown it there before entering the store detectives' office. The case is laboriously presented by the prosecution including providing the jury with diagrams of the store to show the location of the key items.

As far as Keith can tell, the judge is sound asleep. Yet he realises that this is impossible because every so often, he interrupts and stops the trial for a moment while he writes down precisely what has been said, mostly the words given in evidence by the store detectives.

Before all the evidence has been presented by the prosecution the judge decides that it is time to stop for the day. It is 3.30 in the afternoon. Perhaps the judge needs some ore sleep. He explains to the court that the jury needs to be fully awake to follow the evidence being presented so it's time for them to rest until tomorrow morning.

Keith is surprised by the early end to the day's proceedings but he is delighted. It gives him a chance to catch up on some shopping and to put his house in some semblance of order. It is the next day before all the prosecution's evidence has been presented. Most of it consists in cross examining the store detectives. The defence lawyer chooses not to ask them anything. Then the defence counsel makes his case. He shows how the route from the outside of the store does indeed pass the gardening equipment but suggests that it is entirely plausible that there is an alternative explanation of what took place. The petty officer, he suggests, picked up the screwdriver and went downstairs intending to pay for it at the ground floor pay point. He then changed his mind. Lazily, and rather naughtily, he threw the screwdriver in among the gardening tools because he was in a hurry to get back to base. He did not steal it; rather he never had it on him when the store detectives stopped him outside the shop. Keith notices that the defence counsel, whilst offering an entirely different explanation of events inside the store, does not dispute that the petty officer has falsified naval documents to come into town. He only disputes what is said to have happened in the shop. He chooses not to put the petty officer on the stand. Again, the judge has been taking careful note of a few points whilst apparently continuing to doze away most of the hours.

At several times during the day reference is made to what was said "on another occasion". Keith wonders what the other occasion is but nobody seems willing to enlighten him or the other jurors. On the morning of the next day the prosecution counsel summarises his case. It is a dull and uninspiring presentation. The defence counsel then summaries the case for the defence. He turns on a magnificent performance.

Defence lawyer: "Ladies and gentlemen, the prosecution has the task of proving beyond doubt that my client is guilty. Clearly, they have not come within a country mile of doing so. The events as I have outlined are obviously far more likely than the far-fetched story that the prosecution has presented. I hope you will do your duty and find him not guilty, for surely this is the only possible verdict."

Keith thinks he is tremendous. He wants to applaud the performance but decides that this is unlikely to be appreciated. He has yet to hear the judge's summing up. Although at this stage, he has little doubt of the petty officer's guilt, he recognises that the speech is magnificent. Oh, for this kind of passionate brilliance from lecturers in Barmouth. Some of his colleagues there rush through their dull classroom delivery in order to get back to some pointless 'research'.

After hearing from the prosecution and from the defence counsel it is the judge's task to sum up what has taken place. He plans to do this the next day. Keith is keen to return to hear the judge. It is now day three of the trial. The judge's summing up is a masterpiece. He now looks fully awake. He reminds the jury of the key points of the evidence presented to the court. They are taken from the spoken testimony. They are the precise ones that the judge wrote down word for word. The jury listens spellbound by his conclusion:

"Ladies and gentlemen of the jury, it is now for you to decide. You must decide solely upon the evidence presented to you. Let us put aside rhetoric. You can either believe these fine law-abiding detectives, men with no axe to grind against the defendant, or you can choose to believe the word of the defendant, a man perfectly prepared to lie and falsify navy documents concerning his work, perfectly prepared to lie and falsify documents concerning the use of the vehicle. You can choose to believe him. It is for you to decide. I do not want to countenance a majority verdict at this stage. I would like a unanimous verdict but it is for you to decide".

On the third day of the trial the twelve jurists retire to make their verdict. It is about 11.30 am. The jury meet and speak to each other for the first time. One of the jurists immediately says that he has experience as a jury foreman and is willing to do the job if everyone agrees. At least there is a unanimous verdict on this. The newly elected foreman suggests that before the evidence is discussed they may as well have each one in turn declare their position. If everyone thinks the same there will be no further need of discussion. Everyone agrees with his proposal. He goes around the room looking at each one in turn.

"Guilty, guilty, guilty...."

At the end of the round there are eleven, including Keith, all of whom are sure beyond reasonable doubt that the petty officer stole the screwdriver as charged and have said so. However, one young lad, about the age of one of Keith's students, says that he is not sure and wants to discuss it.

Another juror says with a grin that the judge has made it totally plain what he wants and is likely to find us in contempt of court if we do not return a guilty verdict. The lad holds his ground. There follows a two-hour discussion, going fully over the evidence. This time includes a short break for lunch when the court usher provides sandwiches and, astonishingly, expects the jury to pay for them. At the end of the two hours the lad finally agrees that the right verdict is guilty. The foreman goes to tell the usher that are ready to come back to the courtroom to deliver their verdict and that, as the judge has asked, it is a unanimous verdict.

Despite the length of discussion in the jury room, the jury does not, indeed cannot, give reasons for its decision.

Following the jury's announcement of their verdict Keith discovers why the petty officer opted for trial. As a result of having a criminal record he will be reduced to the ranks. He had opted for trial in a desperate attempt to avoid this, even though he would be treated less leniently if found guilty. Keith is disappointed not to hear the sentence. The judge announces that this will be passed at a later date. The judge then turns to the jury.

"I would like to thank this most EXCELLENT jury." He beams. Keith and the others, it appears, have avoided being found in contempt of court. On the way out of the court Keith passes the prosecuting counsel and asks him what the references were to "on another occasion".

Prosecuting counsel: "This was a retrial. The jury at the first trial could not agree on a verdict, even a majority one. You were not allowed to know this in case it affected your decision. The decision had to be based entirely on the evidence presented at this trial."

Keith finds it extraordinary, yet somehow comfortingly British, that they could take almost six days to make as sure as humanly possible that the right verdict is reached about the theft of a power screwdriver valued at just six pounds. He then chases after the young lad who had been the only one to express doubts about the guilty verdict and invites him around the corner from the courtroom for a cup of coffee. His name is Sean.

Keith: "Did you really have serious doubts about the case?"

Sean: "No, not at all. I was always totally convinced of his guilt, pretty much from the outset".

Keith: "Then why did you keep us there for two hours arguing about it?"

Sean: "I am a law student. My professor said he has always wanted to know and to discuss how a jury reaches a verdict. I could not possibly go back next term and tell him that because he was so obviously guilty there was no discussion. I needed something to give him. As it is he will be delighted."

And so, thinks Keith, another twenty-four hours of court time are wasted, two hours for each of the twelve jurists. Then again, perhaps it was not a waste. The education of a group of students will be enhanced in due course. Keith has always tried to show his students the relationship between economic theories and the real world. He has now discovered that law lecturers are keen to do the same thing for their students also.

As he returns to the car park where he has left his Lexus Keith sees a girl whom he recognises from the jury. He has not spoken to her before and she hardly uttered a word in the jury room, although he was intrigued that her very few words seemed to have been pronounced in a notable French accent. He approaches her as she is about to get into her car. She recognises him and smiles. It is only two o'clock on an unusually warm day. She is struggling to remove her coat and Keith, ever the gallant Englishman, helps her to do so. She speaks:

"Thank you. When it is 'ot I like to 'ave it off."

She clearly has no awareness of this unintended double entendre, but Keith just smiles enigmatically and agrees that it is now very warm. He is not inclined to laugh at her English accent, given his own abominable, virtually non-existent French. He suggests that they might go for coffee and she readily agrees. They walk around the corner to the coffee shop. He discovers that her name is Monique. She comments herself upon her French accent and explains that she has lived in England for many years and now has English citizenship, hence she qualifies to sit on a jury in this country. Keith has never much believed in helping the environment by appeals to people's altruistic sense.

He decides that this is a good time to try a present that he has brought with him today and to use it to be environmentally friendly. In general, he believes that it is more efficient to change people's behaviour through changing prices, as has happened so successfully with the introduction of a compulsory charge for a plastic bag. However, the wife of his neighbour, Ben, has encouraged him to be more environmentally aware and she has bought him a special mug for his recent birthday. He takes this out of his bag for the barista and orders coffee for himself and one for his new French friend. The barista makes coffee in the usual way for Monique. He then makes the coffee for Keith in a disposable cup, tips the coffee into Keith's mug and throws the disposable cup in the bin. He will have to decide whether to report this to Ben's wife. He looks on in disbelief but says nothing.

The jury was warned not to discuss the case while the trial was taking place but now it is over he and Monique share a few thoughts on the case.

Monique: "I am amazed that we could spend so long discussing such a small crime. This could never happen in France."

Keith: "Really? What would happen there?"

Monique: "Serious offences would be dealt with by a jury, but such minor matters would always be decided by a magistrate. Such a lot of court time over something costing six pounds seems crazy."

Keith feels that he needs to know a little more. He is uncertain whether he prefers the French or the English system. They part company, thinking that they may meet again in a few days since they are both required to attend for possible jury service for another week. It is not often that he gets home so early but before he spends a while catching up with the inevitable pile of emails, he decides to research a little more on the practice of a jury system in other parts of the world.

He is surprised to discover that few countries now use juries, and most of them are former British colonies, such as the US, Canada and Australia. In the US, their use is rapidly declining as a result of the use of plea bargaining where justice is in the hands of lawyers negotiating with each other. Keith hopes that he might have the chance to discuss some of these things with Sean, although it is unlikely that they will be on another jury together.

He then returns to his emails. A lecturer's work, like the proverbial housewife's is never done. He finds one from the excellent administrator at UCS in Sofia, thanking him for his visit. She comments upon his recent promotion from Senior lecturer to Principal Lecturer. This was a promotion he was lucky to get. Although the University gets ninety percent of its income from teaching, it continues to be the case that most promotions go the ones engaged in research, an area where the university probably sustains a loss. Keith's teaching record is better than his relatively thin research record.

Dear Keith,

It was so good to have you here again. As always, the students are delighted whenever you come. It makes them feel that they are not forgotten when you spend time with them. You really should have told us that you had been promoted. The notice we put on the board about your visit had the wrong title!

Love Bilyana.

He responds.

Dear Bilyana,

It's always a delight to be with you. The title really doesn't matter. Next time you can refer to me on the notice board as "Keith (gets a slightly bigger pension now). I will try to come again as soon as I possibly can."

Love Keith

There is also another email, this one emanating from Mordor. It is the end of term but the eye of Mordor never sleeps. It is just permanently half closed. This missive requires all staff to sign up for at least one course to attend during the next six months in order that everyone is at the cutting edge of knowledge. This procedure is a well-established piece of nonsense and it is easier to respond than fight for months. There is a list of such possibilities and he chooses the one on "managing your diary". In fact, he always chooses this one. It is the optimal choice. It has several advantages. It takes less time than most of the other courses. By doing this one every year he knows in advance that he can fall asleep while he attends. He can pick the last of several dates offered, because, as last year, there is a decent chance it will be cancelled and there won't be another occasion this year which he can be told to attend. He makes his inevitable choice and responds accordingly.

In the morning, he sets off early to the airport to spend a couple of hours with Ellie before her flight to Algeciras. He does so with mixed feelings. He is thrilled to be seeing her again. His thoughts have been with her more and more. Yet he is uncertain whether the problems about her son's cheating in exams will mean that something of a barrier still remains. The last few emails, though, have given him encouragement, but to use an expression which seems especially pertinent, the jury is still out. He enters the airport cafe at the agreed time and discovers that she is there already. She catches sight of him, stands up, and comes towards him. There are tears in her eyes. She throws her arms around him and hugs him so long and so tightly that he fears for his ribcage. With her head on his shoulder, he thinks he hears her whispers quietly:

"I love you".

The kiss is everything it should be, long, warm, gentle, caring, affectionate. Each of them reciprocates, neither escalates. Neither of them notices the crowds around them. Sit opposite each other at a small table and order some breakfast but Ellie is keener to talk than to eat. Their long embrace has caused her to look a little more dishevelled than normal. He thinks she looks magnificent.

Ellie: "I am so very sorry I accused you unfairly. It was a shock to me to discover that Peter had been dishonest with me. I am trying to hang on to my relationship with him but it is even more difficult now. Have I lost you through all this?"

Keith: "My dear Ellie, you got it wrong and there is no point pretending otherwise but you have made a mistake that so many of us have made before. It's so easy to misunderstand things. I same close to a girl a few years ago and lost her out of a misunderstanding although in this case it was also because of my jealousy."

Ellie is intrigued and wants to know what happened:

"Please tell me about it".

Keith: "It was quite a while ago. It did not involve anyone else at the university. We were getting on very well but she started seeing another guy more and more. I saw rather less of her for a while and I thought she really preferred him. She seemed quite secretive about this guy and this confirmed to me that she was hiding another relationship from me. I broke it off. It was very painful."

Ellie: "But your reaction was entirely reasonable."

Keith: "I thought so too until I found out through a mutual friend some months later that the other guy was her brother and because he was having trouble with the police at the time she was trying to help him while keeping it all quiet. She had never told me any of this. When things became clear she was so upset that I hadn't trusted her and she just walked away. I never saw her again."

Ellie: "Do you still think about her?"

" I got over her but it took me ages to realise something. Of course, I knew that everyone makes mistakes but I discovered what an unpleasant emotion jealousy is and how costly it can be. So, my dear Ellie, I know just how it feels to misjudge something. Let's forget it. You have become so precious to me. I don't want to lose you, over this or over anything else."

They reach across the table and kiss each other tenderly. Then she excuses herself to go to the loo. She is wearing a close fitting black trouser suit and it does nothing to hide her gorgeous figure. He watches her as she walks away from the table. There are not a lot of people around but there is a guy at one of the tables nearby finishing his breakfast. As Ellie passes him, he turns his head and stares at Ellie's retreating figure. He continues to stare until she disappears from view. Keith finds it highly amusing. He is torn between the delight of watching Ellie and the fun of watching the guy enjoying the sight of her. When she returns the man has paid for his breakfast and has gone. Keith tells her about him and she finds it hard to believe what he tells her:

"Ellie, you are a very gorgeous woman. People notice when you arrive and notice when you leave. You really should not be surprised."

Ellie: "Thank you. You know, I truly hate spiders but your so-called pet played quite a part in developing my feelings for you. You were very gracious when I screamed in your bathroom."

Keith: "Did I ever tell you about the time the students played a trick on one of the lecturers using a spider, although it was not my pet?"

Ellie: "No, go on, I think I just have just time to hear it."

Keith: "It must have been soon after you left Barmouth. We had a lecturer that I don't think was very good. He is still there. I do not think you could have met him. His name is Edward Stoneham, or as he is known by some of the staff, Mr Death. The students decided to play a trick on him. He would come in to one of the lecture rooms each week and would always stand in front of the lectern to talk. He would never move. You have seen me wandering around the front of the lecture theatre. He was very different. He made a statue look mobile. So, one day the students mocked up an enormous spider out of an old wig. They then set up a kind of pulley system so that there was a piece of string hanging down from the light right above the lectern where he stood. To this they attached their spider. Can you imagine, the spider is now above the lectern but right up against the ceiling. The other end of the string came down near the back of the room where a few of the students were sitting. After the lecture started, they let the string down so that the spider was just above his head. They thought it was very funny and couldn't hide their laughter. The lecturer was clearly deeply irritated that he had no idea what they were laughing at. At the end of the lecture, he left the room. The story went around the department but as far as I am aware no one has ever told Mr Death what provoked the laughter."

She finds the story hard to believe but Keith insists that it is true. Edward Stoneham would find it harder still to believe should anyone ever tell him. The time is rapidly approaching when she must go through departures to catch her flight and so they must say goodbye. Ellie has still to buy a return ticket. There are too many uncertainties about her business opportunities to know precisely when she will be home. However, she expects to be back in about a week. By then Keith expects his jury service to be over so he makes clear his hopes he can meet her at the airport on her return.

Ellie: "Keith, I think that would be wonderful."

Keith: "Stay in touch. When you come back, I may not ever let you out of my sight again – except possibly when you go to the loo. I found it amusing to discover one more guy this morning who was reluctant to see you go."

He hates to see her go but he is aware that it will create huge problems for her if she misses her flight. There is one last long hug between them, one final lingering kiss and she has gone.

A key idea in the teaching of economics is that of efficiency. He doesn't always practice it himself. He wanders around the car park for some while, convinced that someone has stolen his Lexus, before finally finding it, paying the car park fee, which he thinks is only marginally less than Ellie has paid for her flight to Algeciras, and driving back home. He chooses to listen to Nat King Cole again. He is held by the haunting melody of "The very thought of you".

"The mere idea of you, the longing here for you,
You'll never know how slow the moments go till I'm near to you.
I see your face in every flower, your eyes in stars above.
It's just the thought of you, the very thought of you, my love.

Sunday is a quiet day to relax and recover from the long term. Ellie has contacted him to say all is well and she will have her first exploratory meeting tomorrow. Keith looks to see if there is any email he cannot immediately delete. There is one from Dan Billings that pleases him. Mordor had surprisingly made a decision a while ago to make available to each faculty a sum of £50,000 specifically to be spent on e-learning projects. Each faculty would decide how it should spend the money but if there were not enough projects that were deemed to be worthwhile the money was to be returned to Mordor. The Business School had decided upon a date by which applications for the money should be made. Keith had made a bid for £10,000 of it to enable him to undertake a small filming project for use with his students. Dan attended the meeting of the small group of Business School staff appointed by the dean to make the decisions. The meeting had been on Friday. Dan was now emailing with the outcome of the discussion.

Dear Keith,

You have your money! All the Business School bids taken together amounted to just under £50,000. The committee wanted to examine each one of the bids in turn to determine its suitability. It took an economist to point out that this was a waste of time. Any money not allocated had to be returned so I proposed that we give everyone who bid everything that they have asked for and suggested that we all go home. The meeting was torn. Somehow, they didn't like this rational approach but on the other hand it was Friday afternoon. The thought of finishing earlier on Friday afternoon than they had anticipated won the day. You, and indeed everyone else, have got what you asked for.

Dan.

He replies to Dan with his grateful thanks and spends a bit of time in the rest of the day mulling over how exactly to use the funds in the coming months.

At the beginning of the second week Keith is again blessed with being chosen to be on a jury for another trial. This time there are several defendants, all women. They are charged with theft. They are all from the same family and have been employed as waitresses at a transport cafe on an A road some miles outside of Barmouth. They are accused of theft by serving a number of friends and family with meals and not charging for them. This, the prosecution claims, has been going on for some time. The owner has become suspicious of their activities and has paid a private detective to sit, watch and make notes of what has been happening.

Any jury can be quite a mix of people. Keith looks around him and is appalled at the thought that if he were on trial for something serious a bunch of people like this lot could be deciding whether or not he is guilty, especially as this might involve going to jail for some time.

Before the trial gets under way Keith notices that the juror to Keith's left has very little hair but still insists on smothering it with some kind of greasy substance. Could it be Brylcreem? This was a substance that was popular when he was a boy. Are people still using it? Keith recalls the jingle they used to sing on the TV adverts "Brylcreem, a little dab'll do you. Brylcreem, the girls will all pursue you. They love to get their fingers in your hair". This guy clearly doesn't believe the first part. A bathtub full of it seems about right to him. Maybe he thinks that in this way it won't be a few girls who will pursue him but a whole harem. Keith remembers fondly his father who had so little formal education. He used this stuff and always called it "Byrlcreem". But then again when he painted some bare wood, before he used the undercoat, he always applied a coat of primer which he insisted on calling primo, which was a make of cabbage that he grew. The thought of putting a cabbage onto a piece of bare wood and then adding undercoat to it is something he has occasionally called to mind over many years.

The juror to Keith's right has an industrial strength smell that could permeate an air raid shelter. Clearly, if he is a typical example of the town's adult population the directors of the country's soap manufacturers will not be riding around in a Rolls Royce any time soon. Neither of these people sitting either side of him is necessarily unfit to assess the evidence but Keith is not optimistic.

The judge, who is again a white Caucasian male, is of an earlier generation than last week. He looks no more than ninety this time. After the trial has been going on for half an hour his lordship is becoming increasingly irritated. The prosecuting counsel makes the mistake of saying that these women have 'purloined a quantity of beverage'. The judge interrupts, making no attempt to hide his irritation:

"If you mean they stole a cup of tea, why can't you just say so, for goodness' sake?"

Prosecuting counsel: "Yes, m'lud."

Half an hour later Keith is finding things a little uncomfortable. The evidence seems quite conclusive. They must surely be guilty. However, he has to remind himself that this is no time to make up his mind. He is yet to hear from the defence. At this point the judge interrupts and Keith finds it hard not to laugh.

Judge: "This is all quite ridiculous, a waste of the court's time. I have had enough of this. I want these people found not guilty."

The court usher stands up and approaches the jury. He asks which of us the foreman is. Keith points out that we have not even spoken to each other yet and have had no chance to choose someone for the job. The usher points to a man at the front:

"You, you are the foreman. Stand up."

The man seems bewildered but does as he is told.

Usher: "Now, do you find these defendants guilty or not guilty?"

Foreman: "Er, um, well.... not guilty."

"Excellent," says the judge, "Case dismissed".

At this point Keith's work for the day is over and it is another triumph for the system of British justice. He leaves the court overhearing a lady muttering to her fellow juror something to the effect that these women seemed guilty to her. He looks back on those days at university when he had discovered that he could have applied to study law instead of economics. He cannot make up his mind whether at that point he had missed his calling in life or had been mercifully spared.

The next day Keith is back at the courts. Some people never get to sit on a jury. Others are instructed to come but never get called. Keith is about to be serve for a third time. This time the directors of a small interior design company are standing trial for fraud. The case against them is that they have been taking large deposits with the intention of defrauding their customers. It is claimed that they have taken the money but have not done the interior design and building work that customers had the right to expect. Over two days evidence is presented and challenged with a significant number of documents being produced including accounts of the interior design company. This time the judge looks closer to two hundred. He cannot have much time left in this world. Since a person is considered too old and presumably gaga at seventy-five when it comes to sitting on a jury this seems somewhat odd.

He remembers hearing of a man who goes to the doctor for a check-up and is told that, sadly, he only has ten to live. When the horrified man asks whether the doctor means ten months or weeks, or years, the doctor says:

"Nine, eight, seven, and six......"

Despite the weight of years heaped upon this judge, he finds the man so very knowledgeable and helpful. The judge's wisdom and patience are considerable; nevertheless, when the jury retires to consider a verdict Keith is very uncomfortable. The prosecution and defence lawyers seem to have specialist knowledge. It seems that the only people who do not have such knowledge are the jury. He looks around at the lay people who have been asked to follow this complex material. He is an economist and this has helped a little but he is no accountant. When he did his economics degree many years ago, he did a one-year course in accountancy. He struggled so hard to cope with it that on the morning of the exam he went to the exam room and repeated the mantra to himself over and over again: PUT THE DEBITS NEXT TO THE WINDOW. Somehow, he is not clear how, he passed the exam.

Yet although he feels unqualified to make a judgment he looks around at the others in despair. One of them is a young woman with yellow stained fingers. She is shaking somewhat. When the jury decision is heading towards a guilty verdict, she immediately agrees with it. It is patently obvious that it is not out of any conviction that this is the correct verdict. She has no idea what the issues are. She is just desperate to get out of the place to have a fag. Some people say that having a jury of your peers to decide your fate is an essential right, a matter of principle. When they return a verdict of guilty, Keith is pretty sure they are correct in this instance but he wonders whether this is really a decision for those with some accounting training, an expert bench of judges and magistrates who are skilled in identifying fraud when they see it. Being on a jury has been a great experience but he is glad it is over.

Before he leaves the court for the final time, he catches sight of Sean and offers him another cup of coffee. He immediately asks Sean if his law professor has spent time discussing the costs and benefits of a jury system. He is surprised to discover that the law professor is a supporter of trial by jury. Sean is clearly a good student and is well able to summarise the arguments that his professor has used in support of what seems to Keith to be strange and inefficient system.

Sean: My prof came up with a number of reasons. Let me see if I can remember his key arguments. He says that the jury system acts as a check against potential abuses of state power. It prevents the arbitrary use of authority by government officials, who may have an agenda which is not the dispensation of justice.

He also thinks that jury trials educate jurors about the justice system. He feels that people who serve on juries have a greater respect for the system when their time of service is over., that serving on a jury gives people insight into what takes place in a courtroom.

Keith: But surely there is less likelihood of a wrong verdict when made by professionals.

Sean: My professor says that a legal education does not confer upon someone the wisdom of Solomon.

Keith remains unconvinced. It is an important part of the training of an economist to weigh up the costs and benefits of an action and to come to a reasoned conclusion. He is still inclined to the view that the costs of a jury system outweigh its benefits but he promises to reflect further on the topic.

They part and Keith wishes his new friend every success in his future study and career.

At home, he reflects on his time in court and the jury system but also upon how lawyers are generally viewed. The public generally has a low view of them, seeing them as grasping individuals caring nothing for anyone except themselves. He recalls the story of the lorry driver who enjoyed looking out for lawyers as he was driving. When he saw one, he would swerve across the road to try to hit him. One day, as the lorry driver was driving along, he saw a priest hitching a lift, so he decided to stop for him. Inevitably, soon after, the lorry driver saw a lawyer walking down the road and instinctively swerved to hit him. At the last minute, he remembered there was a priest with him, so he swerved back to the centre of the road, narrowly missing the lawyer. He turned to the priest and said:

"I'm so sorry, Father. I only just missed hitting that lawyer".

"Don't worry about it, my son," replied the priest. "I got him with the door."

Keith likes the story, but it is quite untrue to his impression of the layers he has seen in public in recent days, who seem keen to enjoy a difficult job to the best of their ability.

He also reflects on how the particular cases in which he was involved concerned people from lower income groups than those people he usually mixes with. His small circle of friends and the majority of his students are, to use a common term, more middle class than those who were on trial. He is keen to process this aspect of his time on jury service and hopes to get a chance to share his thinking with Ellie. He recalls that, as part of her studies in Barmouth years ago, she had done a course in law. She probably has much to contribute to his thinking.

Keith hasn't looked at his email for a few days but he now finds one from Helen, the student he visited in the French tourist office. It comes with a picture attached. The picture shows her wearing trousers and a high cut top. She looks very demure and very attractive.

Dear Keith,

I took your advice and invested in this outfit. Whilst the boss didn't seem exactly thrilled, she seemed less irritated with me than on most previous days. I hope you approve. Thank you for your visit. I appreciated your coming.

Helen

He writes straight back but thinks he had better not say just how good looking he thinks she is.

Dear Helen,

I think the outfit is absolutely ideal. It sounds at least as if things are a bit better with the boss. Try saying a few complimentary things to her. My impression of her is such that I don't think you need be very subtle about it. Keep me posted.

Keith

He goes to bed thinking what an excellent day it has been. He has finished an interesting time at the court which has given him much food for thought. He feels close again to Ellie. However, as so often in recent days he finds himself wondering if his relationship with her is going to be different from relationships in the past. He comes to a conclusion. His love for Ellie has also given him much food for thought. He has been too risk-averse before. Perhaps not in investment choices. Perhaps not in decisions about job opportunities but in matters of the heart. then it comes to him with great clarity: In all my previous relationships it was fear that held me back. For the first time in my life, I have found a woman about whom I have no fear. "So, Keith'" he says to himself out loud, "what are you going to do about it?"

It seems only right to conclude the day with a large glass of milk.

CHAPTER ELEVEN:
THESE FOOLISH THINGS

*'You see things; and say "Why? "But I dream things that never
were; and I say: "Why not?"*

- George Bernard Shaw.

It is Sunday. Keith has decided to be brave and has made a last-
minute decision that he wants to fly out to try to meet up with
Ellie. He is planning a trip to Gibraltar which is just a few
miles from where Ellie is in Spain. He plans to leave tomorrow.
He has already taken a risk and has been shopping for the things
he wishes to take. He now emails her to see what she thinks of the
idea.

Dear Ellie,

*I could be in Gibraltar from tomorrow around midday. You will
be just a short bus ride away in Algeciras. If it sounds like a good
idea to you and if you haven't visited the rock before, can you
catch a bus and meet me there? The bus from Algeciras goes to
La Linea and you can then get a taxi to the hotel I am staying in.
I will message the name of the hotel and I will explain what is
going on if you would like to meet up.*

Much love,

Keith

He does not have to wait long for a reply.

Dear Keith,

*It sounds a wonderful idea. I am in the process of finalising the
arrangements with the Spanish about the business proposition.
We have just agreed a deal! We have planned a common website
and are sorting out details about the languages to use. I have now
checked out the possibilities of coming to you. I could be with you
for a few hours in the afternoon tomorrow but I have promised to
be back here in Algeciras in the evening to have a Spanish
celebratory meal sealing our business deal. Then, from the*

following morning I am free and we can spend whatever time you have wherever we can be together. How does that sound?

Love you, Ellie.

He replies immediately.

Dear Ellie,

This sounds great. I will be so glad to meet and to hear about the deal. Give me a time and I will be at the bus station in Gibraltar to meet you. Do you have your passport and birth certificate with you? If so, can you please bring it?

Keith xxxxx

He is able to book somewhere he is happy to stay and able to get a seat on the plane, but all this means an early start and he is not at his best in the mornings, especially Mondays. Later that Sunday morning he attends a church service. The sermon is well constructed and interesting although this has not been his universal experience. A friend claimed that he was in a service where the vicar had been droning on and on interminably. One of the choirboys, in a momentary lapse of grace, had thrown his hymnbook at the vicar. He said it missed and struck an old chap sitting in the front row. The old man fell to the floor and other members of the congregation gathered around him. The worried vicar was in the process of asking how he was when the old chap's voice could be plainly heard coming from the middle of the crowd that had gathered:

"Hit me again, I can still hear him."

He has the afternoon free to watch the men's rugby international. A few minutes before the kick-off he changes into his rugby outfit and comes running into the lounge, turns the television on, sits on the settee where he had so recently sat with Ellie, puts the ball between his feet and watches the game. He loves the match but finds it so tedious to listen to the endless discussion before and after the match. He refers to all this talk as the "well Johns ". At half time he prefers to make himself a coffee and think of his coming meeting with Ellie rather than endure the well Johns.

During the rest of the day his thoughts often turn back to her. He thinks about some of the places he has visited on his own: Venice, walking through the Lake District, the incomparable majesty of the Norwegian fjords, picking blackberries and making blackberry and apple pie with custard, wandering through the Scottish Highlands with the smell of wild mountain thyme. Would he love to do these things again and share them with her? It takes him very little time to know that he would. But would she? The words of the Scottish song come to mind:

> *Oh, the summertime has come*
> *And the trees are sweetly blooming,*
> *And the wild mountain thyme*
> *Grows around the blooming heather*
> *Will ye go, Lassie go?*

Would she go with him? I guess, thinks Keith, I will never know unless I ask her. They say that the things you regret most in life are the risks you didn't take. He plans to test this theory. The next day the alarm goes off. He scrambles for his watch. He speaks to himself in his semi-awake state.

"Ummm the little hand is on the six and the big hand is on the nine, so it must be quarter to nine, or maybe quarter past six or...oh I don't care. Yes, I do! I am going to find Ellie!"

He drags himself out of his bed. He has a quick shave, shower and breakfast. He has ordered a taxi to take him to Heathrow for the early morning flight. If he can't spend all the time with Ellie, he will just enjoy Gibraltar for a while. While he is waiting at Heathrow, he observes a number of pilots looking very self-assured in their smart uniforms and on their way to flights around the world. He doesn't particularly like the experience of flying. Some people dislike it because they are not in control. They have put their lives into the hands of another. For Keith, not being in control is what keeps him sane. He would be terrified if he had to fly the thing himself. He knows that pilots are not so self-confident in all circumstances. Last year he had been given a ride in a hot air balloon as a birthday present. He had never been in one before. His friend, Chris, drove him to where the balloon lifted off. There were eight or nine people on board. Once the balloon had risen from the ground one man started screaming hysterically and insisted on being put down. After this character got out it was a glorious flight in perfect conditions. When the balloon came down, he was met by the friend with the car who had followed them. Keith has asked whether Chris knew any more about the terrified guy.

Chris: "Yes, I spoke to him. He was an airline pilot."

Keith: "But that's ridiculous; he spends large parts of his life in the sky."

Chris: "This is what I said to him. He replied that flying a plane felt fine because it had four enormous engines to power it. The insubstantial basket had none".

Keith tries to take comfort in the four enormous engines to which he will be trusting his life. Before taking off he finds a message from the student he visited in Brighton.

Dear Keith,

Greetings from Brighton. I spoke to my girlfriend about it. She was not terribly happy but I guess we can both see the wisdom of it. We come to work together in the morning and leave together in the evening. We only see each other at lunchtime if we leave the premises. No one has complained since we started this arrangement so I hope we have found a compromise with which we can all live.

Andrew.

He sends a supportive reply and boards the aircraft. It's a trouble-free flight, made more interesting by the people sitting in his row. They are a Scottish couple, Malcolm and Lorna, taking a few days' holiday there. It will be their first trip to Gibraltar. He asks them what brings them to the Rock.

Malcolm: "It's somewhere to be where we can feel the sun on our backs. As Billy Connolly says, there are only two seasons in Scotland, June and winter. We have no plans to do much, just enjoy being warm."

The man is a keen football supporter although he doesn't think highly of his national side. He repeats another Billy Connolly line:

"The Scots are the only football team in the world to finish a match with a lap of disgrace."

Since he thinks so little of the Scottish football team, Keith asks him if he has heard what happened when England played Scotland at the time that David Beckham was the English captain. The man does not think he has so Keith tells him the story.

The English team go up to Hampden Park for the match. David Beckham says that he doesn't need the whole team to take on this lot and suggests they all go off to do some shopping while he takes on the Scottish team by himself. He assures them that all will be well. When his team mates return after the match, they find David in the English dressing room looking very downcast:

"What's the matter David? Did we lose?"

David: "Oh no, we won two nil."

Team mates: "So why are you looking so glum?"

"Oh," says David. "I got sent off after twenty minutes."

Fortunately, his new friends find this funny. Keith has his reasons for staying in touch with them so when the flight lands they swap contact details and say goodbye. As soon as possible he looks at his email. There is one for him.

Dear Keith,

This is getting ever more intriguing. Yes, I do have those things. I needed the birth certificate, along with many other pieces of paper, to help set up the business deal. I am not sure why you need it, though. I thought you already knew how ancient I am. The bus will get me to the airport and from there I will pick up a taxi. I should be at your hotel by twelve thirty this afternoon.

Ellie xx

This is ideal. He has time to get to the hotel he has booked, sort out some other things he wants to do and still be ready for her.

Dear Ellie,

This is perfect. I will be there. Can't wait. The weather is very good, so wear the shortest skirt you have!

Much love,

Keith xxx.

He goes to the carousel to collect his luggage. After a while the belt starts to move. For a while there is no baggage. Finally, one sock appears. He hears a voice behind him speaking in an American accent:

"Now that's what I call travelling light."

He immediately thinks about Cliff Richard singing the song "Travelling light". He recalls the less than awe inspiring lyrics:

"Travelling light, travelling light, I just can't wait to see my baby tonight".

Even better he doesn't have to wait until tonight. He expects to see Ellie this afternoon.

One of the advantages of being single is that the huge expense of raising a family is avoided. No one goes into a teaching career for the money but Keith is comfortably off and has booked himself into a high-class hotel experience on a permanently-moored luxury yacht, located in at heart of the Ocean Village development in Gibraltar. By the time he has arrived and checked in he will only have sufficient time to do a couple of short jobs before going back to the hotel to meet Ellie. He is able to complete his tasks quickly and is sitting in the sunshine on a beautiful afternoon when Ellie's taxi arrives. With such warm weather he is not surprised to see her dressed accordingly. She has a thin white blouse and a short black skirt. He thinks she looks sensational. Oh gosh, did he really have the nerve to ask her to wear something like that? They hug and kiss and Keith promises shortly to tell her what he is doing in Gibraltar, although he has been admitting to himself at times that he is unsure about this himself. He says they have time for a quick coffee before he wishes to share something with her. The waiter comes with the order. He is good, but not good enough that Keith cannot tell he spends rather longer looking at Ellie than is necessary for the performance of his duty. Ellie doesn't seem to notice but she must be used to such things now. She takes his hand and smiles.

Ellie: "Keith, I am so delighted that we are here together but there is something going on that you are not telling me. I have some things to share with you about the business but that can wait. I am dying of curiosity."

Keith has a speech rehearsed. He has forgotten it already. His carefully rehearsed speech has gone out of the window. He is a teacher of many years' experience. He is used to being able to convey thoughts in words that say precisely what he intends. Now his heart is beating on overtime. He is stumbling over every sentence. He keeps hold of her hand and blurts out:

"Ellie....in such a short time I have fallen so much in love with you. I hate being apart from you. I have been here only a few hours but I have been to a jeweller and chose this ring and then I went to the registry office here and they said if we come back by two o'clock today to sort out a few formalities we could be married at one o'clock tomorrow. "

He gets down on one knee:

"Will you marry me.... tomorrow?"

He pauses and looks up at Ellie. He has never seen such an expression on her face. She looks stunned.

Keith: "Look, I am so sorry; I shouldn't have said these foolish things...."

Ellie: "Keith..."

Keith: "Sorry, it was stupid of me, please forgive me. I......."

"Keith..."

Keith: It's far too sudden and unexpected. I cannot imagine what your son...

"KEITH..."

He lifts his eyes and looks at her again.

Ellie: "Yes."

It's Keith's turn to look stunned:

"You mean… Really? You will have me? And tomorrow?"

"Yes, let's do it, but we need to be at the registry office if we are to make tomorrow work."

In a daze of disbelief they embrace and he wants to rush for a taxi for the short ride to the registry office. She remains motionless. She is grinning from ear to ear:

"I thought you meant me to have the ring?"

Keith is still shaking:

"Oh, yes. I did."

He tries it on her finger and it fits tolerably well.

Keith: "The jeweller said he can easily adjust it."

Ellie: "It's beautiful. I love it. Keith, have you really worked out all the details?"

Keith: "Yes, really. We have to fill in a bit of documentation now. Oh, and one other thing, by local law we have to spend the night here, either before or after we are married. I rather hoped that, when you come back tomorrow from Algeciras and we are married, you will be willing to stay the night with me……."

Ellie: "Oh, I think this can be arranged."

They arrive at the registry office and the formalities are over with very quickly, although he only has twenty-four hours to find two witnesses that will be needed. So much of his planning has been filled with uncertainty but he is quietly confident that Malcolm and Lorna will oblige. Only now does it become clear that he is fortunate that the registry office has space to marry them. He had already established that twenty-four hours is sufficient notice on Gibraltar. They have time for a short walk before Ellie must return to Algeciras. This time Keith is confident that it will not pour with rain, although the memories of the walk in the rain are still precious to him.

Ellie: "I have much to tell you about Spanish underwear and lingerie but I want to ask you something. I really do not mind what you say but I would like to know your answer. You are plain

Mister Stokes. You never did a PhD and so never became Doctor Stokes. Was there a reason for that?"

Keith: "I guess when I started my career it did not seem necessary. Only a few colleagues had one. It seemed like you could only acquire one if you spent four years doing nothing else and the cost of that seemed too high. Alternatively, you had to do it as a hobby whilst doing a teaching job. That didn't seem a great choice either. Several years studying the import of bananas into Nicaragua during the nineteen sixties or some similar topic just did not appeal. Looking back, I probably got it wrong. In higher education today to be without a PhD is to be marked as a second-class citizen. Only people with PhDs are esteemed colleagues. I wanted to be a good teacher. Does it bother you that you are joining yourself to a second-class citizen?"

Ellie: "The title of the lecturers was of no concern to us. We wanted to be taught by people who could explain things clearly and inspire us to learn. I am sure that there are occasions where someone's research has helped students understand things but I never came across anyone like that when I was in Barmouth."

Keith: "I remember some final year students talking to me about a professor who had taught them very little. He said the same things and used the same stories to any group whatever level they were at. They said they thought he was a great teacher in the first year, okay in the second year and rubbish by the time they were in their final year when they realised that he had nothing new to say. I was desperate not to be thought of like that."

Ellie: "But you did find time to write some books...."

"I did but it did not make me an estimable fellow. The day after I signed a contract to write my first academic text there was an announcement by the Barmouth directorate that a new system would now be in operation to adjudge the quality of published work by academics. The announcement included the statement that textbooks would have no value in the new system. So, my timing was not great, although I am rather good at the timing of placing pet spiders in the bath."

Ellie: "I was very embarrassed that evening in the bathroom. Would you not have been embarrassed if I had come in to find you naked?"

Keith: "Well let me answer your question like this. When I was a schoolboy, we all hated PE lessons – physical education. We had to change into shorts and prance around the gym. I once tried getting out of it by telling the master that I had forgotten to bring my shorts. He just turned and said: 'Wear a long tie, boy'. I suppose that we got over embarrassment among other boys, but yes, I think I am sure that I would have been embarrassed with you. The only difference is that you looked magnificent. Now, my fiancée, do we have time for coffee before you must return to Algeciras?"

Ellie: "Only just. I cannot miss the evening meal. And I might think of one or two other things I would like to do in the morning before coming back here. I am not sure who of us is the crazier of the two?"

Keith: "You are sure you don't want to change your mind?"

Ellie: "Absolutely not and neither must you!"

Keith: "But you have had so little time to think about it."

Ellie: "I didn't need any time at all."

Keith: "None of our friends and family will be there tomorrow to celebrate with us."

Ellie: "We will arrange a celebration back in the UK."

Keith: "You haven't told your son?"

Ellie: "I will let him know very soon. I really want to try to heal our relationship."

Keith: It's a registry office, not a church."

Ellie: "We can discuss a church blessing in the near future."

Keith: "We haven't...."

Ellie smiles that heart-melting smile again:

"Are you withdrawing your proposal already?"

Keith: "No, you beautiful lady, I am not. I have never been more certain of anything in my life."

As they hold hands over coffee it's hard to know what to talk about first, but it quickly becomes clear to Keith that the business deal has been sealed. Ellie's company and the Spanish company will remain separate entities but share everything and widen their market. Everyone seems very pleased.

Ellie: "I do not regret for a second what we are doing. It was you that taught me to assess costs and benefits in decision making. In that way you helped re setting up a business. In that way you helped with decisions about Spain. Yes, in that way you even helped me to assess whether I wanted to spend the rest of my life with you. But there are decisions we must take about the future. One of them is my business and, in particular, my link with the Spanish. I do not want to give this up."

Keith: "My dear Ellie, I do not regret my decision to ask you to spend your life with me but I think I should say this to you. I hold you in my hand, my little bird. But my hand is open so that you are free to fly. I want our relationship to be one in which you can develop, not one in which you feel constrained and restricted."

Ellie: "Thank you, Keith, but I am hoping that we can grow together. I love being with you, but I long to work with you too. You are an economist. Years ago, you opened my mind to all kinds of possibilities in business. I think you can continue to do this."

Keith: "I would love to try, although I have to confess that I have not spent much time considering how to use economic principles and insights to aid the sales of Spanish lingerie and underwear. Had you thought about how you might use your business insights to help economics and business students? If you can stop from blushing, you can come into a few classes and give one or two seminars on pricing and marketing in your own particular area of expertise. We may have to think carefully about what pictures you use to illustrate those principles. We mustn't overexcite my male students."

They are sitting at a table opposite each other. Her hand moves slowly across the tablecloth towards his. His hand inches towards her. Time stands still. Finally, their fingers touch. She raises her hand above his. Then, finally she lowers her hand onto the top of his and looks down at the ring:

"Keith, what made you so sure?"

Keith: "I realised that I had never met a girl with whom I felt so at ease and yet found so desirable at the same time. Perhaps the nearest I came was a few years ago. There was a girl I got to know that I met at one of those dreadful parties that are obligatory at Christmas time. We got talking and found our views on many things, including obligatory Christmas parties, coincided. Our friendship blossomed from there. She was really rather attractive. I guess our friendship lasted the best part of two years and during that time, I think I can say, we became quite close. We really seemed to take pleasure in one another's company. Somehow, for reasons I never fully understood, neither of us felt inclined to take things further. We gradually drifted apart. I do not recall there being harsh words, there was just an absence of magic. But I learned a lot from our friendship. There was warmth in our companionship that I have not often felt with others. Yet there was not that spark of magic I felt with you immediately we got together again."

Ellie: "It sounds rather platonic. Did you never find anyone where there was some heat?"

Keith: "There was one other very different girl where we saw things about me so differently. Whereas that other relationship had warmth, this one had, in your words, heat. But it was a heat that would have burned us. I am easy going and she saw that as idle. I thought I was giving in to her and she thought I didn't care about things. She seemed to be frustrated about me over things I thought were my strengths! But you are entirely unique in my experience. I find you incredibly desirable and yet it is so easy to be with you. I don't want to lose you."

Ellie: "I hope you will lose me for only a few hours. I will be back tomorrow with my suitcase and, when we are ready, we can fly back together. There will be a lot to sort out. It will come as something of a surprise to my son. At least moving in with you will be relatively easy since the business is an online one.

Keith: "Did you really never find anyone else after you so tragically lost your husband?"

Ellie: "Like you, there were a few but it never seemed right. I even tried finding someone through a dating agency."

Keith: "Oh do tell. I have never done that but I had begun recently to think about it."

Ellie: "What made you decide not to try?"

Keith: "You came into my life. So, tell me now about your experiences with the agency."

Ellie: "I hope you won't need to go to one ever again but there isn't much positive to say. I had a few conversations with guys who seemed pretty desperate and a few with whom I spent a relatively short time of irredeemable tedium online. One guy kept pet hamsters and wouldn't stop talking about it. He kept sending me pictures of them. It took ages to persuade him I wasn't very interested. I once read a Japanese saying: if you get on the wrong train, get off at the next station. The longer it takes you to get off, the more expensive the return trip will be. " Good advice, never more relevant than in the context of a dating agency experience.

Keith: "What about a guy who keeps pet spiders and even knows how to train them to sit still in the bath?"

Ellie: "Now that is an art. I could get very interested in somebody like that."

Keith: "Did you ever get as far as meeting any guys?"

Ellie: "I met two or three but none seemed remotely like they claimed to be online. One or two others cancelled at the last minute. Another gave a strong impression that I was the fallback position if something else didn't work out. In the end I realised that I was spending time just scrolling through names as a way to relieve boredom. It was just replacing Facebook. Another guy sent me, entirely unsolicited, a few pretty explicit pictures and that was after a thirty second chat. While I am not an expert in wildlife, I am sure they were not pictures of a hamster. I guess I tried a dating agency because here are very few opportunities to meet people in the normal course of life, especially if you have an online business like I do. Even meeting you wasn't a new meet, although it's true we hadn't seen one another for a long time. Keith, you are not one I have found on the rebound. You are very different from my first husband and I am glad about that. "

He knows she has to leave, although he is reluctant to see her go. He calls her a taxi.

Ellie: "I love you, Keith".

Minutes later she has gone. He then rings Malcolm and Laura and asks if they might possibly be willing to be tomorrow's witnesses that they must have. Malcolm at first seems dubious but Laura is immediately utterly enthusiastic and within minutes it is agreed. They will be at the registry office tomorrow at twelve forty-five.

While he waits Ellie's return tomorrow, he decides to check up on one or two places to which he can bring her in the next few days.

At the southern tip of Gibraltar's peninsula he finds Europa Point, with its historic 19th-century lighthouse and superb views across Algeciras Bay and the African coast. He decides that it's time for coffee and finds another guy who is sitting on his own, although he is clearly not another Englishman. They fall into conversation and it turns out that he is a Spaniard but one who speaks very good English. Keith discovers that he is the general manager of a bullring in Spain, although he has never been in the ring himself. He tells Keith a story about bullfighting. It is obviously one he has told before and he is relishing sharing it again.

An American tourist is looking at the menu in a restaurant in a Spanish bullfighting town. He notices a delicious looking plate of food being served at the next table. It not only looks good but it smells good too. He asks the waiter what the meal is that he is admiring.

The waiter explains:

"Ah senor, those are bull's testicles from the bull fight this morning."

The American thinks that as he is on holiday he will go for that too. The waiter apologises:

"I am very sorry, senor. There is only one serving each day because there is only one bull fight each morning. If you come tomorrow, I can reserve this special delicacy for you"

The American returns and orders this special dish with a carafe of sangria. A little later he calls the waiter over and says:

"These were delicious, but I noticed that they were much smaller than the ones you served yesterday."

The waiter shrugs his shoulders and says:

"Si, Senor. Sometimes the bull wins."

Keith has little time for bullfighting but he can appreciate the humour. The Spaniard asks Keith what he is doing coming to this part of the world and he explains that he has come to meet his girl and they are to marry tomorrow.

The Spaniard: "Then I recommend a game for the two of you. It can be part of your wedding celebrations. You each drink two bottles of tequila and then you have to guess which one of you went out of the room."

He says goodbye to his Spanish friend and goes back to his hotel for a lonely evening. He hopes it will be the last one for some time. He uses the fitness centre but steers clear of the casino. For a very risk-averse character he has risked enough of himself in the last few days. He finds a young couple, Gill and Mark, at the hotel. They look well to do and give every appearance of being on holiday. They fall into conversation and confirm that this is so. He tells him his story about being married tomorrow. They seem very pleased for him and they have a drink to celebrate. Gill seems to want to say something but is also hesitant to do so. Finally, she says:

"Do you have two people who can act as witnesses to the marriage?"

Keith explains about his Scottish friends.

Gill: We would have been delighted to do the job. We have plenty of time. We are on holiday."

Keith: "You would be very welcome. As you can appreciate, there will be plenty of room."

Gill: "When Mark and I were married we had a poem read which was very special to us. Would you like me to read it at your ceremony? It is one of Shakespeare's sonnets. It's the one beginning 'Let me not to the marriage of true minds Admit impediments.' We would be delighted if you agree."

Mark looks dubious about her suggestion. He wears an expression that says: 'I am not so sure, but if my wife says we would be delighted, then we would be delighted.'

It is a long time since Keith has read the sonnet that Gill has in mind but thinks it would be lovely. He decides to take a chance that Ellie will think so also. He agrees warmly and they make arrangements to meet at the registrar's office tomorrow. He then spends most of the last part of the evening thinking of Ellie who is anything but lonely this evening. At least the Spanish cold milk is tasty.

When she appears at the hotel later the next morning he is again amazed by this remarkable lady. Somehow, she has spent the previous evening celebrating a business deal and still found the time today to look stunning. She has had her hair done. It is the first time Keith has seen it up. The carefully arranged wispy bits that hang don loose are very fetching. She is wearing a lightweight cream coloured trouser suit that fits her perfectly. How in the few hours at her disposal she could look so like a bride adorned for her wedding he has no idea. All he has done is to don the suit that he brought with him just in case she agreed to his proposal. They put her suitcase in what has until now been occupied only by Keith and take a short taxi ride to the registry office. He relaxes when he sees Malcolm and Laura who seem honoured to be asked to be the witnesses and Gill and Mark. He introduces Ellie to them and explains that they are his new but very recent friends. Ellie is quite unflustered to discover that Gill will be taking part.

The wedding ceremony is short but unhurried. There are so few people present but Ellie doesn't seem to mind. The vows are exchanged, the register is signed and Gill reads the sonnet delightfully.

"Let me not to the marriage of true minds

Admit impediments; love is not love

Which alters when it alteration finds,

Or bends with the remover to remove.

O no, it is an ever-fixèd mark

That looks on tempests and is never shaken;

It is the star to every wand'ring bark

Whose worth's unknown, although his height be taken.

Love's not time's fool, though rosy lips and cheeks

Within his bending sickle's compass come.

Love alters not with his brief hours and weeks,

But bears it out even to the edge of doom:

If this be error and upon me proved,

I never writ, nor no man ever loved."

During the reading Keith looks across at Ellie. She is moved to tears of joy.

After the ceremony, Keith and Ellie spend a while with their new friends, offering them warm thanks for their friendship and support. They all make vague and unrealistic promises to stay in touch and Mr and Mrs Stokes leave for their hotel which is, unsurprisingly, only a few minutes taxi ride away. During the short journey Ellie asks Keith what he thinks his students will make of his new married status.

Keith: I think that if you recall your student days you will conclude that most of the students will never know or care what has happened. I get taken out of the cupboard for a couple of hours a week and get returned there until another week has passed.

Ellie: "I guess that's true but I do remember having a few conversations with my fellow students in which we decided that you were a crusty bachelor, set in your ways and never likely to change."

As they arrive at their hotel room Keith wonders how much he might change in the coming days. Ellie wraps her arms around him:

"Husband, I am hungry but can we take a shower first? I am hot and would be glad to change."

Keith: "Of course, I will do the same. Who is to go first?"

Ellie: "Ummmm, we just got married...."

Keith: "Oh yes, right."

Ellie: "Give me five minutes start and come and find me in the shower."

Obediently he waits the full five minutes which seems to take approximately three hours. He once saw an ancient clock in a church. It would be showing the correct time at, say, six o'clock. The minute hand would then fall downhill to six thirty in less than twenty minutes. It would then climb uphill to seven o'clock taking something over forty minutes and be showing the correct time on the hour. Keith looks at his watch and sees that it is just after the half hour. No wonder the five minutes is taking so long.

He undresses and enters the shower to find Ellie. She is not quite fully undressed. She is wearing a shower cap to protect her hairstyle.

Ellie: "Don't you dare laugh at me. If you do, I will never speak to you again."

He laughs out loud. She throws a bar of soap at him. She can hardly miss. Now that they are both in the shower, he is no distance away at all.

Keith: "I hope to laugh with you a great deal in future but I will never laugh at you. I am more than ten years older than you. You are young and beautiful. Soon I will struggle to balance on one leg while I put the other one in my pants, even if the pants are made in Algeciras."

Ellie: "You are kind and gentle with a marked sense of humour. I could not ask for more. "

Keith: "So you ignore my other great features: my magnificent physique in general and my finely honed pectorals in particular? "

The gorgeous smile reappears on her face:

"Oh, that was the clincher. Of course, we must not forget that. Indeed, I have no doubt that you will not allow me to ".

She wraps her arms around him.

Keith: "Mmmmm... Last time it took my pet spider to achieve a hug that."

Ellie: "I think you may be cleaner than I am so I think you should begin by washing me."

He fills his hands with suds and begins on her neck. He then moves to her arms. He lingers long over the rest of her body before kneeling in front of her to wash every part. He then stands, turns her round and begins on her back, slowly massaging and at the same time unhurriedly moving downwards. He drops to his knees and caresses every millimetre of skin on her lower half until he finishes at her feet.

Ellie: "Thank you. I think I now have the cleanest breasts in Gibraltar. I think I Should now begin washing you."

Now that it is finally Ellie's turn she is as unhurried as Keith has been. It surprises Keith that when they have finished, the hotel still appears to have a supply of hot water. Drying each other also takes time and by the time they are dressed again they are both feeling hungry. They sit at a table in the hotel. Keith has already booked a table. The view out of the window is delightful but Keith finds it hard to take his eyes off the lady sitting opposite. She has changed again. She is wearing an off-the-shoulder royal blue dress and has let her hair down again. They order some food and then a celebratory bottle of champagne. Keith doesn't yet admit that he doesn't like the stuff much. He has never seen the point in ruining good wine by forcing bubbles into it. They toast each other and it is only then that Keith asks her whether she actually enjoys the champagne. They confess to each other they don't much, and so they order a decent bottle of St Emilion to accompany the meal. The waiter arrives with it and, after spending a little too long looking at Ellie, he lightly brushes her bare shoulder as he leaves for the kitchen. Keith is amused that she decides to make nothing of this outrageous and inappropriate behaviour.

Keith: "I shall now make my wedding speech to this somewhat limited, albeit rather special, audience. I would like to begin by thanking the bride who not only said yes to my proposal but turned up to the wedding on time. Not only did she turn up on time but looked almost as magnificent in her wedding outfit as she looked the first time, I saw her in my bathroom. Now, it is customary to recall in wedding speeches the first time the groom met the bride. In this case I shall ignore the early occasions in Barmouth and recall our renewed acquaintance when she came to my home. In recent days I have read the epic poem of little Miss Muffet and the spider to a couple of delightful children. I shall now recall in poetic form the story of Miss Ellie and the spider, but this time for a rather older audience.

(Ahem. Ahem.)

Little Miss Ellie, her legs turned to jelly

When for her life she had feared.

No surprise there,

For what caused the scare?

A miniature spider appeared.

She had walked for an hour,

Then undressed for a shower,

And all on her own, of course.

But she saw a small spider,

Keith's pet had espied her,

So, she screamed and screamed herself horse.

She'd called out in fear

But Keith was quite near.

He quickly appeared to save her.

While her mind was a blank

Keith paused to thank

his pet for such a great favour.

While he studied her charms,

She was wrapped in his arms.

Now she really could not be braver.

It had shredded her nerves,

But, for Keith, Ellie's curves

Made a wonderful sight to savour.

Then he left her alone.

The occasion had shown

The moral he always would treasure.

If a spider's your pet,

You must never forget

To train it to maximise pleasure. "

The poetic genius falls somewhat short of the Shakespearian sonnet they had heard read earlier. Ellie does not seem to mind:

"That's ridiculous. Funny. but ridiculous"

Keith: "But I haven't finished my speech yet. I want to tell you two stories to show you how much I believe in equality between the sexes. The first story shows a dominant male. A couple had been married for fifty years and no one had ever heard a cross-word pass between them. The local newspaper reporter came around for an interview to discover their secret. 'It all goes back to the day of our honeymoon when we went pony trekking', said the wife. My pony stumbled and my husband said quietly, 'That's once.' A bit further along, the poor pony stumbled again. My husband said quietly, 'That's twice.' Soon afterwards the pony stumbled again. My husband didn't say anything this time, but he pulled out a shotgun and shot the pony. I said to him: 'You can't behave like that. That was an awful thing to do.' My husband turned to me and said quietly, 'That's once.'

Ellie laughs but wants to hear the other story.

"Sometimes it's the female who is the dominant one. Three friends married women from different countries. The first man married a woman from France. He told her that she was expected to do all the cooking, the dishes and the house cleaning, as well as have his slippers warmed and by the fire when he came home. From the first day that's exactly what he got.

The second man married a woman from Spain. He gave his wife the same orders as the first man. The first few days he didn't see any results, but after that it got better and better for him. By the fourth day, he saw that his house was clean, the dishes were washed, there was a meal on the table and his slippers were warmed by the fire.

The third man married a girl from England. He also gave these same orders to his new wife. He said the first day he didn't see anything and the second day he didn't see anything either, but by the end of the week.......... the swelling had gone down enough so he could see a little bit out of his left eye."

Ellie: "Oh, I like that one best. I suppose that it's unusual to have a celebratory wedding meal for two, but when we get to celebrate with friends, I think you should tell both those stories."

They finish the meal and retire to their room. There is a CD there and Keith plays Eric Clapton singing "Wonderful tonight". They dance and Keith tries, not altogether successfully, to avoid treading on Ellie's toes.

"I feel wonderful because I see
the love light in your eyes
and the wonder of it all
is that you just don't realize how much I love you...."

They move in closer and he can feel the shape of her body moulding against his. The music has stopped for some while before they finally untangle. Keith gazes into her eyes:

"Ellie, now it's time I read you a poem. Actually, I am not going to read it. I shall recite it. I was fourteen when I was first introduced to this poem at school and expected to learn it. It's a touching love story and at fourteen such love was of no interest to me, certainly nowhere near as interesting as playing football. But we change with time. I didn't make much effort to learn it then but as I got older, I tried to learn at least some of it and now I would like to recite it to you."

Ellie: "I would like that very much."

Keith: "It took Alfred Noyes two days to write this and it took me forty years to learn it. Maybe he wasn't all that interested in football. "

Keith begins to read.

The wind was a torrent of darkness among the gusty trees,

The moon was a ghostly galleon tossed upon cloudy seas,

The road was a ribbon of moonlight over the purple moor,

And the highwayman came riding—

Riding—riding—

The highwayman came riding, up to the old inn-door.

He'd a French cocked-hat on his forehead, a bunch of lace at his chin,

A coat of the claret velvet, and breeches of brown doe-skin;

They fitted with never a wrinkle: his boots were up to the thigh!

And he rode with a jewelled twinkle,

His pistol butts a-twinkle,

His rapier hilt a-twinkle, under the jewelled sky.

Over the cobbles he clattered and clashed in the dark inn-yard,

He tapped with his whip on the shutters, but all was locked and barred;

He whistled a tune to the window, and who should be waiting there,

But the landlord's black-eyed daughter,

Bess, the landlord's daughter,

Plaiting a dark red love-knot into her long black hair.

"There's a reference now to Tim the ostler, the only reference in the whole poem but he plays a critical part."

Ellie: "Remind me, what is an ostler?"

Keith: "It was someone whose job is to look after the horses of people who are staying at an inn."

And dark in the dark old inn-yard a stable-wicket creaked

Where Tim the ostler listened; his face was white and peaked;

His eyes were hollows of madness, his hair like mouldy hay,

But he loved the landlord's daughter,

The landlord's red-lipped daughter,

Dumb as a dog he listened and he heard the robber say—

"One kiss, my bonny sweetheart, I'm after a prize to-night,

But I shall be back with the yellow gold before the morning light;

Yet, if they press me sharply, and harry me through the day,

Then look for me by moonlight,

Watch for me by moonlight,

I'll come to thee by moonlight, though hell should bar the way."

He rose upright in the stirrups; he scarce could reach her hand,

But she loosened her hair I' the casement! His face burnt like a brand

As the black cascade of perfume came tumbling over his breast;

And he kissed its waves in the moonlight,

(Oh, sweet black waves in the moonlight!)

Then he tugged at his rein in the moonlight and galloped away to the West.

He did not come in the dawning; he did not come at noon;

And out o' the tawny sunset, before the rise o' the moon,

When the road was a gipsy's ribbon, looping the purple moor,

A red-coat troop came marching—

Marching—marching—

King George's men came marching, up to the old inn-door.

They said no word to the landlord; they drank his ale instead,

But they gagged his daughter and bound her to the foot of her narrow bed;

Two of them knelt at her casement, with muskets at their side!

There was death at every window;

And hell at one dark window;

For Bess could see, through her casement, the road that he would ride.

Keith: "I hate the thought of a woman being treated badly by men who think they have such a right as a result of being bigger and stronger. But I hate the thought more now when I think how much I have come to care for you."

They had tied her up to attention, with many a sniggering jest;

They had bound a musket beside her, with the barrel beneath her breast!

"Now keep good watch!" and they kissed her.

She heard the doomed man say—

Look for me by moonlight;

Watch for me by moonlight;

I'll come to thee by moonlight, though hell should bar the way!

She twisted her hands behind her; but all the knots held good!

She writhed her hands till her fingers were wet with sweat or blood!

They stretched and strained in the darkness, and the hours crawled by like years,

Till, now, on the stroke of midnight,

Cold, on the stroke of midnight,

The tip of one finger touched it! The trigger at least was hers!

The tip of one finger touched it; she strove no more for the rest!

Up, she stood up to attention, with the barrel beneath her breast,

She would not risk their hearing; she would not strive again;

For the road lay bare in the moonlight;

Blank and bare in the moonlight;

And the blood of her veins in the moonlight throbbed to her love's refrain.

Tlot-tlot; Tlot-tlot! Had they heard it? The horse-hoofs ringing clear;

Tlot-tlot, Tlot-tlot, in the distance? Were they deaf that they did not hear?

Down the ribbon of moonlight, over the brow of the hill,

The highwayman came riding,

Riding, riding!

The red-coats looked to their priming! She stood up, straight and still!

Tlot-tlot, in the frosty silence! Tlot-tlot, in the echoing night!

Nearer he came and nearer! Her face was like a light!

Her eyes grew wide for a moment; she drew one last deep breath,

Then her finger moved in the moonlight,

Her musket shattered the moonlight,

Shattered her breast in the moonlight and warned him— with her death.

He pauses and looks at Ellie. Her eyes are glistening with tears. He gently squeezes her hand.

He turned; he spurred to the West; he did not know who stood

Bowed, with her head o'er the musket, drenched with her own red blood!

Not till the dawn he heard it, his face grew grey to hear

How Bess, the landlord's daughter,

The landlord's black-eyed daughter,

Had watched for her love in the moonlight and died in the darkness there.

Back, he spurred like a madman, shrieking a curse to the sky,

With the white road smoking behind him and his rapier brandished high!

Blood-red were his spurs I' the golden noon; wine-red was his velvet coat,

When they shot him down on the highway,

Down like a dog on the highway,

And he lay in his blood on the highway, with the bunch of lace at his throat.

He looks at her again. Tears are running down her cheek now. She squeezes his hand.

And still of a winter's night, they say, when the wind is in the trees,

When the moon is a ghostly galleon tossed upon cloudy seas,

When the road is a ribbon of moonlight over the purple moor,

A highwayman comes riding—

Riding—riding—

A highwayman comes riding, up to the old inn-door.

Over the cobbles he clatters and clangs in the dark inn-yard;

He taps with his whip on the shutters, but all is locked and barred;

He whistles a tune to the window, and who should be waiting there,

But the landlord's black-eyed daughter,

Bess, the landlord's daughter,

Plaiting a dark red love-knot into her long black hair.

She clings to him and says:

"I don't know whether I love that poem or hate it."

Keith: "I am still astonished that you said yes to me."

Ellie: "I never believed that you would ask me to spend my life with you. But I had already decided that, if you did, I would say yes. It's an enormous decision but I felt sure it was the right one. When I had to commit in business there came a point where I knew that if I said no, I would always regret it. I knew that I would regret it even more if you gave me a chance to be with you and I turned it down. That's why I responded so quickly to your proposal. You had made me think through what I wanted for my future and I became confident that whatever I wanted I could find it with you. Yes, I was shocked about the problem at Barmouth with my son. In a very short time, I thought I had come to understand you so well. That problem made me think that I had misunderstood who you were. I am so grateful; to you for giving me the chance to rethink what happened."

They turn the lights down low, undress and climb into bed. The bed is enormous. It is so huge that if they each kept to separate sides, they would need a phone to communicate. They find a way to avoid such a need. Their attention is fully focused on each other. There is no need for more words now. Keith, like Postman Pat, feels that he is a very happy man. He had a loving home as a child, he has been fortunate to be able to teach. He has been able to appreciate good things in life as well as to laugh at its absurdities. Now, however, he feels that, maybe, just maybe, the best is yet to be.......

www.ingramcontent.com/pod-product-compliance
Ingram Content Group UK Ltd.
Pitfield, Milton Keynes, MK11 3LW, UK
UKHW020652200525
5970UKWH00051B/347